A winner of the William Saroyan international Prize for Writing, **Margalit Fox** trained as a linguist and was a senior writer at *The New York Times*. As a former member of the newspaper's celebrated Obituary News Department, she wrote the front-page public send-offs of some of the leading cultural figures of our age. She has written three previous books, *Conan Doyle for the Defence*, *The Riddle of the Labyrinth*, and *Talking Hands*, and lives in Manhattan with her husband, the writer and critic George Robinson.

Praise for *The Confidence Men*

'Fox, a former senior obituary writer for *The New York Times* and the author of three previous books, unspools Jones and Hill's delightfully elaborate scheme in nail-biting episodes that advance like a narrative Rube Goldberg machine, gradually leading from Yozgad to freedom by way of secret codes, a hidden camera, buried clues, fake suicides and a lot of ingenious mumbo jumbo. At moments, *The Confidence Men* has the high gloss of a story polished through years of telling and retelling'
The New York Times

'*The Confidence Men* couldn't have come along at a better time. This story of two unlikely con artists – young British officers who use a Ouija board to escape from a Turkish prisoner-of-war camp – is a true delight, guaranteed to lift the spirits of anyone eager to forget today's realities and lose oneself in a beautifully written tale of an exciting and deeply moving real-life caper'
Lynne Olson, author of *Madame Fourcade's Secret War*

'Margalit Fox is one of the premier narrative storytellers we have today, and *The Confidence Men* is a wonderfully entertaining brew of history, thrills and ingenuity, one that highlights the rare occasion when con artistry is employed for the greater public good'
Sarah Weinman, author of *The Real Lolita* and editor of *Unspeakable Acts*

THE CONFIDENCE MEN

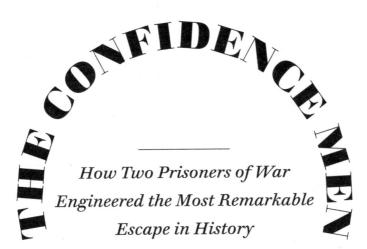

THE CONFIDENCE MEN

MARGALIT FOX

*How Two Prisoners of War
Engineered the Most Remarkable
Escape in History*

P

PROFILE BOOKS

This paperback edition first published in 2022

First published in Great Britain in 2021 by
Profile Books Ltd
29 Cloth Fair
London
EC1A 7JQ

www.profilebooks.co.uk

First published in the United States of America by Random House,
an imprint and division of Penguin Random House LLC, New York

Maps by Jonathan Corum. Used by permission.

Book design by Simon M. Sullivan

1 3 5 7 9 10 8 6 4 2

Printed and bound in Great Britain by
CPI Group (UK) Ltd, Croydon, CR0 4YY

A CIP catalogue record for this book is available from the British Library.

ISBN 978 1 78816 272 2
eISBN 978 1 78283 560 8

For my teachers:
Mark Aronoff
Sandy Padwe

Somehow, what we would not believe in reality, we will believe in a work of art.

—NORMAN N. HOLLAND,
"The 'Willing Suspension of Disbelief' Revisited," 1967

Contents

BOOK THREE · **DEMONS**

Author's Note

In 1928, by an act of the Turkish Parliament, the Turkish language began to be written in a version of the Roman alphabet; the change was part of efforts to modernize the country. Before that date, Turkish had been written in a modified Arabic script. As a result, when pre-1928 Western writers rendered Turkish words in print, their attempts at Romanization produced a welter of competing forms. A single example will suffice: The name "Yozgad," which denotes both the prisoner-of-war camp at the heart of this story and the Anatolian town in which it lay, appears variously as "Yozgad," "Yozgat," "Yozghat," and "Yuzgat."

Although many pre-1928 Romanizations are anachronistic today, in the interest of reflecting the era in which our story is set, I have generally retained the spellings most commonly used by British writers of the period. I also refer to the region's towns and cities by the names they bore in the West at the time: "Angora" for Ankara, "Constantinople" for Istanbul, and the like.*

In addition, many English-language memoirists of the Ottoman theater, our heroes E. H. Jones and C. W. Hill included, used the generic term "Turks" to refer collectively to their Ottoman opponents, be they Turkish, Arab, Jewish, Kurdish, or otherwise, conflating a diverse range of ethnic identities under a single, imperial rubric. For linguistic economy, and in keeping with the diction of the early twentieth-century Britons on whom this book centers, I have occasionally employed "Turks" and "Turkish" in generic references

---

* Constantinople was for centuries the capital of the Ottoman Empire. In 1923, with the formation of the Republic of Turkey, the city's name was formally changed to Istanbul and the capital moved to Ankara.

throughout the text, although such terms would be considered ethnographically insufficient in modern scholarly discourse.

It is also vital to note that Western accounts of the campaigns in Ottoman lands can be fraught with a type of rhetoric—imperialist, exceptionalist, essentialist, Orientalist—that is unacceptable today. Such rhetoric, born of what one modern historian calls "romanticized misrepresentations of places like the Ottoman Empire as sites of mystery and despotism," and which "bolstered ideas of the backwardness of their societies and . . . the superiority of the Western European world," appears at times in this book in quoted matter.

The currency conversions in the footnotes, which translate early twentieth-century pound sterling values into contemporary pound sterling and contemporary U.S. dollars, reflect the historical inflation rate and contemporary exchange rate of late 2020, when this book went to press.

Introduction

—————

THIS IS THE true story of the most singular prison break ever recorded—a clandestine wartime operation that involved no tunneling, no weapons, and no violence of any kind. Conceived during World War I, it relied on a scheme so outrageous it should never have worked: Two British officers escaped from an isolated Turkish prison camp by means of a Ouija board.

Yet that scheme—an ingeniously planned, daringly executed confidence game—was precisely the method by which the young captives, Elias Henry Jones and Cedric Waters Hill, sprang themselves from Yozgad, a prisoner-of-war camp deep in the mountains of Anatolia.

The plan seemed born of a fever dream. Using a handmade Ouija board, Jones and Hill would regale their captors with a tale, seemingly channeled from the Beyond, designed to make them delirious enough to lead the pair out of Yozgad. The ruse would also require our heroes to feign mental illness, stage a double suicide attempt that came perilously close to turning real, and endure six months in a Turkish insane asylum, an ordeal that drove them to the edge of actual madness.

And yet in the end they won their freedom.

I first encountered this story several years ago, through Jones's 1919 memoir, *The Road to En-dor*. Long after I finished it, two things haunted me. The first was that this astounding tale, rife with cunning, danger, and moments of high farce that rival anything in *Catch-22*, had slipped into a crevice in history, where it languished unknown to most of the twenty-first-century public. The second was that it had at its center an enduring mystery: How in the world was this preposterous plan actually able to succeed?

Jones's book dwelled minutely on *how* his ruse worked, detailing a web of plotting, rehearsal, and performance. But there remained the question of *why*—the precise ingredients of the psychological cocktail that transformed his captors into "clay in the potter's hands." Hill's posthumous memoir, *The Spook and the Commandant,* likewise favors exposition over explanation.

The passage of a century has made it possible to solve the mystery at the story's heart. Besides chronicling one of the most ingenious hoaxes ever perpetrated (and one of the only known examples of a con game being used for good instead of ill), *The Confidence Men* explores the strategy that underpins all confidence schemes: the subtle process of mind control called coercive persuasion, colloquially known as brainwashing. The answers to this book's central questions— *How does a master manipulator create and sustain faith? Why do his converts persist in believing things that are patently false?*—also illuminate the behavior of present-day figures such as advertisers, cult leaders, and political demagogues.

Above all, *The Confidence Men* is the story of the profound friendship of two men who almost certainly would not have met otherwise: Jones, the Oxford-educated son of a British knight, and Hill, a mechanic on an Australian sheep station. Vowing to see the scheme through if it cost them their lives, each was sustained throughout its myriad hardships by the steadfastness of the other.

"For a brief period," Jones would write, recalling their six-month confinement in the madhouse, "Hill was put in the bed next mine. It seems a little thing, that we should lie there three feet apart instead of ten, but it meant much. . . . We did not attempt to talk—we were too closely watched for that—but at night, under cover of darkness, sometimes he and sometimes I would stretch out an arm, and for a brief moment grip the other's hand. The firm strong pressure of my comrade's fingers used to put everything right."

THE CONFIDENCE MEN

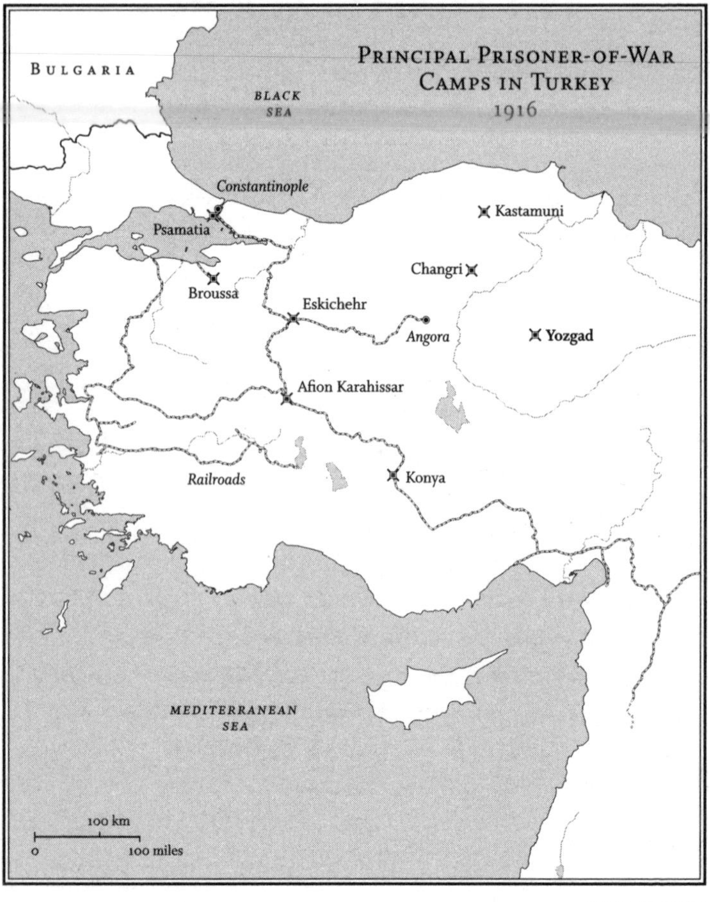

Principal Prisoner-of-War Camps in Turkey
1916
Bulgaria
Black Sea
Constantinople
Psamatia
Broussa
Kastamuni
Changri
Eskichehr
Angora
Yozgad
Afion Karahissar
Konya
Railroads
Mediterranean Sea
100 km
0
100 miles

Jonathan Corum

A Wraith at the Top of the Stairs

THE MEN HUDDLED in the passageway in the flickering candlelight. Some were wrapped in blankets against the Anatolian winter; others wore pajamas. Still others were dressed in British military uniforms, very nearly the only clothing they had. The passage in which they gathered each night, at the top of a dark staircase in a drafty old house, was their de facto sitting room. The house had once been a private home, but the family who lived there had been murdered more than a year before. Since the summer of 1916, when the men were remanded here, this house, with its woeful food, furniture, space, and sanitation, had been their only home. Merely to reach it they had withstood battle, capture, and, for many, a two-month forced march through desert and over mountains, on which scores of men would die.

Every evening, after their sentries locked them in, the men had watched keenly as two fellow officers faced each other across a table, built, like most of the furniture in the house, from disused packing crates. On the table lay a sheet of polished iron; atop the sheet was a raised wooden ring to which the letters of the alphabet had been randomly affixed. The board, too, was made from salvage: the planchette that slid across its surface was an inverted drinking glass, which had begun life as a jar of potted meat.

The sitters at the table closed their eyes and placed their fingers lightly on the glass. Like almost everyone there, they had little faith that they could raise the spirits: They hoped only that a night of "spooking" would help fill their long, empty hours in confinement. They had already tried chess, poker, and roulette, with a wheel made from a discarded door, but all had paled over time. "In spite of the outward cheerfulness, the brave attempts at industry, and the gallant struggle against the deterioration that a prison environment brings, an atmosphere of hopelessness pervaded the whole camp," one of the sitters, Elias Henry Jones, would write at war's end.

For weeks, pairs of officers had taken turns manning the Ouija board, but each time the board refused to speak. At first the glass wouldn't move. When it did—seemingly of its own accord—that caused a ripple of excitement, but still the board was mute: The glass touched only meaningless strings of letters.

"Mere movement was no longer satisfying," Jones wrote. "We were tired of our own company, and knew one another as only fellow-prisoners can. We wanted a chat with somebody 'outside,' somebody with ideas culled beyond our prison walls. . . . It did not matter who it was—Julius Caesar or Socrates, Christopher Columbus or Aspasia . . . but any old Tom, or Dick, or Harry would have been welcome."

As days went by with no results, men dropped out. On this winter night in early 1917, only four remained. They agreed to give the spook-board one last try, and on this night, in Jones's hands, it began to speak.

"For the last time," Jones's companion, William O'Farrell, intoned, addressing the board, "WHO—ARE—YOU?"

"S," the board replied. "A-L-L-Y."

A ghost—and a woman! And a most welcome spirit Sally proved to be, teasing, cajoling, and flirting as the glass spelled out her every word. From then on, Sally was joined nightly by a panoply of shades, including the gentle Dorothy, the cantankerous American Silas P. Warner, and a commanding presence known only as the Spook. At each séance, more and more men pressed eagerly round the table.

IT WAS ALL just a lark, a prank pulled by Jones to pass the stagnant time. But in the coming months, as his humbuggery gained real converts, he began to dream that he could parlay their newfound faith into a far more serious enterprise. "If I could do to the Turks what I had succeeded in doing to my fellow-prisoners," he wrote, "if I could make them *believers*, there was no saying what influence I might not be able to exert over them. It might even open the door to freedom."

And so it would, by virtue of impeccable planning, immense per-

The handmade Ouija board used by Jones and Hill in their early séances.
It would ultimately lead them to freedom.   JONES, THE ROAD TO EN-DOR (1919)

sonal risk, and no small amount of luck. Had Jones not possessed a stellar visual memory; had Cedric Hill, who would become his confederate, not been a sleight-of-hand artist of uncommon prowess; had both men not had a keen aptitude for secret codes; and had they not managed to con their way out of a catastrophic turn of fate that threatened to capsize the entire scheme, they would never have gained their freedom and might well have forfeited their lives. Above all, had any of Jones's fellow prisoners taken the trouble to notice his left thumb, the plan would have been over before it began.

BOOK ONE

DEAD MEN WALKING

CHAPTER ONE

For King and Country

THERE WAS NO barbed wire around Yozgad, nor did there need to be. One of a constellation of World War I prison camps spread over Turkey, it was among the most remote. More than 4,000 feet above sea level, it had been earmarked for incorrigibles—those British officers deemed most likely to escape. The town of Yozgad, in which the camp was set, lay 150 miles south of the Black Sea and 300 miles north of the Mediterranean. The nearest railway station, Angora (present-day Ankara), was five days' journey by cart through forbidding terrain: jagged mountains round the camp and the Anatolian desert beyond. As a result, Yozgad was considered escape-proof, the Alcatraz of its day.

If an inmate did manage to get out, he would have to contend with the cutthroat brigands, believed to number in the hundreds of thousands, who roamed the surrounding countryside. "A solitary traveller, however well armed, would not have stood a dog's chance," Major Edward Sandes, interned at Yozgad, would write in 1924. Men who had fled other camps and been set upon by brigands had been known to beg the nearest Ottoman official they could find to take them back.

But for the British officers at Yozgad, something else precluded escape even more forcibly: On orders of the camp commandant, an attempt by any one of them would bring down severe reprisals—including lockdown, isolation, and even execution—on those who remained, a punitive rite known as strafing.* Men of honor, the prisoners swore to one another that they would not flee.

As Eric Williams, who in 1943 escaped from the Stalag-Luft III

---

* As the modern historian Yücel Yanıkdağ notes, some commanders of Russian POW camps in which Ottoman prisoners were interned discouraged escape by threatening similar reprisals.

The desolate landscape around Yozgad.   JONES, THE ROAD TO EN-DOR (1919)

prison camp in Silesia, would write, "The exhausting . . . march to Yozgad . . . so told on the survivors that once they had settled down the opinion grew among them that it was wrong to escape, that the loss of privileges by those who stayed behind far outweighed the slim chance of the few who might get away."

Yet some, including Jones and Hill, dreamed of liberty. The question was how to attain it without compromising their countrymen.

THE WAR WITH the Ottoman Empire has been called the forgotten theater of World War I, yet it was as brutal as anything on the Western Front. It spanned four principal arenas: Mesopotamia, including modern-day Iraq, where Jones was captured; the Sinai Peninsula and Palestine, including present-day Syria, Israel, and Egypt, where Hill was taken prisoner; the Caucasian Front, where the Ottomans fought Russia; and the Turkish Straits, where Allied forces suffered a devastating defeat at Gallipoli in 1915–16.

The Ottoman Empire had entered the war in the autumn of 1914 after allying itself with the Central Powers: Germany and Austria-Hungary.* The Allies—including Britain, France, and Russia—formally

---

* Bulgaria would join the Central Powers in 1915.

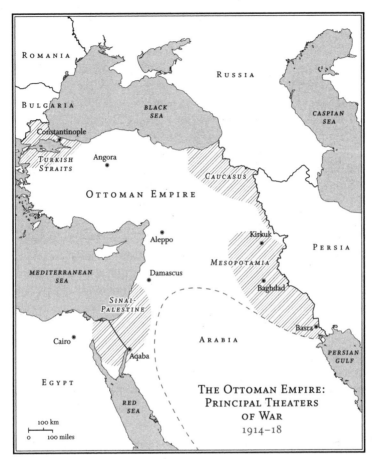

ROMANIA

RUSSIA

BULGARIA

BLACK
SEA

CASPIAN
SEA

Constantinople

TURKISH
STRAITS

Angora

CAUCASUS

OTTOMAN EMPIRE

Kirkuk

Aleppo

PERSIA

MESOPOTAMIA

MEDITERRANEAN
SEA

Damascus

Baghdad

SINAI-
PALESTINE

Cairo

ARABIA

Basra

PERSIAN
GULF

EGYPT

Aqaba

RED
SEA

100 km

0   100 miles

THE OTTOMAN EMPIRE:
PRINCIPAL THEATERS
OF WAR
1914–18

JONATHAN CORUM

declared war on Turkey, as the empire was known in Allied short-hand, soon afterward. For Britain, a crucial imperative was to ensure continued access to its oilfields in Persia (present-day Iran), which bordered Mesopotamia.* In 1913, the First Lord of the Admiralty, Winston Churchill, had urged the Royal Navy to convert its fleet from coal-burning vessels to oil-fired ones: Oil burned hotter and gener-

---

* The Anglo-Persian Oil Company was established in 1909 after the discovery of an immense oilfield in Masjed Soleiman, in what is now Iran, the year before. Urged on by Churchill, the British government became the majority shareholder in the concern in the summer of 1914. The company later became British Petroleum, now BP.

ated steam faster, affording greater speed. Once the Ottoman Empire joined the conflict, Britain moved swiftly to protect its Persian assets.

"The British attitude and policy towards the Ottomans was a variable mixture of Orientalism and racism, on the one hand, and *realpolitik* on the other," the contemporary Turkish historian Yücel Yanıkdağ has written. "From the Ottoman perspective, the Great Powers, including Great Britain, were only interested in carving away the empire." What was more, he wrote, "the British [viewed] the Ottoman Empire as weak and degenerate [and] underestimated what it would take to defeat it." T. E. Lawrence, a British Army officer dispatched for a time to Mesopotamia—he would later become renowned as Lawrence of Arabia for his work in the Palestine campaign—called the British operation in Mesopotamia a "blunderland."

Of all Britain's campaigns in the region, very likely the most disastrous was the five-month siege and ultimate capitulation at Kut-al-Amara, on the banks of the river Tigris some 200 miles upriver from the Persian Gulf. In April 1916, after a siege of 147 days entailing three unsuccessful relief attempts and 33,000 British casualties, the British surrendered. It was, in the words of one twenty-first-century historian, "arguably . . . Britain's worst military defeat since the surrender of Cornwallis's army in 1781 during the American Revolutionary War." More than 12,000 men were taken prisoner at Kut.* Among them was Jones, who with his fellows had endured five months of shot and shell, aerial bombardment, flood, disease, and starvation.

"Harry is home," Jones's father would write at war's end, after his son had come through the siege, the march, two years in Yozgad, and confinement in the madhouse. "He has suffered terribly. I did not think it was possible to suffer so much and live."†

---

* "Kut," as Kut-al-Amara is informally known, rhymes with "foot."

† Of the 8 million to 9 million prisoners of war in World War I as a whole, nearly 300,000—from both sides—were taken in the Ottoman theater. Roughly 35,000 of these were Allied prisoners, held in Ottoman camps throughout Asia Minor. The Allies took more than 200,000 Ottoman prisoners, interning them in camps in Egypt, India, Burma, Cyprus, Iraq, and Russia. Conditions in Allied camps were no better than those on the Ottoman side: Of the estimated 65,000 to 95,000 Ottoman prisoners held in Russia, for instance, some 43 percent died during transport or captivity.

•••

JONES'S JOURNEY TO Yozgad began in Burma. Elias Henry Jones, familiarly known as Harry or Hal, was born in Aberystwyth, Wales, on September 21, 1883, the eldest of six children of a Welsh father, Sir Henry Jones, and a Scottish mother, the former Annie Walker. Sir Henry (1852–1922), a cobbler's son who had left school at twelve to work as his father's apprentice, won a scholarship to Glasgow University in the 1870s and went on to become one of the world's foremost moral philosophers. He was knighted in 1912.

Elias Henry Jones, circa 1915.
JONES, *THE ROAD TO EN-DOR* (1919)

Harry—"his father's double in inventive daring," one of Sir Henry's biographers would write—spent his boyhood in Wales. In 1891 he moved with his family to Scotland, where his father took a post at the University of St. Andrews. Three years later they settled in Glasgow, where Henry Jones had been awarded a professorship in moral philosophy at the University of Glasgow, a chair once held by the eighteenth-century economic philosopher Adam Smith. But to the end of his life Harry remained deeply invested in his Welsh heritage and was fluent in Welsh, a skill that would help turn the machinery of his confidence game.

Harry graduated from the University of Glasgow, where he studied psychology, along with Greek, Latin, mathematics, and history; after earning a master's degree from Balliol College, Oxford, he was admitted to practice as a barrister. In 1906, he joined the Colonial Service and was posted to Burma, then an administrative department of British India. Based in Kawkareik, near the Thai border, he worked as a magistrate, overseeing the judicial affairs of a large province.

During these years, Harry's family would know great loss. His sixteen-year-old brother, Will, described by their father as the most gifted of the Jones children, died in 1906 from appendicitis; in 1910, his sister Jeanie died, at twenty-five, of complications from surgery. Despondent and isolated in the Burmese jungle, Harry became addicted to opium. After several false starts, summoning the resolve that would serve him sublimely in Yozgad, he weaned himself from it. "When I wrote to you . . . the first time . . . I promised you I would never, whatever happened, touch that dreadful drug again," Jones declared in a letter to the woman he loved, Mair Olwen Evans. "I have kept that promise."

Visiting Harry in Burma in 1908, Henry Jones sent accounts of the trip to his wife. His letters betray genuine paternal pride ("He is well and strong and full of courage") and a touch of reflexive paternalism:

> Hal is winning the people hand over hand—*that* is evident. . . . I wish you could see him at this moment. Not in the least conscious of what he is doing, he is sitting on the floor with a fellow-sportsman, a sunburnt, sweaty, dirty old headman from the midst of the jungle. They are chatting away in Burmese like two brothers. The old fellow twenty minutes ago came up, . . . Hal half sternly asking who he is, what he wants, etc. He wants the renewal of his gun licence. "What good did he do with his gun last year, when he had his licence?" He killed two tigers. "With what sort of gun? Where did he shoot them? Would you like to see *my* gun?" and so on. . . . The old fellow's face is sun-wearied with much working in the heat on the fields, and his mouth is all red with chewing betel; but these items, no more than the rags, have not the least influence on the mutual and most sudden love of Hal and the old headman.

In 1913, at twenty-nine, Jones married Mair, a daughter of the eminent Welsh bacteriologist Griffith Evans; he had met her when they were both thirteen. "I have loved you since we were boy and girl together," he would write, "and I love you more with every day that passes." Photographs of the couple around the time of their marriage depict Mair as demure, dark-haired, and slender; Jones, with his raw-boned good looks, deep-set eyes, and long fingers languidly holding a cigarette, has a touch of the dreamy poet about him. After their wedding in Wales, Mair returned with him to Burma; their first child, Jean, was born in December 1914.

By then Britain was at war with the Ottoman Empire, and Indian Army troops commanded by British officers had been dispatched to the region. A call for volunteers soon went out to Burma. Jones obtained a leave of absence from the Colonial Service and in April 1915 enlisted as a gunner* in the Indian Army Reserve of Officers. He became a member of Indian Expeditionary Force D and was assigned to the force's Sixth Division, charged with capturing Baghdad. Mair, pregnant with their second child, sailed back to Britain with baby Jean.

The Sixth Division had been in Mesopotamia since the autumn of 1914 and had enjoyed early victories there, occupying Basra, near the head of the Persian Gulf, in November. Advancing up the Tigris, it took Kurna the next month. Under Major General Sir Charles Townshend, who assumed command of the division in April 1915, it captured Amarah† that spring. Shipping out from Rangoon in the summer of 1915, Jones joined Townshend's troops at Amarah in late July.

Despite its early successes, Force D proved spectacularly ill equipped for a long campaign in a land that was itself a hostile foe, though some sources described it as the site of the biblical Eden. Furnished with imprecise maps, the force had to make its way through barren, seemingly featureless country punctuated by marshes and desert and disarrayed by sandstorms and mirages. In an era when the average summer temperature in London barely exceeded 60 degrees Fahrenheit, troops in the Mesopotamian summer of 1915 endured temperatures that could reach 130 degrees in the shade. "If this is the Garden of Eden," one British soldier remarked, "it wouldn't have needed an angel with a flaming sword to keep *me* out of it."

In this impassable country, the easiest method of transport was by water, but the British had few shallow-draft ships able to negotiate the rivers in the low-water season. Nor were other supplies remotely sufficient, a situation that owed partly to British imperial hubris, which had led commanders to underestimate the extent to which a war in Mesopotamia would consume men, matériel, and time.

Then there were the bugs, a relentless plague of biblical propor-

---

* Equivalent in rank to a private.

† Not to be confused with Kut-al-Amara, Amarah lies on the Tigris about 90 miles southeast of Kut.

tions recalled by nearly every British memoirist of the campaign. There were bugs that crawled; bugs that bit and stung; bugs that swarmed into men's eyes, noses, and mouths; bugs that invaded their food and drink; bugs that tossed their slumbers; bugs that rose up in clouds; bugs that caused lingering sickness, and every one of them— flies and sandflies, fleas, mosquitos, and lice—was, one chronicler said, "of a clinging, affectionate nature." Some men grew so desperate to repel them that they smeared their bodies with crude oil, resulting only in burned skin.

Throughout the late summer and early fall of 1915, Jones, who had been promoted to corporal, remained with the garrison at Amarah, while an advance guard from the Sixth Division worked its way upriver. Writing to Mair from Amarah on September 2, he told her that he was making good progress in the daily Arabic lessons he was taking from a local Syrian priest. On September 21, his thirty-second birthday, he wrote from Amarah again: "The life suits me, and has hardened me up. . . . There is no need at all for you to be more anxious about me here than if I had been in Burma. So far as I know the chances of our being in a scrap are remote. . . . Garrison work—which is our primary duty—naturally means that we take over positions which <u>have been</u> captured. It is monotonous and inglorious but necessary."

THE ADVANCE GUARD entered Kut-al-Amara in late September, capturing the town in a battle of September 27–28. Kut stood on a peninsula, two miles long and a mile wide, in a loop of the Tigris. A largely Arab town of about 7,000, it comprised mud houses, narrow alleys, a mosque, a bazaar, an old fort, palm trees, poverty, and dust. To imperial eyes, it was an unprepossessing sight—"a veritable East End," one British officer called it sourly—but the British did not plan to stay there long. They conceived of Kut as a rear base from which to support a northwesterly press toward Ctesiphon, an ancient city 200 miles upriver. Ctesiphon was the gateway to Baghdad, their most coveted prize.

By mid-November, Jones was stationed at Kut, where he was helping erect gun emplacements. He was now a junior officer—a second

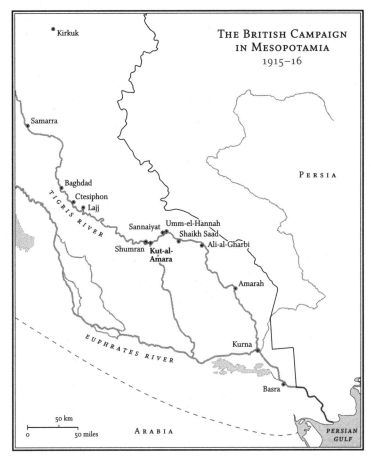

THE BRITISH CAMPAIGN
IN MESOPOTAMIA
1915–16

Kirkuk

Samarra

PERSIA

Baghdad
Ctesiphon
Lajj

TIGRIS RIVER

Sannaiyat Umm-el-Hannah
Shaikh Saad
Shumran **Kut-al-Amara** Ali-al-Gharbi

Amarah

EUPHRATES RIVER

Kurna

Basra

50 km
0   50 miles   ARABIA

PERSIAN
GULF

JONATHAN CORUM

lieutenant—though he assured his brother gunners, "I'm still one of you." To prove as much, his constitutional roguery coming to the fore, he engaged in hijinks most unbecoming an officer, filching a wing from one of Force D's airplanes and using it to shore up his dugout. (The loss of the plane would not have mattered much. Throughout the siege, the Ottoman lines were so close to the Kut garrison that it was considered too risky for the British to take flight.)

On November 14, from Kut, he wrote to Mair, now seven and a half months pregnant:

If the good God grant us a long life together, if he will bring me safe to you at the end of this trial, you must just go on being your own sweet self. And if the fates decree otherwise, my dearie, it will be all the same, and you will be to Sian Fach Fechan* and to the little unknown the same bright star as you always have been to me. I hope I am not to be wasted, as better men than I have been, by a conscript's bullet, but if I am, carissima mea, be of good cheer, and of great courage. . . .

I <u>am</u> coming back, Mairie bach,† back to you and Sian Fach Fechan and the little unknown, for we have had enough of separation, and waiting, and solitude. . . .

And perhaps in six months, perhaps when the Little Unknown is a toddler, perhaps still later, we shall meet, you & I, and when we meet the war will be over and there will be a mighty peace over the world. And wee Jean and the Little Unknown will grow up, and as they grow their mother will tell them how Daddy became a soldier in the time of the Great War, and how Mummy waited at home for him to come back when the war was finished.

As it transpired, he would not see his family for three years.

BY LATE NOVEMBER 1915, part of the Sixth Division—some 14,000 troops—was fighting its way toward Ctesiphon. (Jones was among those who remained behind in Kut.) Ctesiphon was just 18 miles downriver from Baghdad. If Ctesiphon fell, the British believed, Baghdad would not be far behind. But Ctesiphon would not fall. On November 26, Townshend withdrew his men from Ctesiphon 10 miles south to Lajj; on the twenty-eighth, after the British had suffered nearly 50 percent casualties, he gave the order to retreat to Kut. The Ottomans pursued them southward, and the British knew that a siege was inevitable. But they did not despair. They would be out, the consensus went, by Christmas.

---

* "Little Jean."
† "Little Mair."

CHAPTER TWO

Besieged

THE TROUBLE WITH a peninsula is that it can easily be turned into a bottleneck, and that, on the British return to Kut, is what the Ottoman Army proceeded to do. As the enemy closed in from the north, the garrison's most urgent imperative was to dig. They dug three lines of combat trenches, together with the perpendicular communication trenches that ran between them; built a vast series of dugouts (the trenches, roofed with galvanized iron, in which the men would live); laid telephone and telegraph cable; dug gun pits and latrines; and strung miles of barbed wire. Some 30 miles of trenches were dug in all. Jones and his countrymen would spend the next five months living largely within their confines, underground, at times in darkness. It was, one officer recalled, much like being buried alive.

By December 7, Ottoman forces had sealed off Kut entirely, blocking the top of the loop in the river and positioning men all around it on opposite banks. Trapped inside the loop were some 12,000 British and Indian troops; about 6,000 remaining townspeople; some 3,000 camp followers; a bevy of support animals (horses, donkeys, mules, camels); and an array of armaments, including forty-three big guns. Outside were thousands of Ottoman soldiers, with big guns of their own and small arms sometimes superior to those of the British. The Ottomans started shelling on the seventh, with thirty British casualties. As Jones would recall, they were excellent marksmen. He and his fellow gunners were positioned directly in harm's way, at Townshend's first line.

From their trenches, which crawled with slugs and scorpions, the men kept their ears tuned to the savage symphony that played daily in Kut: the crash of palm trees felled by enemy fire; the *crack-crack* of sniper rifles; the *brrp-brrp-brrp* of the Ottomans' 40-pound guns; the deep *krump-kr-rump-sh-sh-sh-sh* of falling shells and the incongruously gentle *swissssh* of flung-up earth that followed; the bee swarms of bullets that swelled till they sounded like hail; the screams of the starlings that wheeled overhead; the howling of jackals on the plain nearby. By December 23, Kut was surrounded by 25,000 Ottoman troops with fifty big guns.

Yet Townshend's men remained hopeful. There was enough food to permit the British soldiers a substantial daily ration: "a pound of meat, a pound of bread, three ounces of bacon, four ounces of onion, six ounces of potatoes, three ounces of jam, one ounce of tea, and two and a half ounces of sugar, plus salt, butter and cheese." Plans were under way for a British relief force to bring troops and supplies from the south. The besieged men of Kut felt certain they would be out soon after New Year's.

Just after 5:00 A.M. on December 24, 1915, the Ottomans began a ferocious assault, attacking Kut's old fort, and the town itself, with heavy rifle and machine-gun fire. They lobbed grenades across the British lines; one of their land mines exploded nearby. Palm trees fell, men fell, bullets came down like hail, and Kut was enveloped in smoke, dust, blood, and shrapnel. Breaching the fort, Ottoman fighters commenced hand-to-hand combat with bayonets. The British returned fire with rifles, machine guns, and howitzers. Equipped with few proper hand grenades, they resorted to lobbing homemade ones, jury-rigged from shrapnel bullets and old jam tins, across the Ottoman lines.

A second Ottoman assault followed that night, and a third on Christmas Day. In the end, the British suffered more than 300 casualties. The Ottoman figure was at least three times that, with masses of dead and wounded lying just outside the walls of the fort. Though fighting would continue daily through the end of April, the Christmastime assault was the last colossal battle the Ottomans waged. They had come to the unassailable conclusion that the best way to rout the British was simply to wait, and starve them out.

As 1916 DAWNED, the passage of time was marked increasingly by the advancing relief date, mounting casualties, and dwindling rations. By

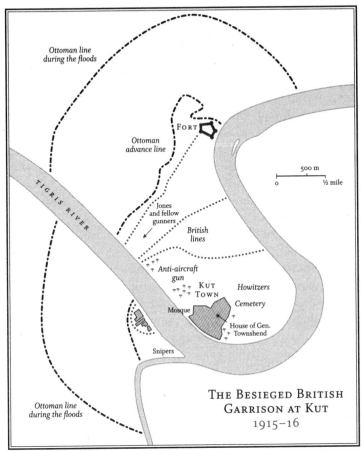

Ottoman line
during the floods

FORT

Ottoman
advance line

TIGRIS RIVER

500 m

0   ½ mile

Jones
and fellow
gunners

British
lines

Anti-aircraft
gun

KUT
TOWN   Howitzers

Cemetery

Mosque

House of Gen.
Townshend

Snipers

THE BESIEGED BRITISH
GARRISON AT KUT
1915–16

Ottoman line
during the floods

January 10, the men's daily food allotment had been cut by one-third. Later that month, it was reduced to half the original amount. In late January, the first of the garrison's horses was slaughtered for food, and in the coming months, British soldiers worked out a rigorous taste taxonomy of the animal kingdom. "For dinner we had a very excellent roast joint of horse and some rice," one officer wrote. "I find that first-class horse is better than second-class mule, and only second to second-rate young donkey. It beats camel and eclipses buffalo altogether." Mule stew was pronounced delicious; likewise mule's tongue in aspic, which "was really first class and disappeared in less than no time." But the men could not bring themselves to eat Mrs. Milligan, a hen that a group of gunners had bought on the way back from Ctesiphon, intended as dinner but kept instead as a pet. As if aware of her precarious position, Mrs. Milligan quickly cleared out of camp.

As rations dwindled, deficiency diseases including scurvy and beri-beri appeared, as did tetanus, cholera, dysentery, colic, jaundice, malaria, and tuberculosis. In the field hospital, with its beleaguered doctors and impoverished supplies, the sick lay side by side with the wounded. Conditions there—damp, dark, dirty, and well within range of enemy shells—"would make a London surgeon speechless with disgust," a British officer observed. Men remanded to the hospital were reported to beg to be sent back to the front lines.

Morale was sinking. British casualties were running 150 to 200 a day; during lulls in the fighting, Townshend's men emerged from the trenches to bury their dead in the palm grove outside of town. Auctions were held for dead men's things: soap and cigarettes, whisky and tobacco, a shaving mirror, a chocolate bar. When enemy fire kept the British from burying their countrymen, the dead remained where they had fallen. "We got accustomed to the dead things in the trenches, and ate by them and slept by them," one British officer wrote. "After all, they are only earth, full of memories as is an old coat."

Providentially, the British relief force was now assembled at Ali-al-Gharbi, 56 miles downriver. Commanded by Lieutenant General Sir Fenton Aylmer and numbering 19,000, it would start for Kut on January 3. Then the rains came.

In January 1916, cataracts of rain began falling on Mesopotamia, and soon the men could scarcely remember a time when it had not rained. The land turned to mud, and as the relief force inched its way up the Tigris, horses sank up to their withers, men to their waists. "No one who has not experienced Mesopotamia mud can have any conception of what it is like," a member of the force said. "It sticks to the feet like glue, making them heavy as lead, and it is slippery as ice to walk on." To fall down was to have one's mouth, and one's rifle, instantly choked.

The relief force, too, lacked adequate land and water transport. Relievers' maps were crude, and under the influence of lightning—

and the men's steel bayonets—compasses went wild. As it struggled upriver, the force was engaged by Ottoman soldiers at nearly every turn. By late January, the first attempt to relieve Kut was over. Aylmer's men had suffered some 8,000 casualties and were still 25 miles away.

On February 13, the men of Kut heard an airplane—and an explosion. Then came a strange, pulsating whining they hadn't heard before, culminating in a loud crash and a column of black smoke that rose from the town. Kut was being bombed. The box around them had closed: shooting and shelling from the sides, mines in the land below, and now, overhead, this "demon bird," as an observer called it, "with its unhappy trick of laying, in mid-air, eggs that explode on reaching the earth."

Flown by a German pilot, the bird visited Kut each night at dusk, bombing the trenches, the town, and the hospital, where it showered the already wounded in metal, bricks, and blood. By the end of the month, Kut's casualty figure stood at 2,927, including 846 killed in battle or dead from wounds, 443 dead from disease, 1,608 wounded, and 30 missing.

Logistical problems delayed Aylmer's second relief attempt until the first week of March, and in Kut, quiet optimism began to be supplanted by quiet fatalism. "We know we have got to be killed sooner or later," one British soldier said, "but we hope it will be later." Food grew scarcer. After the tinned milk ran out, the sugar went, then the eggs and the jam and finally the tea. Menus broadened to include local wildlife: Roast sparrows were not too bad, roast starlings even better, though they had to be beheaded right away or else they turned bitter. Hedgehog fried in axle grease was surprisingly palatable. Stray dogs found their way onto the table.

But when Mrs. Milligan returned unexpectedly, no one had the heart to eat her: She had become, in a manner of speaking, a war bride and arrived trailing a brood of chicks. Awash in admiration for "the way she had found herself a rooster, sat over her eggs, hatched them out and returned through shot and shell to her original home," one chronicler wrote, the gunners looked on with tender propriety as she taught her children to peck in the mud for bullets.

In the garrison, an infantryman noted, "officers and men were now so thin and weak that to walk a few hundred yards required a great effort." One day in mid-April, some black-humored wag in the officers' mess set out a dessert dish with nothing in it but an awl. NOT TO BE EATEN, an accompanying sign read. MAY BE USED FOR MAKING ANOTHER HOLE IN YOUR BELT.

Desperate for nutrients, men of the garrison took to eating weeds and other wild plants. Some proved poisonous, causing violent enteritis, whose symptoms included severe abdominal pains and vomiting. Men died, and Townshend forbade the eating of wild greens. Kut's horses—those that remained—were starving and had begun to eat their head ropes, their saddle cloths, and one another's tails.

IN MARCH, AFTER a battle at the Dujaila Redoubt, 7 miles southeast of Kut, resulting in 3,474 British casualties and 3,100 on the Ottoman side, Aylmer's second relief attempt ended. He was replaced by Major General Sir George Gorringe, who began the third relief offensive on April 17. On the twenty-second, some 16 miles below Kut, Gorringe's men came under a rain of enemy bullets while swamped in mud up to their armpits. The third and last relief attempt was over.

But before Townshend would surrender, the British tried two last-ditch gambits. The first, a perilous attempt to supply the garrison by water, foundered when the ship, a steel-clad vessel carrying 250 tons of food, ran into an enemy cable strung across the Tigris and was seized. The second was a bid by Townshend to pay Enver Pasha, the Ottoman minister of war, £2 million in exchange for the garrison's freedom after a British surrender.* Enver refused.

The garrison was now down to emergency rations: "4 oz of flour or biscuit, about 6 oz of mule meat and a morsel of chocolate." Fifteen to twenty men were dying of starvation each day. The gunners ate Mrs. Milligan and found her tough.

TOWNSHEND SURRENDERED ON April 29, 1916; the Union Jack that had flown over Kut throughout the 147-day siege was lowered and the

---

* £2 million in 1916 is the equivalent of more than £200 million, or more than $270 million, in today's money.

white flag raised. The five-month debacle had produced nearly 9,000 Ottoman casualties and cost the British a total of 33,000—23,000 in the relief force alone. There had also been almost 900 casualties among the Arab townspeople.

As they smoked the last of their tobacco in the mess, some officers pondered fleeing Kut that night, their last before the victors took over. If they were to cover themselves in a protective film of oil and, with the aid of a ship's lifebelt, slip into the water in darkness, what were the chances of floating downriver to safety, undetected by the enemy or Arab brigands? In the end, they concluded, their diminished physical state would not let them survive the six or seven hours in the water.

Only resignation remained. "Kut was in the hands of the Turks," a British officer wrote, "and we were prisoners."

CHAPTER THREE

Destination Unknown

THE EXECUTIONS BEGAN after the Ottomans marched into Kut: Anyone believed to have collaborated with the British was in peril. As one British officer recounted, scores of Arabs who had weathered the siege inside the garrison were rounded up and shot in the town square. The sheik of Kut was hanged, along with his son and nephew. A local man named Sassoon, an Ottoman Jew who had sold the British provisions, was hanged as well.

There was also looting, with some Ottoman troops, who arrived in Kut poorly clad and equipped (many lacked boots, water bottles, and even shoes), lifting the belongings of their new British captives. Expecting to be body-searched after the formal surrender, the men of the garrison had already thrown their most vital small items—watches, cameras, compasses, pistols—into the river. But no search was forthcoming, and they realized bitterly that they could have secreted those things, all of which would have been of immense use in captivity, safely on their persons.

On the morning of April 29, British officers were issued their last army pay, in gold sovereigns. Trapped afterward by entering Ottoman soldiers in one of Kut's narrow passageways, Jones and a group of his countrymen were forced at gunpoint to hold up their hands as the soldiers relieved them of their money. By squeezing his sovereigns tightly between his fingers behind his hands, Jones was able to retain five of them.

The prisoners had eaten the last of their rations on April 28; the Ottomans brought no food when they took over Kut the next day. On April 30, the first echelon of British officers, including Jones, was dispatched by steamer to an Ottoman army camp at Shumran, 8 miles upriver. The rank and file were made to walk. "Like the other belligerents, Ottomans treated officers differently than the rank and file, no matter the ethnicity or nationality," Yücel Yanıkdağ has written. "Officers were assigned orderlies and paid a salary, whereas the other ranks were expected to work."

A barren, dusty patch of desert near the river, Shumran was the staging area for the journeys into captivity—to a half dozen prisoner-of-war camps across Turkey for the officers, to labor camps for the rank and file. At Shumran, they were at last given something to eat: a pile of the hardtack known among Britons as Turkish army biscuits, dumped in a heap in the dust. Roundish, hard as stone, and made from coarse wholemeal flour, the biscuits were, along with bulgur, a staple of the Ottoman soldier's diet. To the British, they resembled dog biscuits and were, more than one Kut survivor later wrote, patently unfit for any dog to eat. "Unfortunately," a British officer said, "they contained so much dirt, husk and extraneous matter that it required a powerful and unimpaired digestion to cope with them."

The biscuits further taxed the health of the Kut captives, many of whom were already suffering the violent symptoms of enteritis. "A man turned green and foamed at the mouth," one observer recalled. "His eyes became sightless and the most terrible moans conceivable came from his inner being, a wild, terrible retching sort of vomiting moan." During the week at Shumran, some 300 men died from enteritis, dysentery, or starvation, along with ailments such as cholera. Desperate for something safe to eat, prisoners bartered what little they had with local villagers—a pair of boots for some rice, an overcoat for a few dates.

ON MAY 4, a steamer carrying Jones's echelon left Shumran for Baghdad on the first leg of the voyage to the camps. They were not told where or when their journey would end. Aboard ship were nearly a hundred British officers, at least sixty Indian officers, and scores of orderlies, selected by the British from their rank and file. As the boat slid upriver, the prisoners watched as bands of Arabs on shore jeered and drew their fingers expressively across their throats. On May 6,

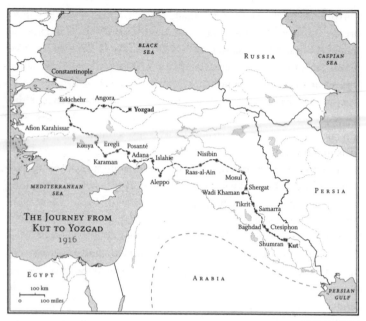

THE JOURNEY FROM
KUT TO YOZGAD
1916

JONATHAN CORUM

they passed Azizieh, and on the eighth, Ctesiphon, the site of Townshend's pivotal defeat five and a half months earlier.

On the ninth, the boat reached Baghdad, where the captives were taken ashore and paraded through the center of town "as in a Roman triumph," one later wrote.* Marched a quarter mile beyond the city, they were deposited in disused Ottoman cavalry barracks. On May 11, they were allowed into the city, under guard, in groups of twelve. They called at the American consulate, where the consul, understanding what they would need most in captivity, slipped each of them three Turkish gold lira from his private store. Two of Jones's lira would become playing pieces in his confidence game.

The next day they received their salaries: Under the terms of their captivity, British officers were to be paid monthly at Ottoman army rates. With their carefully husbanded coins they would be able to buy food—oranges, chapattis, small cakes, and the thick yogurt known as labneh—from hawkers along the trek.

---

* The British did likewise with captured Ottoman combatants.

On May 12, the echelon boarded a train for Samarra. This leg, 70 miles, was one of the few that could be made by rail. Germany had plans to build a railroad stretching from Berlin to Baghdad, a feat of engineering that would greatly help the Ottoman war effort. But in the summer of 1916 the project was more vision than reality. "At the moment the railway was merely a series of disjointed sections across illogical patches of desert," a later chronicler explained. "Wherever there were mountains, or structural difficulties to be overcome, there was no railway."

Arriving in Samarra that night, the prisoners awaited further transport. For three days they remained at the station, with little water, bedding down each night on the gravel platform. On May 15, the transport came: donkeys in varying states of physical fitness. The men loaded them with their remaining baggage and, flanked by armed Arab guards on horseback, embarked on the 370-mile desert trek to Raas-al-Ain, where the railway reappeared. Most of the prisoners walked. There weren't enough donkeys for baggage and men.

"We had not marched for many months, and for months we had been on reduced rations; and as, hour after hour, we continued our journey . . . every one began to get very weary," Major Edward Sandes, who would be dispatched to Yozgad with Jones, recalled. "Once we were allowed to fall out to fill our water-bottles from the Tigris when we were near it; and later again, during a ten-minutes halt, we found ourselves on the banks of a pond of stagnant water which many of us sampled, driven to it by our thirst."

The lack of fresh water would plague them throughout the trip. The Tigris was polluted; when they occasionally passed a fresh stream, the guards would herd the donkeys into it, letting them foul the water before the captives drank. Once, after a day's desert march, they were ordered to bivouac in a dry, dirty site. When an officer protested that a site near water was close at hand, a guard lashed him with a whip.

There was danger outside the column, too. Along the trek, stronger officers kept their eyes on weaker ones, making sure they did not falter and get left to the mercies of marauding brigands. But many— exhausted, ill, and frail after Kut and Shumran—fell anyway. From time to time the column stopped to bury its dead.

They reached Tikrit on May 16, having made the 35 miles from Samarra in a day and a half. The column pressed on to Mosul, 120 miles northwest, arriving on May 25. That afternoon, Enver Pasha, the war minister, swept up to their barracks in a grand motorcar. Surrounded by staff, he addressed the captives in elegant French, reiterating what he had assured Townshend upon the surrender: Prisoners of war would be treated "as Precious and Honoured Guests of the Ottoman Government." *

If they were the precious and honored guests, the officers remarked acidly to one another in the years that followed, then God help the ordinary prisoners.

THEY LEFT MOSUL on May 27 for the desert trek to Raas-al-Ain, in what is now Syria. For this leg, they were given four-wheeled carts, drawn by ponies, but there were so few carts that each man could ride just one hour in every four. And so they marched, tongues swollen, throats aflame. By June 1 they had marched through the worst of the desert and passed into a series of ghost towns: The Armenians who had lived there had been murdered by the Turks in the genocide of 1915. As the column passed through, officers saw the remains of men, women, and children in the village wells.†

The column reached Raas-al-Ain on June 8 and bivouacked near

---

* As Yanıkdağ points out, "The 'prisoners as the guests of the Sultan' mantra [is] a phrase that originally comes from Ottoman soldier training manuals. These instructed officers to tell their illiterate enlisted men that the captured prisoners did not belong to them but were the guests of the Sultan."

† At the start of the twentieth century, there were more than 2 million Armenians living in the Ottoman Empire, most in Anatolia, including the town of Yozgad and its environs; tensions between the empire's Christian Armenian minority and its Muslim Turkish majority had existed to varying degrees for generations. After the war began in 1914, Ottoman authorities, fearing that many Armenians would be loyal to the Russians, and dreading the possibility of an independent Armenian state, deemed the Armenian population a threat to empire. In early 1915, under the command of Enver Pasha, the Ottoman military demobilized and murdered its ethnic Armenian soldiers. The systematic murder of Armenian civilians, or their deportation to concentration camps in the desert, soon followed. Modern historians estimate conservatively that by 1916 between 600,000 and 1 million Armenians had been killed outright or had died along the forced marches to the camps. By war's end, murder and deportation had eliminated 90 percent of the Armenian population in Ottoman lands.

the railway station. Except for the two days in Mosul, they had marched continuously for twenty-five days. There had been 370 miles between Samarra and Raas-al-Ain, and Sandes estimated that he had walked for nearly 270 of them.

On June 10 their train came, pulling a single passenger coach joined to a string of boxcars meant for horses. The senior officers took seats in the coach; Jones and the other junior officers rode in the horse cars. Crossing the Euphrates on a steel girder bridge, they bumped west toward Aleppo. There the captives met with the U.S. consul, who wired their names to officials in London, the first word their families had that they were alive. On June 13, they boarded a train, arriving at Islahie, 90 miles north in Turkey, later that day. There the railway ended, with the mountains ahead.

At Islahie, they got carts again. These were larger, letting each man ride every other hour. Setting off on June 14 in bare, stony country, they began to climb. The carts had no springs, and as they jolted painfully over the Anti-Taurus range, many men, despite worn boots and ravaged feet, got out and walked. Night fell, and they negotiated tight mountain roads, bounded by sheer drops of hundreds of feet, in darkness. Attaining a summit, the column began to wind its way down, and that, Sandes wrote, posed new problems:

> The descent of a caravan of Turkish carts down a mountain road is a wonderful sight, but to be a passenger in one of those carts is too exciting for the average European. The gradients are as steep as will allow a pony to get a foothold, there is no parapet wall to prevent a cart from falling headlong to the bottom of the ravine, and *there are no brakes*. Add to these facts that the harness is largely of string, that the ponies are only half trained, and the driver is a fatalist of fatalists, and you can picture the state of mind of the unhappy passenger unused to the ways of the country.

After several days' travel by cart, truck, and foot, they reached Posanté, in the Taurus range. The railway resumed there, and on June 17 they left by train, rattling through the mountains on the four-day journey north to Angora—present-day Ankara. On the eighteenth, the train stopped briefly at Konya, where the Hindu officers disembarked and were remanded to a segregated prison camp. Farther north, at Eskichehr, the Muslim officers were removed to another camp. The train, now carrying only British officers and their orderlies, continued toward Angora. There they would be told their final destinations.*

JONES'S PROMOTION TO second lieutenant, which had come just weeks before the Kut siege began, may well have saved his life. As harrowing as the officers' trek was, the odyssey of the rank and file—known in British military parlance as "other ranks"—was far worse. Unlike the officers, they were made to walk nearly the entire way, flogged ever onward by their guards. Officers in later echelons could see the remains of the rank and file who had gone before them, the victims of brigands, jackals, and vultures. Those who survived the trek were placed in labor camps, assigned to build the Berlin-to-Baghdad railway. Working in brutal heat and bitter cold, they were soon ravaged by pneumonia, malaria, typhus, and cholera. An Austrian officer who came upon a band of British laborers described what he saw as "a scene from Dante's 'Inferno.'"

There are no precise casualty figures for the other ranks' forced march: It is nearly impossible to ascribe deaths to the march per se as opposed to the conditions of battle, starvation, and disease that preceded it. However, Yanıkdağ writes: "It is documented that of the 2,680 British rank and file taken captive in Kut in April 1916, 1,306 (48 percent) had died by 25 October 1918, and another 449 were untraced

---

* The voyages into captivity of Ottoman prisoners of the Allies were just as arduous. For Ottomans taken by the Russians, for instance, "the journey to the interior from the front started on foot, sometimes with no shoes," Yanıkdağ has written. "Once near a rail junction, prisoners were loaded onto boxcars and sent to either points north-west in European Russia or east to Siberia. Especially for the ranks [non-officers], the travel in unhygienic, lice-infested, overcrowded, and bolted shut boxcars spelled disaster. Some died from wounds, exposure, disease, or even suffocation during travel and were unceremoniously left by the railway tracks at the next occasion of unbolting the doors. Some others, numbering at least a few hundred cases that have been recorded, froze to death or died of hunger when Russian transportation officials separated some boxcars at connection points and left them locked and unattended for days."

therefore believed dead, bringing the likely mortality to 65 percent. Indian mortality rates for the same period, with 1,773 untraced, ranged from 12.3 to 59.5 percent."

As for General Townshend, whose decision to stand at Kut in the winter of 1915 brought death, injury, or exploitation to tens of thousands—he passed the remainder of the war confined to the scenic island of Prinkipo, in the Sea of Marmara. There he was billeted in a waterfront villa that had once been the summer home of the British consul, a house that resembled, in the words of a later writer, "an English country vicarage." He was, for the duration, very likely the Ottomans' only precious and honored guest.

ARRIVING IN ANGORA on June 21, Jones's echelon was allowed to write postcards of four lines to their families. (The length restriction had been instituted to avoid overtaxing Ottoman censors.) In his postcard to Mair, dated June 25, Jones wrote:

I am in excellent health en route for an unknown destination. Tell father that all is well as I am only allowed to write one postcard of 4 lines. Keep cheerful, and apply to our War Office for my address. Much love to my dear one.

Harry

In reality, Jones would write afterward, "we were then travel-worn, footsore and starved":

The memories of the awful desert march, . . . the misery of being herded and driven and clubbed across the wastes like so many stolen cattle, and sheer weariness of body had nigh broken our spirit. Long afterwards a British officer, captured on the Suez front, who saw the Kut prisoners pass through Angora, told me, "When we saw your mob being driven along I turned to my neighbour and said, 'By God! Those fellows have been through it! They're broken men, every one of them!' You all looked fit for nothing but hospital."

They were given their destinations soon afterward. Senior officers and their orderlies would be dispatched to the prison camp at Broussa, in northwest Asiatic Turkey near the Sea of Marmara. The rest would go a hundred miles inland to Yozgad, one of the most isolated camps in Asia Minor.

CHAPTER FOUR

A Hundred Springs

ON JUNE 25, 1916, the junior officers and their orderlies left Angora for the journey to Yozgad, five days by cart through wild, rocky, gorge-filled country. In a letter to his father from captivity later that year, Jones would offer a characteristically stoic description of his voyage from Kut, writing, "The only thing that kept us going—in my case certainly—was the knowledge that every step was a yard nearer home." But the English writer Dorina Neave, who interviewed Jones for her 1937 book on the siege, wrote that during the five-day trip from Angora "his depression increased as they proceeded farther and farther from all signs of civilization."

About a hundred British officers would eventually spend the war in Yozgad. As a 1918 British government report observed drily:

The Turkish Government has announced that in its zeal for the comfort of the British officers in its hands the finest situations in Asia Minor have been chosen for their internment; and if a prisoner of war were in the position of a summer tourist in peace-time this consideration would be admirable. Yozgad, Kastamuni, Afion-Kara-Hissar, Gedis [Kedos], are places of interest and beauty: the mountain scenery of Central Anatolia is very striking, the summer climate excellent. Unfortunately this attractive landscape is buried deep in snow throughout the winter; the cold is intense, the places named being from three to four thousand feet above sea-level; communication with the outer world (Afion alone is on the railway) becomes difficult or almost impossible; and the picturesque towns, with their streams and valleys and mediaeval citadels, have none but the most primitive provision against the rigour of the season. This would be so even in the time of peace. The difficulties of life under such conditions in war-time can hardly be imagined.

On June 30, just after dawn, Jones and his comrades—many ill, all exhausted and painfully thin—began their approach to Yozgad after a journey of sixty-two days and nearly 2,000 miles. The town, whose name means "a hundred springs," was ranged over the steep slopes of a high plateau, surrounded by barren hills; before the war, it had had a population of about 20,000. Within the town there were fruit trees and poplars; a mosque, whose slender minaret, Sandes wrote, looked "for all the world like a sharpened pencil pointing to the sky"; and whitewashed houses with red tile roofs.

Sketch of the prisoner-of-war camp at Yozgad, made by one of the British officers interned there. JOHNSTON AND YEARSLEY, FOUR-FIFTY MILES TO FREEDOM (1919)

The camp comprised two of these houses, a typical accommodation for prisoners of war in the region. "Ottomans did not use barbed wire camps," Yanıkdağ explains, "but placed the prisoners in houses, school buildings, hotels and other buildings." The houses at Yozgad were empty thanks to the murder of their Armenian owners the year before; inside, Sandes found himself haunted by absence. "In various rooms and landings of our upper house were small niches with traces of sacred pictures pasted on the walls," he wrote. "Soon after our arrival I found a number of old exercise-books of children, containing translations from Armenian into French and vice versa. . . . The simple exercises in a childish hand . . . made pathetic reading when one thought of the cruel fate of the innocent little writer."

Situated on a hillside one above the other, the prisoners' residences became known as Upper House and Lower House. Each was set in a garden flanked by high stone walls and guarded by elderly local gendarmes, whose geriatric aspect was rivaled by that of their weapons, breech-loading rifles from about 1870. Though the houses were large, they could scarcely accommodate the initial cohort of more than fifty officers, plus orderlies. In Upper House, to which Jones and Sandes were consigned, as many as seven officers shared a single room. This gave each man a personal space of just over 42 square feet, about the size of a prison cell.

Upper and Lower Houses were thin-walled, barren of furniture, and almost entirely lacking in sanitary arrangements, a situation aggravated by the arrival of a second contingent of officers on July 16. "The conditions under which we lived for the first month were very bad," recalled Lieutenant Arthur Holyoake, a member of the second contingent, which also included Jones's future co-conspirator, Cedric Hill. "The sanitation was disgraceful for 89 persons. There were two long rooms each with a hole in the floor and everything fell down into a huge pit under the house which was never emptied. The smell was appalling. Our water supply consisted of a small trickle, which was fed from an open stream. When any gardener higher up the stream decided to irrigate his garden our supply ceased." For these accommodations, the captives had to pay rent to the Ottoman government; Jones recalled the tab as having been £5 per month, equivalent to more than £500, or nearly $700, today.

The conditions the prisoners faced were typical for captives of both sides throughout the region. "Far less prepared for war and not nearly as modern or industrialized as its enemies, the Ottoman Empire suffered from major problems of logistics, shortages of food and medical personnel," Yanıkdağ has written. "Ottoman transportation was primitive, incomplete, or non-existent in some regions of the Empire.

From all these shortcomings, prisoners suffered greatly, [and] so did the Ottoman soldiers themselves." Illuminating these deficiencies, he added, "does not excuse or explain away any possible ill-treatment or sufferings of Kut or any other prisoners, but places it in the context of a larger problem experienced by Ottoman civilians, officers, soldiers, and enemy prisoners alike."

Upper House at Yozgad, where Jones held his first séances.

SANDES, *IN KUT AND CAPTIVITY* (1919)

FOR WEEKS, THE prisoners were confined to their houses almost twenty-four hours a day. The camp commandant, Binbashi Kiazim Bey,* feared they would attempt escape and was terrified of censure from his superiors in the Turkish War Office. An Ottoman artillery officer, Kiazim had long since completed his active service. The command of a prisoner-of-war camp in an isolated town, where he could do largely as he pleased, far from Constantinople's direct supervision, was a nice soft posting; he was determined that nothing should com-

---

* "Binbashi" ("Bimbashi," in Jones's Romanization) denotes the rank of major. "Bey" is an honorific title, roughly comparable to "Mr.," which traditionally follows a Turkish man's given name.

promise it. "As a specimen of the Turkish officer of the older generation, the commandant . . . deserves special mention," Sandes would
write in 1924, in an evocative if Orientalist depiction:

> Imagine a man of middle age, tall and erect, dressed always in a
> uniform frock-coat of light grey, and wearing a woolly Turkish
> kalpak (cap), gold-braided on top. His features aquiline, his hair
> white, and his movements always extremely slow and deliberate.
> A semi-invalid, who doubtless had been recalled to service for the
> war, he led a life of seclusion and indolence. His face was remark-
> able for its pallor, and from this mask looked a pair of eyes which
> glinted like those of a hawk. He seldom raised his voice, yet this
> softness of address was belied by the cruel line of his mouth. His
> most marked characteristics were his extreme caution, his dis-
> trust of all men, his sphinx-like gravity and impassiveness, and his
> superstition. Of respectable birth . . . he was ready nevertheless to
> accept commissions from all shop-keepers trading with the camp.
> In his dealings with the prisoners his line was complete inactivity
> and inaccessibility. He would answer no letters, would grant no
> interviews, and for months was never even seen.

On Kiazim's orders, the prisoners were placed in lockdown for three
weeks from the day the first cohort arrived. "Caged and helpless," they
could do little more than lie on their mattresses—the only amenities
provided—and sleep or smoke. Their brief, dismal meals were served
in Lower House, to which the inmates of Upper House were marched
under guard, the only time they were let out. They were charged ex-
orbitant fees for the food, which was supplied by Ali, a local contractor
who paid kickbacks to the Commandant.

Passable at the start, meals deteriorated quickly. Bad bread took
the place of good, goat replaced mutton, wine was watered. Linen and
dishes were set out unwashed; broken chairs went unmended; portions dwindled. The officers had received no salary since Baghdad,
and Ali's extortion would soon bankrupt them. But if they did not pay,
they did not eat. A delegation of prisoners sent word to Kiazim, asking
him to have the contractor lower his prices. The Commandant sent
back a two-word reply: "Eat less."

It was this cold, remote figure under whom the captives would live for more than two years—and whom Jones and Hill would have the fearsome task of bending to their will. "In the middle of September one of our number got a postcard from a friend in the 2nd Echelon of Kut prisoners at Kastamuni,"* Sandes wrote, "from which we gathered that the treatment of our officers at that place was excellent as compared with ours—in fact, we heard later that some Germans at Kastamuni had objected because the prisoners dined too often with the commandant. We envied our fellow-prisoners at Kastamuni their good-natured commandant. Our own Turkish guards at Yozgad admitted that our commandant, Kiazim Bey, was 'choke fenna' (very bad). . . . It was our misfortune to be under such a man."

Kiazim spoke neither English nor French; all communication was transacted through the camp interpreter, Moïse Eskenazi, a young Ottoman Jewish soldier whom the British called "the Pimple" for his diminutive stature and oleaginous mien.† Sandes offers a memorable description:

> The interpreter was an exceedingly stumpy young man of about twenty, with very short legs encased in breeches and gaiters, and remarkably short-sighted eyes peering through pince-nez. He wore the uniform of a chaoush (sergeant), but was really a species of cadet. . . . He was a good linguist, speaking Turkish and French fluently, English passably well, German slightly, and I believe he had a smattering of Italian. His French he had learnt in Paris, where he had lived for five years as a student previous to the war. . . . He was as sharp as a needle and remarkably observant. Though inclined to be conceited and patronising, he was not averse from being bribed with chocolate or biscuits, or even from asking for eatables and clothes in the most barefaced manner.

---

* Kastamuni (present-day Kastamonu) lies about 120 miles northwest of Yozgad.
† The name may also have been influenced by the British silent-film character Pimple, a baggy-pants buffoon who featured in a string of short comedies released between 1912 and 1918. Played by the well-known stage comic Fred Evans, Pimple was usually depicted as a childlike bumbler who landed himself in a series of scrapes. The Pimple films were widely seen in Britain and were said to have rivaled Chaplin's early pictures in popularity.

*Yozgad's commandant, Kiazim Bey, front row
center, and the Pimple, front row right.*
SANDES, *IN KUT AND CAPTIVITY* (1919)

Like the others of the subordinate Turkish staff, he was in mortal dread of the commandant, though quite ready to disobey his orders if he could do so without risk of discovery.

Imprisoned in their houses, the officers were growing desperate for exercise—even a walk would do. They appealed to the Pimple, who responded with the absurdist logic that was a hallmark of life at Yozgad. "You have completed a long journey, and you are *très maigre*," he told them. "There is no *necessity* that you go out into the country, for you have no business. Therefore, why go? The rooms are clean, and the sun gives heat in them. You have mattresses. You have some books. You have cigarettes from the town. So be patient and restful! *Lie on your mattresses, read your books, smoke your cigarettes, and be happy. You need not do anything. The war will end soon.*"

At last, in late July, Kiazim decreed that prisoners could be taken for walks in small groups. Sandes recalled the scene:

The mulazim* swaggered about with a cheap sword clanking at his side, the chaoush† ran hither and thither roaring abuse at the indolent sentries, and a guard of twelve old Turkish soldiers turned out armed to the teeth. We filed out of the gateway, two by two, with soldiers before, behind, and on each side, and marched solemnly and sedately through the town to the open country beyond. There the mulazim called a halt.

"What's up now, Mr. Moïse?" I asked.

"The mulazim says you have had a good walk, *Effendi*.‡ It is more than one mile. Now you can rest."

"But we don't *want* to rest! Great Scott! Call this a walk? We want to go to that hilltop, and that one, and that one." . . .

The Pimple translated, and the mulazim pondered and replied.

"The mulazim *effendi* thinks," explained the Pimple, "that his boots will be worn out if he walks so far. You cannot go without him. He orders that you sit down and play."

And so they did, the officers of His Majesty's Army launching into a rousing game of leapfrog in the Anatolian hills. "Never shall I forget the sight of an elderly major . . . flying ponderously over his superior officer," Sandes wrote. "It was exercise—glorious exercise. It made the blood course through the veins; it revived drooping spirits, and brought joy, laughter, forgetfulness. Turkish gentlemen from the town stopped to gaze open-mouthed at the mad English. . . . What wonder when, as the newspapers said, their country was collapsing before the might of Turkey."

OVER THE COMING months, once Kiazim was persuaded that escape was impossible, strictures were relaxed a bit. After the success of the walk in the hills, prisoners were allowed to stroll during the day in the gardens outside their houses. In early August, after the food situation had become completely untenable, a few officers were permitted to

* Lieutenant.
† Sergeant.
‡ An honorific term roughly equivalent to "sir" or "master."

visit the bazaar under guard each day to buy food for the whole camp. They found the prices for ordinary items like meat, eggs, potatoes, and bread a revelation: Ali had been charging them three and four times the going rate. Upper and Lower Houses had kitchens with wood-burning stoves, and the inmates took turns cooking meals, though Sandes harrumphed that because there were so few orderlies, officers, too, had to do their part at the stove—"not work which officer-prisoners of war should ever have to undertake." The prisoners constructed serviceable ovens out of mud, bricks, and empty kerosene tins, in which they baked a variety of pies and tarts.

"There was no end to the ingenuity of individuals in supplying their wants or adding to their few comforts," Jones would write. "We had cobblers of every grade. . . . We had knitters who could unravel a superfluous 'woolly' and convert it into excellent socks, heels and all. We had tailors whose efforts (being circumscribed by the paucity of cloth) would have brought tears of delight to the eyes of Joseph. In every house there was an embryo Harrod who kept a 'store' containing everything, 'from a needle to an anchor,' that the Turks would allow him to buy, and an accountant who evolved a system of book-keeping and book-transfer of debts which enabled those under a temporary financial cloud (a thing to which we were all subject, thanks to the irregularity of the Ottoman post) to continue making necessary purchases until the next cheque arrived."

They also made their own furniture. From the bazaar, prisoners procured empty packing crates that had been used to ship tobacco. Tobacco was a state industry, and the crates bore the monogram "ROT" ("Régie Ottomane Turquie").* It also, Sandes remarked, "aptly described the wood of which the boxes were made." Dismantling them, the prisoners were nonetheless able to turn them into beds, tables, chairs, and shelves, using tools bought from the bazaar; for weeks the houses rang with the music of saws and hammers. Hill, who arrived at Yozgad in July, made his bed by nailing legs to a disused door.

The furniture was welcome, but it threw into relief a problem that had plagued the captives since their earliest days in Mesopotamia.

* The phrase roughly translates as "Ottoman Company, Turkey."

"I . . . bought half a dozen planks, and, with a few tools and much hard labour, made myself a bed," Sandes recalled:

> The planks were clean, the room . . . was swept daily, and my bedding was well aired. . . . On the third night in that new bed I was bitten to pieces. I . . . made a paste of insect powder and smeared the bed liberally with it, and hoped that the enemy had been defeated. . . . Two nights later the foe assaulted with renewed vigour. I repeated the process, bought four saucers, filled them with creosote, placed a saucer under each leg of the bed, and turned in with a happy mind. The truce lasted just forty-eight hours. . . . A kind orderly, experienced in these matters, then suggested the boiling-water treatment. . . . Every Monday I carried my bed into the road, got a large kettle of boiling water, poured the liquid into every crack, and gloated over the slaughter of the innocents which followed. A new generation started the next day, but they were mere infants and met their doom on the following Monday before they really knew their business.

The severe overcrowding was eventually eased after Kiazim allocated the prisoners several more empty houses. Among them were Hospital House, where Hill would live, and what became known as Posh Castle—so called not because it was opulent, but because of the raucous "poshings" regularly administered there. (The word, coined by the captives, denoted "a good-tempered cross between a riot and a rugby scrum," Jones explained. "The object of the 'poshers' is conjointly and severally to sit upon the victim and to pinch, smack, tickle, or otherwise torture him until he begs for mercy.")

They also started to get money. In July 1916, the U.S. embassy began sending prisoners a monthly stipend of 3 lira apiece, which over time grew to 15. In September, the Ottomans paid British officers their first salary since May, though at a lower rate than before. But despite these small comforts, their lives were stiflingly empty. "We dragged out our monotonous existence from day to day," Sandes wrote. "We ate, we worked, we played, we slept, and we tried not to drown our sorrows too deeply in 'raki.'" (Raki, an anise-scented local spirit made from fermented raisins, could have strange effects. "For a time," Sandes wrote, "it seems powerless to elate; and then, suddenly, it sweeps away self-control, reason and even consciousness, especially in the novice.")

They sought what diversions their circumscription would allow. After chess, cards, and roulette had had their day, they began a twice-weekly nighttime lecture series. By the light of oil lamps, the audience of prisoners massed on one of the landings amid a haze of tobacco smoke as the evening's speaker delivered a talk on a subject he knew well. Topics included tea planting, trapping in Canada, crime in Burma (this was Jones), beekeeping, cow punching, the Geological Survey of Egypt, sleeping sickness, and wireless telegraphy. "On the whole, the most popular lectures were those dealing with non-military subjects," Sandes said. "We had all had enough of war."

Prisoners also taught continuing-education classes, in subjects ranging from physics and mathematics to agriculture and engineering to French, German, and Hindustani. "We became a minor University, with Professors who made up in enthusiasm what they lacked in experience," Jones wrote. "Memories of their own youth made some of them set 'home work,' and it was no uncommon thing to run across a doughty warrior, most unacademically dressed in ragged khaki, seeking in vain for some quiet corner of the garden where he might wrestle uninterrupted with the latest vagaries of x, or convert into graceful Urdu a sonorous passage from the 'Decline and Fall of the Roman Empire.'"

In October, prisoners began playing field hockey in the garden below Upper House, though there was room for only four men a side. Their sticks were fashioned from branches cut covertly from nearby fruit trees; the ball was anything that could be wadded up and hit. They reveled in the exercise, though several players developed serious infections through abrasions sustained in the game: The camp had only a tiny dispensary, stocked with very few drugs.

They also made music. Sandes, an amateur violinist, bought a small violin of cheap plain wood from the bazaar. Playing from memory (he had no access to sheet music), he serenaded his countrymen with Gilbert and Sullivan, selections from grand opera, and the popular standards of the day as the Upper House landing, the only place large enough to accommodate them all at once, swelled with smoke

The prisoners' "exercise lane" between houses at Yozgad.

JONES, *THE ROAD TO EN-DOR* (1919)

and song. Over time, governed by what the bazaar had to offer, a tiny orchestra was assembled at Yozgad, comprising three violins, a flute, and a guitar.

As DECEMBER APPROACHED, the officers decided to write and perform a holiday musical show, *The Fair Maiden of Yozgad*. The set was made from pasted-together sheets of newspaper—"printed in French and very pro Turk, the only paper we were allowed to have"—gaily painted with aniline dye. The curtain was pinned-together blankets, reeled open and closed with spools of cotton thread. The footlights were candles set in tins, manned by a row of orderlies seated on the floor. Music was supplied by "Don Sandeso's Famous Orchestra," whose entire membership was Sandes, tucked into a corner with his violin. Prisoners—whose roles included the fair maiden Saba, the dashing Captain Vere de Vere, and the Good Spirit Raki (played by Jones)—were outfitted in fantastical getups pieced from scraps of fabric bought at the bazaar. Wigs were made from sheepskins.

The production had to be rehearsed in secret, for it lampooned their captors in terms that left little to the imagination, including unvarnished caricatures of the Commandant and the Pimple. But the Turks got wind that a show was in the works, and Kiazim was eager to see it. The British would have to stall them until after *The Fair Maiden of Yozgad* had played its first and only night. "If any of them had seen the performance," Sandes said, "there would have been an end of such amusements, and solitary confinement for the actors."

On December 16, 1916, after evening roll call, the captives crowded onto the Upper House landing. To their surprise, certain seats in the front row were marked "Engaged"—not something one expects to find in an ersatz theater in the middle of a prisoner-of-war camp. "Their surprise changed to loud applause when a pretty flapper looking most demure was escorted [to those seats] by her mother in a very décolleté evening dress," wrote Lieutenant Arthur Holyoake, who had conceived the show. "The flapper was the Padre (Capt. Willcox) and a very pretty girl he made. Capt. Phillips . . . was the mother, whose ample bosom was a trifle spoiled by his hairy chest. . . . The audience had barely recovered when the curtain went up."

The show, in the style of the romantic melodramas of the day, was a rollicking success. Playing the good fairy, Jones "looked the most repulsive type of elderly female chorister that ever graced the stage of a low class theatre," Holyoake wrote approvingly. The actor playing the Pimple sang lustily of his habit of pilfering food and clothing from parcels sent to the prisoners.

The real Pimple approached them the next day. "There was much noise in the upper house last night," he said. "What was happening?"

"It was only another *rehearsal,*" the prisoners told him.

"When is the final performance?" he asked. "The Commandant is desirous to view it."

"We are very sorry, Mr. Moïse," they replied, "but we must tell you the unfortunate truth of this business. We had another rehearsal last night, as we have already said. This time it was a *dress* rehearsal. You understand? A rehearsal *in costume.* But the acting was so bad that, in spite of all our trouble, we have decided to drop [the show], so you will never be able to see it."

"A thousand pities!" the Pimple cried. "I was hoping for much pleasure. Alas! You English are too easily discouraged."

No DIVERSION COULD leaven the realities of captivity for long. The prisoners' time was minutely regulated: They were counted each day, morning and evening, and locked in each night. Their accommodations were spartan and in constant need of repair: When the rains began in December, every house brimmed with buckets, basins, and jugs, placed to catch the water that poured through holes in the roofs. Visiting Yozgad that month, a Red Cross inspector pointed out an especially large hole. "Let us hope it will not often rain!" was an Ottoman staff officer's response.

Their correspondence was censored, and its length and frequency curtailed. At first they were allowed to write only a single four-line postcard each week; later in 1916 the allowance was increased to both sides of a single sheet of paper. Nor was receiving mail a dependable proposition: A letter from England could take a month or more to reach Yozgad. On a single day in October 1916, after receiving no mail for six weeks, Arthur Holyoake got eleven letters at once, dated from July 22 to September 4. Parcels could take six or even eight months (if they arrived at all) and were sometimes looted by the staff before being turned over to the recipients. "It was obvious," Dorina Neave wrote, "that many of the parcels had been stolen by the guards, who wore socks and garments sent out for the prisoners."

Medical arrangements remained dire. The autumn after they arrived, Captain Claude Bignell, a popular officer, developed blood poisoning after scratching his knee while playing hockey. Despite the efforts of Capt. William O'Farrell, a British Army doctor captured in the Sinai, plus a round-the-clock volunteer team of officers, Bignell died in late November: Wartime shortages had rendered the drugs that might have saved him unavailable. "This was the first death in the Camp and everyone felt very depressed," Holyoake wrote. "We gave him as near to a military funeral as we could manage and he was buried on the hillside just outside the town."

As the year ran its course, with no end to the war in sight, the captives increasingly courted the psychological malady that would soon be named "barbed-wire disease." Identified in 1918 based on studies of World War I prisoners, it is characterized by depression, hopelessness, nightmares, and crushing ennui.

"The last days of the momentous year 1916 ended with Yozgad . . . under snow, but with us, prisoners of war, at last fairly snug and comfortable," Sandes wrote. "Our food was plentiful, though not of the best quality. White bread, wheat porridge, meat, vegetables, honey, apples, figs, prunes, dried apricots, raisins, flour, sugar, and eggs served to keep us fit and even fat, and cost remarkably little. There was hardly any illness, and we should have been happy were it not for the terrible monotony of our life, the uncertainty of the arrival of our letters and parcels, and, above all, the loss of that inestimable boon—freedom. Only those who have suffered imprisonment for a long period can know what loss of liberty means."

Then, in February 1917, a postcard arrived for Jones. "I did not know this innocent-looking piece of cardboard was going to provide the whole camp with a subject for discussion for a year to come," he would write. It would also, he added, "prove the open sesame that got two of us out of Turkey."

BOOK TWO

GHOSTS

CHAPTER FIVE

Spooked

WHEN THE MAIL came that day, Jones was dismayed. There was nothing from Mair, and nothing from his parents. The only thing addressed to him was a postcard from an aunt in Britain. But her message contained an intriguing proposal: Knowing her nephew faced long empty hours in captivity, she suggested that he and his comrades try experimenting with a Ouija board. Though few of the men were spiritualist believers, they held their first séance the next night. "We took it up," Jones wrote, "for the same reason as we took up philosophy, mathematics, French, Spanish, and a score of other pursuits—to pass the time and to break the hopeless monotony of our days."

"TALKING BOARDS," AS the Ouija and similar devices were first known, arose in the 1880s amid the spiritualist fervor that suffused the Victorian age. Previously, spiritualists hoping to channel voices through the ether would spell out communications through a series of audible raps: A member of the séance would chant the alphabet aloud, and a knock would sound when the correct letter was reached. But the chant-and-rap method was agonizingly slow, and the spirits had much to say. Imagine how much faster the dead could speak, late nineteenth-century spiritualists realized, if they had recourse to boards equipped with letters, numbers, and pointing tools—hardware for the original Ethernet.

In 1886, the Associated Press reported that just such boards were being used by spiritualists in northern Ohio. Soon afterward a Maryland man, Charles Kennard (no spiritualist, but a shrewd businessman who knew a sure thing when he saw one), began manufacturing them commercially. In 1890 he established the Kennard Novelty Company in Baltimore with four investors, among them Elijah Bond, a patent lawyer. The next year Bond was awarded United States patent 446,054 for a "toy or game . . . which I designate as an 'Ouija Or Egyptian luck-board.'"*

"The objects of the invention," Bond's patent states, "are to produce a toy or game by which two or more persons can amuse themselves by asking questions of any kind and having them answered. . . . The invention consists of a board of suitable thickness, having the letters of the alphabet printed, painted, engraved, or affixed upon it in any suitable manner, but flush with the surface, and also the numerals . . . and in conjunction therewith of a peculiarly-shaped table [the planchette] having legs and a pointer."

The genius of the board's early marketing lay in its being pitched both as a tool of serious spiritual inquiry and a lighthearted parlor amusement—one with the added attraction of allowing the fingers of respectable Victorian men to touch the fingers of respectable Victorian women as they worked the planchette in tandem. "The Ouija is, without doubt, the most interesting, remarkable and mysterious production of the nineteenth century," an 1891 newspaper ad proclaimed:

> Its operations are always interesting and frequently invaluable, answering as it does questions concerning the past, present and future with marvelous accuracy. It furnishes never-failing amusement and recreation for all classes, while for the scientific or thoughtful its mysterious movements invite the most careful research and investigation—apparently forming the link which unites the known with the unknown, the material with the immaterial. It forces upon us the conviction that a great truth was contained in the statement of the Danish Prince: "There are more

---

* The origin of the word "Ouija" is fittingly enigmatic. While the name has long been believed to be an amalgam of *oui* and *ja*—the French and German words for "yes"—some sources describe it as having been suggested by Elijah Bond's sister-in-law Helen Peters, perhaps in partial homage to the Victorian novelist Ouida. (Ouida, born Maria Louise Ramé, was an associate of Oscar Wilde and Wilkie Collins. Her pen name derived from her childhood mispronunciation of her middle name.)

things in Heaven and Earth, Horatio, than were ever dreamed of
in thy philosophy." Price, $1.49.

The board was an immediate success. By 1892, Kennard was operating six factories in the United States and a seventh in London.
Ouija's popularity continued on both sides of the Atlantic through

*Patent-application drawings for the first commercial Ouija board,
manufactured by the Kennard Novelty Company of Baltimore from
the early 1890s onward.* UNITED STATES PATENT AND TRADEMARK OFFICE

the first decades of the twentieth century, buoyed from 1914 onward by the intense spiritual searching that perhaps only a war can bring.

JONES HAD NEVER used a Ouija board, but his aunt's postcard gave precise instructions. His first order of business was to make the board, and his earliest was simply the top of a table, itself made from a packing crate. William O'Farrell polished the tabletop with the hem of his coat until the glass could slide across it. Other prisoners cut twenty-six squares of paper, labeled each with a letter of the alphabet, and arranged them in a circle on top.

Doc O'Farrell, as he was known, took a seat at the table opposite Jones, and each put his fingertips on the inverted glass. For fifteen minutes nothing happened. Others took turns at the board, with identical results, before Jones and O'Farrell resumed their places.

"Ask it some question," one of the prisoners suggested.

O'Farrell addressed the board soberly: "WHO—ARE—YOU?"

Seemingly of its own accord, the glass began to move. Slowly it traversed the tabletop in widening circles, until it came to rest at the letter B. "B!" everyone cried in awed unison. Circling the board again, it touched the R. "R!" the prisoners chorused. But that was all.

Night after night the men tried to wring sense from the spirits. The table's uneven surface, they decided, was impeding the flow of the glass, so they tried a large enameled tray instead. The glass moved better but still wrote only nonsense. Then a fellow prisoner, Captain Gatherer, showed them another board, one he had built a few months earlier to use in spiritual experiments of his own. Having lost his taste for spiritualism, he gave it to Jones. It was this board, a sheet of polished iron, that would become the foundation of the confidence scheme. The men of Upper House added the raised wooden ring, pasting the alphabet randomly round its circumference.

On the new board the glass sailed smoothly, though it continued writing gibberish. Weeks went by, until only Jones, O'Farrell, and two others remained: Lieutenants Alec Matthews, of the Army, and Edward Price, of the Royal Navy.

"One more shot, Bones," the Doc declared, addressing Jones by his customary nickname.

"I glanced at him, and from him to Price and Matthews," Jones recalled. "Disappointment was written on every face. Success had seemed so near, and we had laboured so hard. Was this to end as so many of our efforts at amusement had ended, in utter boredom?"

"One more shot," Jones echoed, "and as I said it the Devil of Mischief that is in every Celt whispered to me." He closed his eyes, the glass began to move, and Sally appeared.

"GOOD EVENING, SALLY!" O'Farrell boomed. "HAVE YE ANYTHIN' TO TELL US?"

"Sally had quite a lot to tell us," Jones would write. "She made love to Alec Matthews (much to his delight) in the most barefaced way, and then coolly informed him that she preferred sailor-boys. Price beamed, and replied in fitting terms. She talked seriously to the Doc (who had murmured—out of jealousy, I expect—that Sally seemed a brazen hussy), and warned us to be careful what we said in the presence of a lady. . . . She accused me of being unbecomingly dressed. (Pyjamas and a blanket—quite respectable for a prisoner.) Then she complained of 'feeling tired,' made one or two most unladylike remarks when we pressed her to tell us more, and 'went away.'"

Jones intended to come clean and tell his comrades that he had guided the glass himself, having memorized the positions of the letters long before. His humbuggery would be punished by a vigorous poshing; of that he was certain. But he was constitutionally puckish—"an arch leg-puller," Hill would call him—and found Sally and her spectral brethren too delicious to give up. He also felt he owed it to his comrades to keep his ghosts alive:

With the exception of a monotonous melancholic, who butted in at regular intervals to inform us plaintively that he was "buried alive," the spooks were a decidedly jovial lot. They kept us in touch with the outside world. We walked with them down Piccadilly, dined with them in the Troc, and tried to hear with them the music of the band. We conversed with Shackleton on his South Polar expedition, with men in the trenches in France, and with ships on the wide seas. . . . There was no place to which we could not go, nothing we could not see with the Spook's eyes, or hear with his ears. A successful night at the spook-board was the nearest we could get, outside our dreams, to a breath of freedom.

Each night the group round the board grew larger, as Jones and O'Farrell manned the glass and Price and Matthews wrote down its every utterance. Soon Jones was in too deep to confess. A spate of doubters remained, however, and he began to view their skepticism as a challenge—almost a personal affront. He vowed to himself to convert as many as he could.

One of his first successes was Major Sandes. "I decided one evening to attend one of the early séances," Sandes wrote. "It was about nine o'clock on a dark night that I stumbled up the unlit staircase to the little passage-room where Jones and his friend 'the Doc' sat before the polished iron plate with their hands on the inverted glass. A couple of guttering candles cast a ghostly light."

"Hullo! Here's 'Don Sandeso, the Bandmaster,'" one of the crowd cried. "Can he work the glass?"

"Speak to the board," Jones admonished.

"Right oh, Bones," he said, and turned to the board. "Please tell us if Sandes can work the glass."

"Yes, he can," the glass replied.

"Who with?"

"Alone."

Sandes took his seat. "I put two fingers on the glass, closed my eyes, and waited in silence for the oracle to speak. Then, as nothing happened, I asked the spook if he would kindly send a message. Slowly, slowly, the glass began to slide; then more and more rapidly. It shot from side to side of the polished surface, spelling out a meaningless jumble of letters. I opened my eyes suddenly to see who was pulling it hither and thither, but no one was touching either the glass or the table. Yet I could have sworn that someone else had hold of that glass."

Despite the lack of a sensible message, Sandes wrote afterward, "that experience changed me from a sceptic to a believer."

WHAT MADE THE glass move seemingly on its own? The answer centers on an unconscious phenomenon known as motor automatism or ideomotor action. It was first described in 1852 by the English doctor and physiologist William Benjamin Carpenter, who defined it as "muscular movement, independent . . . of volition."

Motor automatism is a product of the altered consciousness that a person attending a séance or religious rite can experience. It is what makes his hands move—and with them a planchette, divining rod, or other lightly held object—without his being aware of having directed them. The result, for the spiritually inclined, is the sensation that the object is being controlled by an unseen force. "The state in question," Carpenter wrote, "is essentially one of reverie, in which the voluntary control over the current of thought is entirely suspended, the individual being for the time (so to speak) a mere *thinking automaton*, the whole course of whose ideas is determinable by suggestions operating from without."

The divided consciousness that typifies this state—the mind simultaneously aware and unaware—was studied experimentally in the late nineteenth century by an American researcher, Gertrude Stein. (Indeed, it was *that* Gertrude Stein, who as an undergraduate at Radcliffe was a disciple of the distinguished psychologist William James.) In a scientific article of 1896—her first published writing—she and a colleague, Leon Solomons, induced the state in themselves. While performing a conscious activity such as reading aloud, they simultaneously let one hand rest on a planchette, in this case a small wheeled plate with a pencil attached.* Over time, they reported, they were able to concentrate entirely on the conscious activity while at the same time writing unconsciously with the planchette, which moved about as if under its own steam.

What is noteworthy about the writing that resulted ("This long time when he did this best time, and he could thus have been bound, and in this long time, when he could be this to first use of this long time") is that it resembles nothing so much as the early twentieth-century experimental prose of Gertrude Stein.

MOTOR AUTOMATISM WAS enough to convert Sandes, but others were harder to sway. Jones put up a hand-drawn poster urging prisoners to attend meetings of "the Psychical Research Society of Yozgad." "The closest inspection was invited," he later wrote. "The poster ended by

---

* Planchettes of this kind were used by some early spiritualists to produce communications written directly on paper.

saying that the mediums each suspected the other and would welcome any enquirer who could decide how the . . . movements of the glass were caused."

A committee of prisoners asked whether he and O'Farrell would submit to a series of tests. "Doc, strong in his own innocence, welcomed the suggestion," Jones recalled. "As for me, it was exactly what I wanted—the *raison d'être* of my notice. . . . If all were discovered, as I expected would be the case, I'd get my poshing, there would be a good laugh all round, and that would be the end of it. If by any fluke of fortune I survived, the testers would only have themselves to blame afterwards. It was now a fair fight—my wits against the rest—catch as catch can, and all grips allowed." Without knowing it, he was laying the foundation for the plot against his captors.

The tests were held over several nights in the Upper House passageway. The first was simple: The mediums were blindfolded. That posed no problem for Jones, who knew the board cold. "Given any one letter, I could visualize the positions of the rest almost automatically, and my hand could guide the glass to them with as little conscious effort as a pianist, given his C natural, finds in hitting the right keys in the dark."

Because the slightest jar of the board could upset his calculations, Jones also cut barely perceptible nicks in its raised wooden ring. As his right hand worked the glass, his left thumb could discreetly confirm the board's orientation. O'Farrell, for his part, was coming to believe that the glass was being moved by a vigorous unseen hand— "a sixty-horse-power, armour-plated spook of the very first quality," he noted approvingly. He remained blissfully unaware that the hand in question belonged to the man across the table.

Handkerchiefs were tied over the mediums' eyes, and Matthews turned to the board. "Who are you?" he asked.

"The glass began to move about," Jones recalled. "I was writing rubbish. Some sceptic laughed."

"Wait a bit," said Price. "It always begins like that. Now who are you?"

"S-I-double L-Y, Silly!" the sceptic read out. "That's rather a poor shot for 'Sally.' The bandage affects the Spook, it seems."

"A-S-S," the Spook went on. "I-T M-A-K-E-S N-O D-I-F-F-E-R-E-N-C-E."

"We'll see!" said the sceptic. *I felt the board being moved under my hand.* "Now who are you?"

As the glass circled under my right hand, I felt for and found the secret nicks with my left thumb.

"U T-H-I-N-K U A-R-E C-L-E-V-E-R." . . .

Mistakes were made, of course, and the glass frequently went to "next-door" letters, but not more so than on ordinary occasions. It became generally accepted by the company that whether the mediums had their eyes bandaged or not, and whether the position of the board was altered or not, it made no difference.

In another test, the board was turned again, but this time Jones lost his bearings: Try though he might, he could not find the nicks. Deploying the preemptive thinking that is the stock in trade of the foremost barristers and confidence men, he began banging the glass repeatedly in the same spot.

"It's getting wearisome," he told the group, pained to be in the grip of a one-note Spook. "Curse it a bit, someone."

"Leave that damned 'D' alone!" one of the men cried.

"-O-N-T S-W-E-A-R," the Spook replied, bearings regained.

A THIRD TEST was almost Jones's undoing: One of the prisoners turned the board upside down. A number was written on the underside of each letter; the men would record which numbers the glass touched. For Jones, it was like being thrust without warning into a hall of mirrors. Exposure seemed assured:

The problem would have been easy enough had it merely meant a reversal of all the motions of the glass . . . as happened when the board was merely twisted round a half-revolution. I was accustomed to that; but this was different. Take an ordinary dinner-plate. Mark the points of the compass on it. Now . . . revolve the plate on the axis of the North-South line, and turn it face downwards. The North point is still in the same position. So is the South point; but while East has changed places with West, North-East has become not South-West but North-West; East-Nor'-East has become not West-South-West but West-Nor'-West, and so on. . . . Imagine the state of mind of a musician who finds the C natural in the usual place, but the bass notes on his right and the treble notes on his left!

To avert suspicion, Jones knew, he would have to move the glass as fast as usual. He bought time by figuring out the location of "N" and "O," and for some minutes the Spook was surly, replying "No" to every question while Jones "thought and thought and thought." Suddenly he had it: Instead of seeing the board in his mind's eye from above, he needed to see *through* it, as if the table were made of glass and he was lying on his back beneath it. Within moments, the Spook was chattering fluently. "I do not think my friends ever realized the difficulty of the task they had set me, or how near we were that night to failure," Jones said. "Certainly I got no credit for the performance. . . . The credit went where it belonged—to the Spook."

"You birds satisfied?" O'Farrell asked the crowd. "Seems to me the Spook has had you cold every time.'"

IN WINNING HIS converts, Jones had the advantage of quick wit, a superb visual memory, and training in legal argumentation, which had schooled him in "the gentle art of drawing a red herring across my questioners' train of thought." He realized early, for instance, that he could deflect suspicion by having the spirits "speak" only when he and O'Farrell worked the board as a team. As a result, he wrote, "suspicion centered not on me, but on the perfectly innocent Doctor. . . . He swore vehemently that he had nothing to do with it, but it was pointed out to him that the glass only wrote when he was there—a fact he could not deny."

Jones also had the times on his side, for in the late nineteenth and early twentieth centuries one could hardly spit without hitting a ghost. By the time he began spooking his way out of Yozgad, the wide popular belief in spiritualism, along with a profusion of literary ghost stories and ghoulish entertainments designed to frighten and delight the paying public, had, as one modern scholar observes, "placed ghostly apparitions and supernatural phantasmagorias at the very core of popular culture" in Britain and the United States.

While the belief that the dead can communicate with the living has been documented since antiquity, modern spiritualism is conventionally said to have begun in 1848, when the Fox sisters—fourteen-year-old Margaretta, known as Maggie, and eleven-year-old Catherine, known as Kate—reported hearing a series of mysterious knocking sounds at their family farmhouse in Hydesville, New York, near Rochester. The knocks, they asserted, were made by a spirit, later described as the ghost of a peddler murdered in the house years before. The ghost could count, and respond to simple questions, by knocking the appropriate number of times; answers to complex questions could be spelled out letter by letter via the chant-and-rap method.

Joining forces with their elder sister, Leah, the girls began displaying their mediumistic skills across the country to immense public attention; they were soon taking in $100 to $150 a night.* The sisters would become international celebrities, and the Hydesville house a tourist attraction. "The excitement in reference to the mysterious knocking in a house at Hydesville . . . still continues," the *Rochester Daily Advertiser* reported in a widely reprinted article from the spring of 1848, "and the revelations which it makes daily are astonishing the multitude." It continued:

A pamphlet has been published, containing a great number of certificates from individuals residing in that neighborhood, who have heard the mysterious knocking, and have propounded to his ghostship a variety of questions, all of which have been answered by *raps*. . . . The ghost not only answers all questions put to it, but readily gives the age of each child in the family, and of others in the neighborhood, but the "spirit's" history of its own affairs is altogether the most marvelous. The "story of its wrongs" runs somewhat thus:

It states the body it once inhabited was that of a pedlar; that it was 31 years of age, and was murdered about four years since by

---

* Roughly equivalent to $3,300 to $4,950 today.

the then occupant of the house, by having its throat cut with a butcher knife; that it left a family of five children . . . that its wife died about two years since; that the amount of money taken was $500. . . .

Sometimes there has been as many as two or three hundred persons at the house at a time, and it is said that all have distinctly heard the noises. . . . According to the unquiet "spirit's" story it was buried ten feet under ground, in a particular part of the cellar designated, and that since, on account of the body affecting the water in a neighboring well, it was removed from its first resting place and buried on the bank of "Mud Creek." . . . It says that it shall keep up the rapping until its remains . . . are discovered. . . . We await further revelations with a good deal of interest.

The "Rochester rappings," as they became known in the press, were exposed as a hoax soon afterward.* "In Buffalo, where the Foxes subsequently let their spirits flow, a committee of doctors reported that these loosely-constructed girls produced the 'raps' by snapping their toe and knee joints," P. T. Barnum, who knew tomfoolery when he saw it, wrote in 1865.† But by then their childish prank had spawned a worldwide quasi-religious movement. The hoax had occurred at a propitious time—the Second Great Awakening, an age of intense spiritual questing that began in the 1790s and lasted through the 1840s. The era gave birth to Mormonism, Millerism (the forerunner of Seventh-Day Adventism), and a spate of other movements.

"Why modern spiritism chose America for its starting-point . . . is chiefly found in the state of our nation's growth," the American neurologist George M. Beard wrote in "The Psychology of Spiritism," an 1879 critique. "America at the time of the Rochester rappings was entering its mental puberty, passing from childhood into youth, feeling the throbs of new desires, champing impatiently for the race; the home

---

* In 1888, Maggie Fox acknowledged the hoax, though she recanted her acknowledgment the next year.

† Barnum, who is erroneously described in some sources as having sponsored the Fox sisters' tour, publicly offered $500 to any medium who "can cause invisible agencies to perform in open daylight many of the things which they pretend to accomplish by spirits in the dark." The reward went uncollected.

not so much of the abjectly ignorant as of the fractionally educated; not of the raw, but of the underdone, the paradise of non-experts."

The hoax also occurred in a propitious place: the "Burned-Over District," the swath of central and western New York so named because of the myriad fire-and-brimstone revivals it had spawned. Mormonism had begun there in the late 1820s, after Joseph Smith experienced a revelation near Palmyra, New York. So, a decade later, did Millerism. A string of social reform movements, arising in tandem with the religious revivals, also sprang to life there—among them abolitionism, the campaign for women's rights, and the Oneida utopian community.

By midcentury, spiritualist believers were flocking to séances in public halls and private parlors throughout the United States. In an era of widespread family bereavement, the chance to "speak" with vanished loved ones was something few could resist.* In the 1860s, the Civil War was estimated to have garnered the movement 2 million new adherents. Mary Todd Lincoln organized séances in the White House ("some of which," the historian Drew Gilpin Faust writes, "the president himself was said to have attended"), in the hope of conjuring the spirit of their son Willie, who had died in 1862, at eleven.

Spiritualism made its way to Britain in late 1852, when the American medium Maria B. Hayden began holding court in the parlors of the London gentry. Ghosts—restless, unquiet, often demanding— suffused the popular fiction of the Victorian age: Jacob Marley from *A Christmas Carol* is a canonical example. A spate of sober journals— including *The Medium and Daybreak*, published in London; *The Spiritual Telegraph*, from New York; and *The Banner of Light*, out of Boston—printed transcripts of "communications" received by mediums. In 1882 the Society for Psychical Research was formed in London to investigate claims of spiritual contact. (Its approach, in the words of a twenty-first-century writer, was "usually skeptical, sometimes credulous.") The American Society for Psychical Research was established two years later.

---

* In 1850, the infant mortality rate in the United States was roughly 21 percent for White babies, 34 percent for Black. Women stood forty times the risk of dying during pregnancy or childbirth as they do today, and diseases such as cholera, scarlet fever, tuberculosis, scrofula, and smallpox collectively killed thousands of Americans each year.

By the late nineteenth century there were reported to be 8 million spiritualists in the United States and Europe. The movement had reached Turkey in the 1850s "via the European and Levantine communities in Istanbul," one scholar notes, and by the 1920s had become "a very popular topic in the press" there.

IF SPIRITUALISM WAS an article of faith, it was also extremely good business, and within short order the medium had emerged as a new breed of solo entrepreneur. "Many spiritualist mediums were virtually indistinguishable from professional performers," the media historian Simone Natale writes in his recent book *Supernatural Entertainments.* "They had managers and agents, advertised their performances in the press, and developed spirit phenomena characterized by a high degree of spectacularism and theatricality." For some mediums, spiritualism was a genuinely well-intentioned calling, abetted by motor automatism, their own susceptibility, and the yearnings of a wistful public.* For many others, it was unreconstructed chicanery, whose sole purpose was to separate spiritual seekers from their pocketbooks.

"The average medium works only for the money he or she can extract from the public," Houdini, who spent years exposing spiritualist charlatans, wrote in 1924. "Spiritualism is nothing more or less than mental intoxication, the intoxication of words, of feelings and suggested beliefs. Intoxication of any sort when it becomes a habit is injurious to the body but intoxication of the mind is always fatal to the mind. We have prohibition of alcohol, we have prohibition of drugs, but we have no law to prevent these human leeches from sucking every bit of reason and common sense from their victims."

In large halls, mere communication—through rappings, pencil-and-paper messages, chalk on slates, or the Ouija—was soon not enough. Patrons wanted to *see* the spooks, or at least experience their presence through a series of onstage "manifestations." Spiritualist

---

* In magicians' parlance, mediums like these are described as "shut-eye" performers, so named because they have blinded themselves to their own deception. Correspondingly, those who know full well that they are deceiving their audiences are called "open-eye" performers.

demonstrations quickly became ripping good theater, a vibrant star in the constellation of late nineteenth-century popular entertainments that included stage magic, mentalism, magic lantern displays, and freak shows.

At public séances, ghostly apparitions could fly above the stage in all their ectoplasmic filminess. Mediums might be tightly bound with ropes and placed in locked cabinets, only to have the audience serenaded by violins, guitars, and other instruments, seemingly played by invisible hands. Even in intimate settings, manifestations were a medium's meal ticket. In darkened sitting rooms, ghostly hands might reach out and grab séance-goers; ethereal bells would ring; voices would wail; tables would tip.

These manifestations, as Houdini knew, were simply magic tricks. "Throughout this period magicians, Spiritualist performers, and anti-Spiritualists purchased their tricks and cabinets from the same catalogues," one historian has written:

> From the mid-1800s, the catalogues of shops that sold magical devices to performers frequently devoted pages to . . . devices . . . such as the "Spirit Bell," "Rising Tables" . . . "Luminous Materialistic Ghosts and Forms," and "Magic Slates." The catalogues also offered entire acts such as "Etherialization"—which enabled a medium "to produce any number of spirit forms, in the perfect dark, which have the appearance of a fine, misty, luminous vapor . . . fading away, producing a weird and wonderful effect." Hands that could rap out messages were also available, as well as the "New Flying Music Box," "Slate Tricks," and "Spirit Lectures," "meant to [be] use[d] in combating spiritualism, or by anti-spiritualists. Are suitable for delivery from the stage, parlor or pulpit."

Renouncing spiritualism in 1888, Maggie Fox, by then an alcoholic, described how she and Kate had hoodwinked audiences for decades:

> Like most perplexing things when once made clear, it is astonishing how easily it is done. The rappings are simply the result of a perfect control of the muscles of the leg below the knee which govern the tendons of the foot and allow action of the toe and

ankle bones that are not commonly known. Such perfect control is only possible when a child is taken at an early age and carefully and continually taught to practice the muscles which grow stiff in later years. A child at 12 is almost too old. With control of the muscles of the foot the toes may be brought down to the floor without any movement that is perceptible to the eye. The whole foot, in fact, can be made to give rappings by the use only of muscles below the knee. This, then, is the simple explanation of the whole method of the knocks and raps.

By the late nineteenth and early twentieth centuries, interest in spiritualism had begun to wane. Among the reasons were the advances in medicine and sanitation that had lowered mortality rates. Then came the Great War, and with it a new spiritualist heyday.

SPIRITUALISM'S REANIMATION IN 1914 is hardly surprising: Susceptibility to an array of popular delusions (cults, con games, paranormal beliefs) increases in times of instability, notably wartime. But what *is* surprising about the spiritualism of the turn of the twentieth century—from our twenty-first-century vantage point it is the single most astounding thing—is that many of the movement's most fervent supporters were eminent men of science. They included Sir Arthur Conan Doyle, a trained physician and the creator of the single most rationalist character in world letters; Alfred Russel Wallace, who independently of Darwin developed the theory of evolution through natural selection; the Harvard psychologist William James;* and the English physicist Sir Oliver Lodge.

Lodge, whose youngest son, Raymond, was killed in action in Flanders in 1915, published a widely influential book, *Raymond,* the next year. In it, he chronicled his repeated attempts—ultimately successful, he believed—to reach his child via spirit mediums. "Death is real and grievous," he wrote, "but it is the end of a stage, not the end of the journey. The road stretches on beyond that inn, and beyond our imagination, 'the moonlit endless way.' Let us think of him then, not as

---

* James was a founding member of the American Society for Psychical Research.

lying near Ypres with all his work ended, but rather, after due rest and refreshment, continuing his noble and useful career in more peaceful surroundings, and quietly calling us his family from paralysing grief to resolute and high endeavour."

Today, most of us view scientific rationalism and spiritualist belief as mutually exclusive. But in the late nineteenth and early twentieth centuries, as one modern observer has noted, "science was to a degree the ally of ghosts." The reason was simple: In order to define what is *super*natural, one must first define what is natural, and in those years the border between the two seemed far more porous than it does now. It was a time of hurtling scientific change, which saw the development of technologies such as radio, in which disembodied voices sailed through the ether; the phonograph, which let bygone men and women speak as if from beyond the grave; and X-rays, which made visible the ghostly scaffolding of the human body. If technology had the power to do all those things—to transcend space, time, and the body's innate opacity—then what was to say, scientists reasoned, that communication across the ultimate divide was not possible, too?*

"That direct telepathic intercourse should be able to occur between mind and mind, without all this intermediate physical mechanism, is . . . not really surprising," Lodge wrote in *Raymond*. "It has to be proved, no doubt, but the fact is intrinsically less puzzling than many of those other facts to which we have grown hardened by usage." Jones used precisely this argument to win converts to his sham spiritualism: "A few years ago," he would cajole his fellow prisoners, "I expect you were saying that wireless telegraphy and flying and all the rest of our modern scientific marvels were impossible."

SPOOKING ASIDE, LIFE in camp in the winter and spring of 1917 went on much as before. The prisoners' evening lectures continued, as did meetings of the Yozgad Debating Society. (Subjects of debate included "That the modern stage is degenerate and that this is a sign of the

---

* Through his work on electromagnetism, Sir Oliver Lodge contributed to the development of radio and held several patents connected with the emerging technology. In the mid-1890s, for instance, he perfected the coherer, a device that detected radio waves, which became an essential component of early wireless receivers.

degeneracy of the times" and "That the progress of civilisation on the present lines is more likely to lead to disaster than Utopia.") The men convened a moot court, in which, Arthur Holyoake wrote, "we tried Capt. Dinwiddy for stealing an egg. I prosecuted and Jones defended. . . . Jones was very good and so was Dinwiddy."

When the first snow fell, Jones built a toboggan from scrap lumber, and others soon followed suit. A track was created on the steep winding path that ran through the camp. "It was a hair raising journey and most people knocked bits off themselves," Holyoake recalled. "There were two right angle bends and to miss either of them meant a head on collision with a wall."

In early spring, a pair of storks built a nest atop one of the Hospital House chimneys and became objects of intense fascination. "Never were birds so closely observed," Sandes wrote. "They were in the habit of serenading each other at intervals, which they accomplished by swinging their heads over backwards and clicking their bills rapidly—a manoeuvre usually productive of applause from their audience. In due time young storks hatched out in the nest, and . . . took their first uncertain flight. I believe a considerable amount of money changed hands as a result of this first effort. When the young ones could fly, the old birds began to prepare for their journey southwards . . . and we saw them no more."

Through it all, Jones kept working the spook-board, making his converts a few at a time. The men delighted in the visits from saucy Sally and demure Dorothy ("Dorothy that's always gentle and sweet! She is the one *I* like," O'Farrell declared), though the Yankee crosspatch Silas P. Warner was less welcome. "Silas had a nasty habit of butting in where he was not wanted—always at crucial and exciting points—and was unpopular," Jones said. A constant presence, towering over them all, was the Spook.

"In matters of belief, as elsewhere . . . it is all a matter of practice and experience," Jones would write. "We in Yozgad had not yet acquired the capacity of an Oliver Lodge or a Conan Doyle, but we were getting along very well for beginners. The stage of 'True-believerdom' was in sight when my little flock would cease from talking about 'elementary details' and concentrate their attention on the 'greater truths of the World Beyond.' Once a medium has been accepted as bona fide he has quite a nice job—as easy as falling off a log, and much more amusing."

It was still no more than a leg-pull, "a rag, with no definite aim in view." But in the spring of 1917 Jones discovered that spiritual charlatanism might be the means to a far more vital end. His epiphany came from a most unlikely source: the Pimple.

CHAPTER SIX

The Uses of Enchantment

ONE APRIL DAY, the Pimple — "the five-foot-nothing of impertinence" — sidled up to Jones. "You are a student of spiritism?" he asked cagily. "The sentries have told me. . . . Have you much studied the subject?"

"So-so," Jones replied cautiously. He wondered whether he was going to be punished.

"I want you to answer by occultism for me some questions."

Needing time to ponder this unprecedented demand by one of his captors, Jones asked the Pimple to join him in half an hour for tea in Upper House. "I walked back, up the steep path, thinking hard," he recalled. "Hitherto spooking had been merely a jest, with a psychological flavouring to lend it interest. But now a serious element was being introduced. . . . Without any clear vision of the future, with nothing but the vaguest hope of ultimate success, I made up my mind to grip this man, and to wait for time to show how I might use him."

At the prisoners' spartan tea, the Pimple dropped off his list of questions. Every one of them centered on his romantic prospects: Though he possessed none of the requisite attributes, he fancied himself a Casanova. The questions were put to the board at the next séance, and the Spook obliged him with just the sort of assurances he was seeking. "The answers created a deep impression on Moïse . . . who, at this time, was not a believer in spiritualism," Jones wrote. "He had only reached the stage of wondering if there might not be something in it. . . . I felt I had a difficult task in front of me and walked warily. I pretended an absolute indifference as to whether he believed in the Spook or not and never suggested that he should come to séances. The result was that he consulted the Spook once, twice and again. Every time, without knowing it, he gave something away. I privately tabulated his questions, studied them hard, and determined above all to hold my own counsel until the time was ripe."*

AROUND THIS TIME, the Spook began issuing regular war news bulletins, obtained, Jones asserted, direct from the Beyond. A first-rate correspondent, the Spook reported authentic information about the progress of the war—intelligence forbidden to prisoners—including the ultimate seizure of Kut by the British in February 1917, and the fall of Baghdad the next month. The actual source of these reports was encrypted messages from prisoners' families, for coded communications in both directions had been making their way between Britain and Yozgad since the captives first arrived.

In August 1916, the Ottoman government had eased the restriction on letters. Writing home, prisoners were now allowed to fill both sides of a single sheet. But since mail to and from Yozgad was still vetted by Ottoman censors, the only way for the prisoners to get war news, and to relay accounts of their own condition, was in code. Jones once sent Mair a postcard that read this way:

> Now Darllenwch dear: Send tea and tobacco, Eno's, underclothes, needles, sugar, Antipon, tabloid ink, soap, Formamint, aspirin, cocoa, toffee, Oxo, razor, Yardley's dental extract, matches, alum, nuts, dates, Euthymol, novels, quinine, uniform. I remain Yozgad for present.

The key word is "Darllenwch." It looks like a term of endearment but is actually the Welsh imperative verb "Read!" And when the initial

---

* In doing this, Jones had already, if unwittingly, adopted an essential trick of sham mediums. As Houdini wrote in his 1924 book debunking such charlatans: "One thing which makes the work of these mediums easier is the fact that many people tell things about themselves without realizing it. I have known people to deny emphatically that they had made certain statements or mentioned certain things in a seance although I had personally heard them say those very things not more than twenty minutes before. Under the excitement of the moment their subconscious mind speaks while their conscious mind forgets. This does not escape the medium who takes advantage of everything which it is possible to."

letters of the succeeding words are read together they spell "State unsatisfactory. Demand enquiry."

In reply, Mair wrote:

Have sent parcels of following, Darllenwch dear: Grape-nuts, oil, Virol, Eno's, razor, nuts, malt, elastic, novels, tea, envelopes, quinine, underclothes, ink, reels, indiarubber, needles, games. Eryl now growing long and noisy. Daisy very energetic. Ruth yesterday saw Ted. Rode over. Nesta going Newnham. Orme Willows empty now. Emma married. I expect spend Christmas Oxford. Llandudno after. Papa says I'll never go. [Government enquiring. England very strong now. Enemies collapsing.]

To alert his family that a letter or postcard contained a code, Jones often addressed them curiously. Writing to his parents at their country home in Tighnabruaich, Scotland, he might mark the envelope "Tighnabruaich, Argyllshire, Scotland *England*," an oddity that would slip past the censors but send an unmistakable signal to the Joneses.

He once sent his father a postcard whose text was entirely blank, with an address reading, "Sir Henry Jones, 184, Kings-road, Tighnabruaich, Scotland." There was no such road in Tighnabruaich, and no such house number. Sir Henry, who had high government connections, brought the postcard to Room 40, the British Admiralty's codebreaking department.* But as Room 40 labored away on the card, it was Mair who spotted its meaning: The address was a reference to the biblical Book of Kings, chapter 18, verse 4. The verse reads, "Obadiah took an hundred prophets and hid them by fifty in a cave and fed them with bread and water," an indication that Jones and his fellows were being held at Yozgad with little to eat.

Prisoners also found covert means of requesting contraband. The Ottoman government had issued a long list of items that they coveted but were not allowed, including cameras, compasses, binoculars, non-safety razors, postage stamps, and currency. Sandes devised an

---

* Established in October 1914, Room 40 would decipher the Zimmermann Telegram (the intercepted communication from the German Foreign Office urging a strategic alliance between Germany and Mexico) in January 1917. The decipherment was a major intelligence coup that helped bring about the United States' entry into the war that April.

ingenious way of asking his family for money, and an equally ingenious way of securing it on arrival:

> I remember one occasion when Kiazim was superintending the
> opening of parcels of food and clothing which had arrived for us
> from England. I was among the lucky few who trooped up to his
> office to get the supplies sent by kind relations and friends. . . . We
> entered a room where Kiazim sat in state amid piles of parcels,
> while behind him hovered the interpreter Moïse. . . . Now, among
> the good things in one of the two parcels addressed to me I ex-
> pected to find a tin of carbolic tooth-powder, and in that powder I
> hoped to discover several golden coins. I had sent a postcard to
> England asking for this tooth-powder, and had added that I had
> heard that it was much improved by the addition of certain yellow
> tabloids "which were made in two sizes only."* Kneeling on the
> floor, I opened the first of my parcels beneath the watchful eyes of
> Kiazim himself. A tin of Huntley & Palmer's fancy biscuits fell out,
> and behind it I spied a tin of carbolic tooth-powder. . . . It was a
> time for rapid action. If Kiazim handled the small tin and was sur-
> prised by its weight, I was lost. Hurriedly I opened the tin of bis-
> cuits. . . . Smiling, I offered it to Kiazim Bey, who saluted, selected
> a few biscuits, returned the remainder to me *and at once turned
> his back,* while I shoveled the contents of both parcels into a sack
> and left the office. He had his half-dozen biscuits and I my golden
> sovereigns.

Prisoners' families also wrote in code. "The news that somebody's father's trousers had come down was . . . the occasion of a very merry evening," Jones said, "for it meant that Dad's Bags (or Baghdad) had fallen at last.† If, as occasionally happened, we found hidden meanings where none was intended, and captured Metz or Jerusalem long before such a possibility was dreamt of in England, it did more good than harm, for it kept our optimism alive." Other messages from

* I.e., sovereigns and half-sovereigns.
† Per the *Oxford English Dictionary*, "bags" as British slang for "trousers" is attested between 1853 and 1927.

home told covertly "of Zeppelin raids, Lloyd George's accession to the premiership,* Romania's entry into the war and the fate of Russia's lumbering armies." Such items quickly found their way into the Spook's dispatches.

In EARLY MAY 1917, an extraordinary memorandum was posted in Yozgad. It forbade prisoners from conveying, in their letters home, *"news obtained by officers in a spiritistic state."* The notice made Jones's heart sing: He suspected it had been issued by Kiazim, and that Kiazim saw the spirit world as a force to be reckoned with. That scenario was plausible, as traditional belief was alive and well in the region. One summer night, the prisoners heard a prolonged firefight outside the camp—hundreds and hundreds of rounds. Yozgad was so remote it would scarcely have become a battleground. Could the gunfire be from the Russians, come to liberate them? No, they learned, it was only the townspeople responding to an eclipse of the moon. The shooting was designed "to scare away the devil who is obscuring her light."

Wanting to confirm his suspicions, Jones took the Pimple aside:

"That's a poor trick of yours," said I, "stopping us writing home about spiritualism. We only want verification of what the Spook says. The matter is one of scientific interest. It has no military significance at all."

"I say so to the Commandant," said Moïse, "but he would not agree! He says it is dangerous."

"Get along, Moïse! The Commandant has nothing to do with that notice. You put it up yourself to crab our amusements."

Moïse probed excitedly in his pockets and produced a paper in Turkish which he flourished under my nose.

"There you are!" he said. "The seal! The signature! He wrote the order. I merely translated. I *told* him how great was the scientific value, how important is the experiment. He said the Spook gives war news. It is his fault, not mine."

---

* David Lloyd George served as the British prime minister from December 1916 to October 1922.

"Is the Commandant also a believer?" I asked.

"Assuredly! He has much studied the occult. He often consults[,] on problematic difficulties[,] . . . witches in this town, but mostly by cards. He greatly believes in cards." . . .

As I went I hugged myself. The Commandant too! . . . How long, I wondered, would it be before I could get him into the net?

It was one thing to convert the Pimple. It would be quite another, Jones knew, to ensnare the remote, wary Kiazim—along with Kiazim's chief henchman, the Cook, whose draconian hold on the camp belied his humble title. ("A limb of Satan," O'Farrell called him. "He'll poison or shoot you as soon as look at you.") Jones realized he would need a lure so tantalizing that even Yozgad's stoniest officials could not resist. He would not find it until September.

TOWARD THE END of May, a new group of British rank and file arrived at Yozgad to serve as orderlies. An additional house was allocated (originally known as the Schoolhouse, it was in short, unruly order christened Posh Castle), and thirteen senior officers, with the orderlies, moved in. Among those moving was Doc O'Farrell, and that put Jones's plans for the commandant on agonizing hold. Because he had resolved to raise the spirits only when he and O'Farrell worked the board together, the Upper House séances came to an end: Visiting between houses was forbidden after nighttime lockdown.

But by this time much of the camp had caught ghost fever. For some months spooking had also been afoot in Hospital House, where two officers, Alfred James Nightingale and G.W.R. Bishop, presided over a homemade board of their own. O'Farrell had broken the news of their séances to Jones early on:

The Doc came up to me as I was walking in the lane. He was all hunched up with glee.

"Faith," he said to me, "the sceptics have got it in the neck. Here's Nightingale and Bishop been an' held a long conversation with the spooks last night."

"I don't see that that will make much difference to the sceptics," said I.

"But I do," said the Doc. "The camp doesn't believe in it now because you're you and I'm me. But who in Turkey or out of it can suspect fellows like Bishop and Nightingale?" . . .

"And why not suspect Bishop and Nightingale?" I asked.

"Ach! Ye might as well suspect a babe unborn. Not one of the two of them has the imagination of a louse. They're plain, straightforward Englishmen—not Celtic fringe like you an' me—an' the camp knows it." . . .

"Whom were they talking to last night?"

"Oh—just Sally, and Silas P. Warner, and that lot. . . . Same crowd of spooks as we get ourselves."

I glanced at him to see if he was joking. He wasn't. Lord! Doc dear, how I longed to laugh!

So those séances were a sham, too, right down to the plagiarized spooks. But the men of Hospital House soon outdid Jones by conjuring a fearsome spook of their own, Millicent the Innocent. With no visible means of support, she smashed a window, upended a washbasin full of water and sent a candelabra crashing to the floor. Millicent was the work of a third officer, Cedric Waters Hill, an airman and master magician whom Jones knew only by sight. Years later, Hill explained how he had rigged the washbasin trick, a manifestation that any nineteenth-century medium-for-profit would have been proud to call his own:

In the bedrooms of most Turkish houses in those days there was a sleeping platform across one end of the room about 18 inches high and 3 to 4 feet wide. The spook room [in Hospital House] had one of these and on it . . . were a couple of home made wooden stands for holding wash basins. One of these, complete with basin half full of water, usually stood in an ideal position for a manifestation. . . .

One night during the evening meal time I arranged the washstand near the edge of the platform. I had a long piece of thin string with a wire hook attached to one end. I hooked the wire under the bottom of the back of the stand and passed the string over the top and laid it round the skirting board to the door, hiding it as much as possible. Giving the string a quick hard pull would make the wooden stand somersault off the platform and throw the basin of water into the room. The whole thing worked beautifully and was even more effective than I had expected, and I managed to gather up the string without being spotted. . . .

We had made the grade. . . . Spooking went on in both houses for the next few months with such success that about seventy percent of the whole Camp were now firm believers.

After Millicent broke the window, showering the spook room with glass and causing the rapid exodus of its spiritual seekers, Jones paid a visit to Hospital House to check out the competition. The window, set in an upper story some 20 feet above the ground, had been broken from the outside, as if Millicent herself had come surging through. It would have been impossible for a man to break it without standing on a ladder, yet no trace of a ladder was evident. But there was, Jones observed, a small enclosed lavatory abutting that side of Hospital House. The lavatory had a tiny ventilation window, high in the wall, with a ledge running beneath it on the inside. It might be possible, he realized, for someone to stand on the ledge, reach a long stick through the little window, and use it to smash the window of the spook-room. And sure enough, when Jones investigated closely he found the one clue that the otherwise careful trickster had left behind: a footprint, clearly visible in the dust on the ledge.

Jones wiped away the footprint and, not wanting to betray either the Hospital House spooks or his own, kept silent. In August, with his own séances in abeyance, he confessed his mock mediumship to Hill and Nightingale (it was Nightingale who had been steering the Hospital House planchette) and received a confession from each in return. The three men vowed to keep their frauds a secret.

In September 1917, Jones found the lure he had been seeking for months. It, too, was supplied by the Pimple, who approached him one day outside Upper House:

The little man glanced furtively up and down the lane, to make sure no one was within earshot, and lowered his voice to a confidential whisper.

"Can the Spirit find a buried treasure?"

"That depends," said I.

"On what?"

"On who buried it, and who wants it, and whether the man who buried it is still alive; or, if he is dead, on whether he can communicate. . . . You want me to find this Armenian treasure?" I went on, risking the "Armenian."*

"You know about it?" the Pimple asked in surprise. . . . "Did the Spook tell you?"

"I have had several communications," I said guardedly. "You've been concentrating on the wrong places." (I did not know whether Moïse had been digging or merely thinking about digging. "Concentrating" covered both.)

"We tried the Schoolhouse garden," said the Pimple, "but did not find it."

"Of course not," said I. "Digging at random is like looking for a needle in a haystack." The Pimple was much struck by the phrase, and made a note of it in his pocket-book.

What finer enticement could there be than a treasure hunt? Jones also suspected that one of the hunters was Kiazim himself: Describing the digging, the Pimple had used the word "we." Jones assured the Pimple that he would ask the Spook about the treasure, provided the Pimple could get permission for him to visit Hospital House at night. This would let him hold séances with Nightingale, a confirmed medium in the camp's estimation.

"I was filled with the growing hope that my door to freedom lay through the Ouija," Jones wrote. *"I intended to implicate the highest Turkish authority in the place in my escape, to obtain clear and convincing proof that he was implicated, and to leave that proof in the hands of my fellow-prisoners before I disappeared."*

JONES WOULD FIRST have to prove the Spook's fitness as a treasure-hunting guide by having him find something small, much as a devious owner salts a barren mine with gold nuggets before putting it up for

---

* It had long been rumored in camp that at least one wealthy Armenian of the town, anticipating the coming genocide, had buried his riches somewhere in Yozgad—and that the Turks had been searching for them in vain.

sale. With this opening stratagem, he had instinctively mirrored a crucial early step of traditional confidence games, known in con men's argot as "the convincer." A standard convincer might involve letting the victim win returns on small investments before soaking him in a stock scam or at the racetrack. Jones had little money and no actual treasure; he would nevertheless have to offer something that his captors would accept as the first step in the grand hunt to follow. His convincer would also need to draw out the Commandant, on whom all his plans depended.

He decided that the Spook would find a revolver, a rusted Smith & Wesson that one of the prisoners had discovered half buried on the grounds; it had probably belonged to a local Armenian. Though it was useless as a weapon, Jones's comrade had held on to it from force of habit. "The magpie instinct was by this time well developed in the camp," Jones said. "At one time or another we had all been so hard up that we now made a habit of collecting tins, bits of string, pieces of wood, old nails, scraps of sacking—in short, everything and anything which might some day have a possible use for some project yet unborn. The sum total, hidden under your mattress, was technically known as 'cag.'"

Jones borrowed the revolver and reburied it in the garden. He told Nightingale and the others only that he wanted to make the Pimple the butt of a practical joke involving a phony treasure hunt. All were happy to help. This time—*and this time only*—Jones informed them, the glass would be deliberately guided by one of the mediums, who would have his eyes shaded but not fully closed. Thus "the Spook" would generate a set of farcical instructions. Of his nascent escape plans Jones said nothing.

In Hospital House, Jones took his seat across the board from Nightingale, with the eager Pimple, paper at the ready, the designated recorder. "My double part," Jones wrote, was "to appear genuine to the Pimple and fraudulent to the rest of the audience." To free himself to focus on this dual acting job, he had arranged for Nightingale to steer the glass and spell the needed responses.

The glass decreed that the treasure hunt would begin on September 12. "The Treasure is by Arms guarded," the Spook reported ominously; the treasure hunters were obliged to find the arms before he would part with another clue. He ordered the mediums to bring cer-

tain items with them on the appointed day, among them wood shavings, a length of cord, ink, and a saucer. (These, as Jones had
orchestrated the event, would lend an air of theatrical ceremony.)
The Spook also told the Pimple to bring a companion—this was meant
to flush the Commandant—and ordered them both to arrive wearing
bayonets beneath their trouser legs. (This was for pure slapstick
value.) The Pimple wrote down the Spook's every word.

On the afternoon of the twelfth, Jones and a fellow prisoner, Stanley C. B. Mundey, met the Pimple as arranged. To Jones's dismay, the
Pimple had brought only the Cook. There was some small consolation
in watching the two men stagger stiff-leggedly about, hobbled by the
unsheathed bayonets down their trousers.

"Do you think there will be danger?" the Pimple asked.

"One never knows in these things," replied Mundey, who had come
along simply to enjoy the joke. "But if we follow instructions it should
be all right."

Jones and Mundey held out their hands, and, as the Spook had directed, the Cook bound them with the cord. Jones then lapsed into a
dramatic trance, as if receiving instructions from an ethereal force
that only he could hear. "South!" he shouted, and dashed off in that
direction, the others racing behind. "South! South!"

Reaching a nearby field, Jones sat down among the cabbages.
"What has happened?" he said. "Where am I?"

"You cannot see it now?" the Pimple asked.

"Quick!" said Mundey. "The Ink Pool! Before it goes!"

The Pimple poured the ink into the saucer, and Jones gazed into it
deeply.

"Can you see which way it is pointing?" Mundey asked.

"West!" Jones cried, and off they went, until they reached the place
where the revolver was buried. Per the Spook's orders, they placed
the wood shavings on the spot and lit a ceremonial fire. "Something is
here," Jones called out. "I feel it. Get a pick!" The Cook raced up the
road to get one as a group of prisoners, stifling their laughter, watched
from behind a nearby wall.

The Cook brought the pick, and Jones set to work. The revolver
appeared, and at the sight of it he swooned to the ground. "It was a
good faint—rather too good," he recalled. "Not only did I cut my fore-

head open on a stone, but one of our own British orderlies who was not 'in the know' ran out with a can of water and drenched me thoroughly. I was then carried by orderlies into the house and laid on my own bed."

Outside, the Cook and the Pimple, wild with excitement, kept on digging, certain that the treasure itself lay within reach. By the time Jones rose from his bed and returned dreamily outdoors, they had made a hole "big enough to hide a mule."

"What happened?" he asked. "How did I get back to my room? Did we find anything?"

"Magnificent!" the Pimple declared. "You have been in a trance. You found the revolver. . . . When you found the revolver you fainted. Then the Cook and I, we digged the ground, but found nothing."

"You've spoiled everything," Jones admonished him. "The Spook ordered you to do nothing without instructions from me."

"You think the Spirit will be angered?" the Pimple asked.

"Tell me, did you find anything more?"

"No," the Pimple admitted. He and the Cook swung into a long conversation in Turkish.

"He is thanking you," the Pimple told Jones. "He says you are most wonderful of mediums. You will know how the Spirit may be appeased. We shall dig no more without orders."

THE PRISONERS WERE delighted with the prank, but Jones was disgusted. The whole production—"the first real step in a considered plan of escape"—had failed to bring the Commandant. And though the Pimple attended séance after séance for months to come, Kiazim, cautious as ever, did not appear. And so the Spook turned nasty. "Nothing but abuse of the Turks emanated from the board," Jones wrote. "The Spook was very angry with them for exceeding instructions and continuing to dig after the revolver had been found. Not one word would It say about the treasure. The Pimple apologized to the board abjectly, humbly, profusely. It made no difference."

Finally the Pimple lost his temper. "Always you are cursing and threatening," he wailed to the Spook, "but you never do anything. Can you manifest upon me?"

It was exactly the opening Jones needed. "To-night," the Spook thundered, "you shall die!"

"No! Please, no!" the Pimple cried. "Nothing serious, please! I beg your pardon! Please take my cap off, or my gloves! I only wanted you to move something!"

"I shall move something," the Spook promised.

And so he did. That evening, the Pimple was invited to Upper House for a cup of cocoa—a cup into which Jones had dissolved 6 grains of calomel, a powerful laxative. Before the night was over, it had done its torrential work. "It was no use sending for the doctor," the Pimple told Jones humbly the next day, "because I knew it was all supernatural."

Kiazim would have been told of the incident, Jones knew, yet still he did not come. Jones would need an even stronger lure—but what? Large-scale séances were now on hold throughout the camp: Without O'Farrell, Jones could not have them in Upper House, nor (with the exception of the covert, private sittings for the Pimple) had they been held in Hospital House after Millicent broke the window. The prisoners craved entertainment; Jones craved escape.

In the autumn of 1917, Jones solved the first problem by developing a thought-reading act with Hill. As Jones sat blindfolded, Hill transmitted by "telepathy" the name of an object—a watch, a coin, a comb—held up by a member of the audience, and Jones would proceed to identify it. Their act, which entailed memorizing an intricate verbal code, was conceived purely for amusement. But it would ultimately help solve the second problem: As the Ouija board had, ersatz mind reading would become a central feature of the confidence game.

TOWARD THE END of January 1918, as the Commandant continued to withhold his presence, Jones tried one last gambit. If it failed, he would abandon his plan to escape via spooking.

"I have only seen one previous instance where the Spook behaved so badly for so long," he told the Pimple confidingly. "A lady asked me to consult the Spirit about a gold watch she had lost."

"Did you find it?" the Pimple asked.

"Oh yes. Quite easily. Then several other people came who had lost other things. The Spook found them all. Then came a man who asked me to find a diamond necklace for a friend of his, whose name he would not give. I tried, and the Spook became abusive—for three months it abused us. Finally a fakir told me the reason. The Spook was angry because the sitter kept back the name of the lady who wanted the necklace. . . . The lady who wanted it was in a very high social position, and she was afraid of being laughed at for consulting the Spook, so she remained in the background. That made the Spook angry."

"I see," the Pimple replied. "And did you find the necklace in the end?"

"Oh yes," Jones said. "Once the lady learned the reason, she allowed her name to be mentioned, and we found it at once."

A few days later Jones was summoned to the Commandant's office.

JONES HAD BEEN at Yozgad for a year and a half and had never met the Commandant. What followed, he recalled, "was an amazing interview between a junior officer prisoner and the Turkish major in charge."

As the Pimple translated, Kiazim cut straight to the point:

"Before we go into any details," he said, "I want your word of honour not to communicate to anyone what I am now going to tell you."

"I will give it with pleasure, Commandant, on two conditions."

"What are they?"

"First, that your proposals are in no way detrimental to my friends or to my country."

"They are not," said the Commandant. "I promise you that. What is your second condition?"

"That I don't already know what you are going to tell me."

"It is impossible for you to know that," he replied. "How can you know what is in my mind?"

I looked at him steadily, for perhaps half a minute, smiling a little. . . . "You forget, Commandant, or perhaps you do not know. *I am a thought-reader.*"

"Well?"

The time had come to risk everything on a single throw.

"Let me tell you, then," I said, "You are going to ask me to find for you a treasure, buried by a murdered Armenian of Yozgad. You want me to do so by the aid of Spirits." . . .

The Commandant leant back in his chair, in mute astonishment. . . .

"Am I correct?" I asked.

He bowed, but did not speak. We sat for a little time in silence, he toying . . . with his pencil, I endeavouring to look unconcerned, and smiling. It was easy to smile, for the heart within me was leaping with joy.

By the time the visit ended, Jones had pledged to use his powers to help the Commandant find the glittering hoard. "What did it matter that I was threatened with death if I sought to betray Kiazim's interest in the treasure to Constantinople?" he wrote. "What did it matter that the Pimple told me how such things are done—how a prisoner's body is produced with a hole through the back—'shot while attempting to escape.' Nothing mattered. The fish was hooked at last."

CHAPTER SEVEN

The Regard of Flight

JONES'S CON GAME would have to be planned to the last detail. He would need time, privacy, props, and the raw materials from which to make them. He would need a narrative so compelling that it would hold his captors' attention for months or even longer. "A well-constructed story," as two modern-day scholars of courtroom argumentation have noted, "may sway judgments even when evidence is in short supply."

He would also need an accomplice: The task ahead was too large for a single con man. Besides, he said, "I had had enough of plotting and planning in solitude during the last six months. I longed for companionship." He chose Hill, who, Jones had learned, longed to escape as fiercely as he. Hill had been training in secret for a solo attempt, only to have his plan thwarted by senior British officers.

"There were probably many men in the camp who would have joined me had they been asked, but there was only one who had given clear proof of his deadly keenness to get away," Jones wrote. "He possessed . . . qualities which would make him an invaluable collaborator for me. He had extraordinary skill with his hands. . . . He could find his way by day or night with equal ease, and he could drive anything, from a wheelbarrow to an aeroplane or a railway engine. . . . He was a wonderful conjuror, the best amateur any of us had ever seen.

"I knew I was choosing well, but I little knew how well. Seeking a practical man, with patience and determination and a close tongue, I was to find in Hill all these beyond measure, and with them a great heart, courage that no hardship could break, and loyalty like the sea."

• • •

THE SON OF Edward Ormond Waters Hill and the former Phillis Clark, Cedric Waters Hill was born on April 3, 1891, at Maryvale, the 20,000-acre cattle station in Queensland that his father managed. His boy-

Cedric Waters Hill, circa 1915.
JONES, *THE ROAD TO EN-DOR* (1919)

hood, he recalled long afterward, "was wonderfully free and happy"; he delighted in "walking miles through the bush with my catapult and shooting at every living thing in sight."

School was a less welcome proposition. Sent to Brisbane, Cedric lived with relatives and attended Brisbane Grammar School. A school report described him as "sluggish at his work, but good natured and honourable." He learned more from building things in his uncle's workshop, he later said, than he ever did in the classroom.

After high school, he moved to New Zealand, where his sister and brother-in-law ran a sheep farm, to learn shearing. Photographs from this period depict a rangy young man whose dark good looks are rendered endearingly gawky by protruding ears. He was painfully shy, he recalled, and lacking in confidence. Intrigued by airplanes, a technological marvel then barely a decade old, he built a biplane glider in his spare time.

Returning to Australia, Hill worked as an apprentice at a Brisbane engineering firm. One night, at the Empire Theater there, he saw Nate Leipzig, the Swedish-born American magician who was considered one of the foremost sleight-of-hand artists of his generation. "The amazing thing" about Leipzig, the magicians Dai Vernon and Lewis Ganson have written, "was that [he] enchanted the audience with a few thimbles and a pack of cards—but then the principal magic was Leipzig's personality, charm and complete hold he had over his audience." They added: "He was deadly sure in every trick he did. Every trick he performed had been carefully analysed, *its weak points so concealed as to seem like strength*—nothing was left to chance."

Magic entails both mechanical and psychological engineering, and those arts, along with the contemplative patience and manual dexterity they required, suited Hill sublimely. Leipzig himself had been a maker of optical lenses before turning to magic; the eminent French illusionist Jean Eugène Robert-Houdin (from whom Houdini took his name) had been a watchmaker and engineer. Entranced with Leipzig's act, Hill bought a string of books on conjuring and, while Leipzig was in Australia, took several lessons from him. He would continue to practice sleight of hand throughout his life.

Moving to Sydney, the young Hill took training in the installation, operation, and repair of the machinery used in large-scale sheep-shearing concerns. On completing the course, he got a job overseeing the machines at a small sheep station in Queensland. He was soon in great demand throughout the state, and before long was supervising the eighty shearing machines at a 220,000-head station.

When Australia entered the war in August 1914, Hill, then twenty-three, wanted to join up as a trainee pilot. But Australia did not have a fully functioning military air corps—the Great War would be the first in which planes played a significant role—so he deferred enlisting to honor his shearing commitments.* Toward the end of the year his sister, who had moved from New Zealand to England, suggested he come to London and join the Royal Flying Corps, the precursor of the Royal Air Force.

Established in 1912, the Royal Flying Corps succeeded a disparate constellation of British military aviation units that included an airship battalion and the Royal Engineers Balloon Section. The idea of using airplanes in warfare was still so novel that even in Britain, a flying corps had been a hard sell, as one historian of military aviation has observed:

In war there is always a demand for reconnaissance, for the soldier can only see as far as the hedge or hilltop in front of him, and yet his commander must know what lies over the hill. Has the enemy got troops, guns, and transports? And where are his re-

* As *The Oxford Companion to Australian Military History* notes, "Australia's early involvement in aerial warfare . . . was modest enough. One aircraft (a BE2c) accompanied the expedition [in 1914] against German New Guinea but was never unpacked from its crate."

serves and depots? He knew about the fringe of enemy activity and sometimes tried to get through this fringe with cavalry patrols, whose vision was also restricted. The young officers pressed for scouting aeroplanes to fly over the fringe, but they were up against some of their masters, who thumped the table and declared that it would be quite impossible to see anything on the ground when flying at forty miles an hour!

As late as 1911, Field Marshal Sir William Gustavus Nicholson, the head of the British Army and a veteran of the Boer War and many prior conflicts, had remarked, "Aviation is a useless and expensive fad advocated by a few individuals whose ideas are unworthy of attention."* But the airplane's champions persevered, and by the time World War I began, Britain's fledgling corps had 179 planes at its disposal.

Hill bought a second-class passage and sailed for England. His mother had outfitted him with the homemade accoutrements with which Australian mothers were sending their sons off to war: a bala-clava, a "housewife" (a small sewing kit), and a cholera belt—a cloth band worn around the abdomen, believed to keep the wearer safe from cholera, dysentery, and other gastric ills.

In London, he reported to the War Office and asked to join the flying corps. He met with officer after officer, answered question after question, submitted reference after reference, and filled out form after form. Then he went back to his boardinghouse to wait for a decision. Weeks went by with no word; each time he called at the War Office he was told to return in a fortnight. His patience began to wear thin, and his funds were running low. He lost a precious £4[†] in the street one day after becoming the target of a confidence game—three-card monte. He began to worry that the war would be over before he could get into it.

During this time, Hill went at least once a week to shows by the great English stage magicians David Devant and Nevil Maskelyne. He

* Nicholson's formal title was chief of the Imperial General Staff, as the position was called until 1964. It has since been known as chief of the General Staff.
† About £460, or $600, today.

also struck up an acquaintance with a lovely young woman whom he often passed near his boardinghouse. He was about to work up the courage to ask her for a date when she asked him whether he had considered doing his part for the war effort.

"I am in the process of joining up," he told her, "but there is a bit of a delay."

Each time he saw her, she asked the same question, and each time he was obliged to give the same answer. On the Friday of his sixth week of waiting, their paths crossed again.

"You haven't joined up yet," she said. "I suppose it's the same old excuse?"

"Yes," he confessed. "I'm afraid it is."

She leaned close to him. Gathering his nerve, he said: "Gosh, you are beautiful. I want to kiss you."

The young woman reached for his lapel, put something in his buttonhole, turned, and departed. Hill looked down to see what she had given him. It was a white feather, the widely recognized symbol of cowardice. He seethed all weekend, and on Monday reported to the War Office, girded for personal battle. To his surprise, he was told to report for pilot's training in two days' time.

"I did not see my beautiful white feather girl again," Hill said. "No doubt my disappearance from her patrol area caused her to think she had scored a victory for her country."

THAT WEDNESDAY, HILL reported to the Brooklands aerodrome, a former auto-racing facility in Surrey that had been commandeered for military aviation. By the time he arrived in 1915, it housed an airplane factory, hangars, maintenance workshops, and classrooms, bounded by a large sewage farm. He and his fellows would learn to fly in Maurice Farman Longhorns and Shorthorns (biplanes with "a top speed of about 50 mph") and a Henry Farman, a circa 1910 biplane well suited to stunt flying.* The planes were too delicate to withstand

* The Farman brothers, Maurice and Henri (known in Britain as Henry), were Anglo-French aviators and aircraft design pioneers. Their company, Farman Aviation Works, established in France in 1908 and active until the mid-twentieth century, designed and built hundreds of models.

much wind, so "if there was the slightest breath of wind," Hill recalled, there would be no instruction.

The Longhorns had no dual controls—there were only two seats, one behind the other. The instructor sat in the front seat as the terrified student, sitting directly behind him, thrust his arms beneath the instructor's to work the controls from a distance. He could see over the instructor's shoulder but could not reach the rudder bar with his feet. "This discrepancy in the instruction made itself felt . . . when the pupil started off on his first solo," Hill wrote. "Hence the very amusing but quite common sight of a pupil . . . sitting in his Longhorn in the middle of the sewage farm watched by an angry instructor."

At the end of June, Hill was ordered to take a plane up alone:

It came as a bit of a shock and I felt horrified for a few minutes, but calmed down by the time I was settled in the pilot's seat. I was in a state of tension with feet glued to the rudder bar as I opened the throttle and ran along the ground for take off. The machine ran dead straight until the wheels left the ground near the sewage farm. Then it did a gentle climbing turn towards the farm.

I had seen so many land or crash on it that I was determined not to do the same. I thought, "If I have to land or crash I will do it on something more pleasant." So I did nothing until I was heading back towards the line of hangars at about half their height. At that point I began to feel the rudder and found that I then had control of the whole machine. I managed to clear the hangars and was very thrilled when I landed successfully after doing a few turns over the aerodrome.

In July 1915, after performing two takeoffs and landings, ten figure eights, and a climb to 900 feet, Hill earned his civilian pilot's certificate. After passing a written exam, he was awarded a probational commission, with the rank of second lieutenant. ("I felt very much like a fish out of water in an officer's uniform," he said.) He was ordered to report to Joyce Green, the Royal Flying Corps base in southeast England, for additional training. There he was taught map reading and navigation and logged more hours aloft, in a single-seat Avro, "which did not seem to have enough power to get above about

200 feet," and a Vickers Gun Bus, a two-seat fighter biplane with mounted Lewis gun.*

In September 1915, after passing more exams, Hill earned his RFC wings and was made a flight instructor at Castle Bromwich aerodrome, in the West Midlands. Toward the end of the year, with forty-two hours and five minutes of flying time to his credit, he was posted to the corps's No. 14 Squadron, soon to be dispatched to the Sinai and Palestine campaign. After sailing for Egypt in December, the pilots spent a month in Alexandria waiting for their planes to arrive by sea. During that time Hill entertained his comrades with a conjuring act almost every night.

After their aircraft arrived (they were flying BE2c's, single-engine two-seat biplanes), Hill's unit was sent to Kantara,† which straddles the Suez Canal in northeast Egypt. Each of their aircraft was fitted to carry three bombs: two 20-pounders and one 100-pounder. The pilot carried a loaded revolver, and the observer, in the second seat, a loaded rifle. Only later was a mount for a Lewis gun added near the pilot's seat. "With this arrangement I was terribly keen to meet an enemy aircraft," Hill wrote. "In fact I was terribly keen to meet one even when I only had a revolver, which goes to show how stupid the young can be."

In late February 1916, Hill was given a demanding assignment: to bomb the Ottoman reservoir at Hassana (or Bir el Hassana), 150 miles east of the canal. Other pilots from his unit had tried to destroy it without success—dropping bombs from an airplane was a new, and inaccurate, endeavor. But Hill had been practicing:

> We had no approved bombing range, so for live practice we had to make do with dropping a bomb now and again at some mark in an uninhabited part of the desert. Eventually I had a bright idea. I would make my own harmless practice bombs and my own bombing range. I decide to copy a 20 lb bomb in shape, size and weight in the form of a bag made of aeroplane fabric and filled with sand.

* Invented in 1911, the Lewis gun was a light machine gun widely used by the British in World War I.
† Now El Qantara.

The tail of the bomb could be made of tin sheet. Having made the prototype I cut out and marked the pieces of fabric to form the bag with the least possible trouble in sewing, etc. And the same with the pieces of tin. I was then able to cut out the patterns by the dozen and the sand-filled bomb went into mass production.

For my bombing range there were lots of small areas of shallow water caused by flooding in the vicinity of the Canal. So, by placing an aiming mark on a wet area one had an excellent self-marking target. The splash from the sand bomb hitting the water could clearly be seen by the pilot. These wet patches, when they dried out, formed hard smooth surfaces which made excellent landing areas. . . . Needless to say I had quite a lot of fun with my sand bombs and I certainly improved my ability to drop a bomb near a given spot. . . . I was so keen on having a go at bombing the reservoir that I almost thought of nothing else.

Every few days a pilot from Hill's unit was chosen to destroy the reservoir, and each time he flew back in defeat. At last, on February 26, 1916, Hill's name was called: He was to bomb the reservoir the next morning. He spent the afternoon practicing, dropping live 18-pound bombs from 3,000 feet. He was delighted to find that he got within 10 feet of his target each time.

At dawn on the twenty-seventh, Hill took to the sky with his three bombs aboard. "I had not flown over this bit of country before except for about the first fifty miles or so . . . but I had no difficulty in finding my way," he wrote. "I had seen photographs of the reservoir and it showed up quite clearly at about two miles ahead as I approached at 3,000 feet."

When he got within a mile of the target, the Ottomans opened up their anti-aircraft guns. Although Hill could hear several rifle bullets hitting his plane, he felt secure in the knowledge that their fire was rarely accurate. He let loose a 20-pound bomb, which fell 20 yards wide of the target. Circling back, he dropped the 100-pounder and watched an immense flume of water rise as it hit the reservoir. A keen photographer, Hill kept the plane level, leaned out, and captured the explosion on film. His second 20-pound bomb landed wide of the mark, but by then it didn't matter. The reservoir had been destroyed.

Hill turned and headed for the base, "making rude faces" at enemy anti-aircraft shells as they pinged off his plane. "I cannot remember exactly my feelings the first couple of times I was fired at when flying," he wrote years later. "I do remember that . . . I was not in the least scared. In fact I enjoyed hearing the rifle fire and the odd bullets hitting the plane and seeing the puffs of smoke in the sky. I felt completely immune and it never occurred to me that sooner or later an odd bullet would hit me or something vital which would stop me getting home. If I had been dangled on a rope under the aircraft and fired at I would have been terrified, but in the machine, which was literally no protection, I felt perfectly safe."

He was quite the hero when he returned to camp, and that night, at the party to celebrate his victory, he got "drunk as an owl" on crème de menthe. To the end of his life, he never touched the stuff again.

THROUGHOUT THE SPRING of 1916, Hill continued making bombing and reconnaissance runs. At 4:00 A.M. on May 3, four days after the fall of Kut, he took off from Kantara in his BE2c. His assignment was to photograph El Arish, 100 miles east on the Mediterranean coast. The British had begun building a trans-Sinai railway line extending eastward from Kantara; El Arish was to be one of the stations. Hill's flight would be his last of the war.

Had the day been clear, he would have photographed El Arish from 6,000 feet, safely out of range of enemy anti-aircraft fire. But on reaching the town he encountered dense cloud cover at about 1,000 feet, forcing him to fly beneath it. As a result, he wrote, "the whole Turkish Army, as it seemed by the noise, turned out with rifles and kept up a continuous fire." Opening the throttle, he turned the plane rapidly backward and forward with one hand while working the camera with the other. After fifteen minutes under fire—he heard several bullets hit the plane—he headed inland for Kantara.

The only damage to his plane, he believed, was one severed control cable, and that could be borne. But at about 7:00 A.M., when he had long since left the coast, the engine began to knock. "I must land and see what the trouble is," Hill thought. There was no site in the desert from which he could take off again afterward, so he turned and made for the coast. "By the time I reached the coast the engine was pounding like a steam hammer and I guessed correctly that I had lost all the lubricating oil. The engine was now so bad it was no longer any use landing with the hope of repairing it so I decided to fly on till it gave its last gasp."

Which way? "It seemed to me that the engine would seize up at any minute and that my best bet was to make every mile I could nearer home. The engine went on for much longer than I expected and . . . I made about another 15 miles before it finally seized up, absolutely red hot."

He landed in the sand near an Arab village and was immediately fired upon. Leaping from the plane, he ducked behind it and found that the engine sump, which held the oil, had been pierced by a bullet. There was no cover anywhere nearby. The sea was some 300 yards away, with a line of thornbushes in front offering the only slender cover between him and the village. Retrieving his Lewis gun, ammunition, food, and water, he knew he would need to keep the aircraft out of enemy hands. Though "it almost broke my heart," he cut a fuel cable, stood back, and tossed in a lighted match. There was a "terrific bang," and the plane was gone. He ran for the thornbushes, "feeling as naked as a new born babe," as the villagers fired behind him.

I was across the open space and before I disappeared among the thornbushes I dropped everything except the Lewis gun and fired a couple of bursts at the place they were firing from, hoping that it might tend to make them stay where they were for a while.

The thornbush area was very narrow, but when past it and in the open I was blanked off from the Arabs by the ground formation nearer them. I was now between 200 and 300 yards from where Mt Casius* . . . sloped down steeply to the water's edge. My immediate idea was to get beyond that point as quickly as possible along the sea shore before the Arabs made any serious move. I would then walk along the coast towards Romani, about 40 miles away, with the hope of being picked up by a relief aircraft soon. If

* The mountain, known in Arabic as Ras Kouroun, El-Katieh, or El-Kas, lies on Egypt's Mediterranean coast, roughly halfway between El Arish and Port Said.

the Arabs mounted the sand dune before I got past I would be done.

Before he could get far, a "big lead bullet" hit the sand near him, and he knew it would be futile to make a run for it. Spying a piece of wood nearby, he grabbed it and used it to dig himself in. "After about an hour's work, with pauses now and again to fire a shot or two at the Arabs when they began to fire too often, I had a hole big enough to sit in with safety provided I leant forward with my head down."

For the rest of the morning they fired at each other, the Arabs from behind their sand dune, Hill from his little hole. He managed to keep them from advancing until midday, when two villagers, looping round from the dune, were able to slip to 20 yards southeast of him. Now he was fired on from two sides. "I had to keep my head well down and when I wanted to shoot I would pop up quickly and fire a burst in their general direction without pausing to aim. This procedure used up rather a lot of ammunition but had the desired effect."

At twelve-thirty, with Hill holding off the villagers from both sides, an Allied plane passed overhead. It did not see him, and flew onward.

It was brutally hot in the sand, and Hill had neither water nor shade. Though he fought the urge, he was lulled into sleep, awakened at intervals by the *whang* of a bullet near his head, which caused him to pop up and fire. And so the cycle went for hours—sleep, *whang*, fire; sleep, *whang*, fire—until, at two-thirty, he was out of ammunition.

At three o'clock, two Arabs waved a white flag from atop the sand dune and began to walk toward him. When they were a few yards away, Hill held his empty gun on them and offered them £50 to escort him to Romani. They agreed. "The Arabs to the south east then fired a shot at me which hit the sand nearby, and the others rushed in, taking the machine gun and all my possessions except clothes."*

After an immense argument among his captors—in which, as best he could make out, they weighed killing him on the spot versus handing him over to Ottoman forces—he was taken to the village. There he

---

* Hill's six-hour stand in the desert was considered so noteworthy that it was even commended in *Hilal*, the Ottoman-controlled French-language newspaper that was the only news source permitted the Yozgad prisoners.

sat in the sand, ringed by Arab men, women, and children, as their chief held a loaded rifle on him. Shortly after three-thirty another Allied plane flew overhead. The Arabs thronged round him to hide him from view, and the plane flew on. An hour later, some of the men took him away on foot, saying they were bringing him to Romani. They set out walking southward. Romani lay to the west.

They had walked only a little way when they were met by a military camel patrol: an officer, six men, and a riderless camel. They had been alerted by an Arab messenger, Hill realized, and had come to collect him. He was now a prisoner of war.

Hill was mounted on the extra camel, and the little caravan began to make its way back toward El Arish, camping for two nights in the desert. He spent a day at El Arish, where he was grilled about British military operations by a German commandant. "I almost blush," he recalled, "when I think of the lies I told." The next morning he was mounted on a camel for the two-day, 70-mile trek east to Beersheba (Be'er Sheva), in the Negev Desert in what is now Israel. "When I dismounted I felt I never wanted to ride a camel again," Hill said. "Having ridden 120 miles in five days I was too sore to sit and too tired to stand."

The next morning, in the charge of an Ottoman officer, he was put on a train to Damascus. "These few days were the most unhappy ones of my life," Hill wrote. "I was so terribly disappointed at being a prisoner of war and out of it all. My one idea now was to escape, but there was never a reasonable opportunity during the journey." After the two-day trip, he was put up, under guard, in "a filthy house . . . alive with bugs of every shape, size, and colour." He was joined the next day by a group of British officers, among them Arthur Holyoake, who had been captured at Katia (Qatia), in the Sinai Desert. They were kept in the bug-filled house for three more days before being dispatched by train on May 12 to Aleppo, where they were billeted in a very dirty building that had once been a prison.

From Aleppo, the journey largely mirrored that of the Kut captives a few weeks before: a train to the Anti-Taurus Mountains, followed by a precarious cart ride across them to Mamourie; a train from there to Kulik, and a trip over the Taurus Mountains by cart and truck; a train to Afion Karahissar, where they were quarantined for five days in an empty house; then a train to Angora, where they were held for six weeks, the senior officers in "a fairly clean hotel" and the junior officers, including Hill, on the top floor of "a filthy one which was full of vermin." They were allowed to come down only for meals, and over time, Hill recalled, they grew so weak that they could scarcely manage the stairs. Finally, on July 11, 1916, the junior officers, all of whom now had lice, were placed in springless carts for the journey to Yozgad. They arrived on July 16.

The prisoners were still in lockdown when Hill arrived, and he spent a week cooped up in Hospital House. His confinement only heightened his desire to break free and walk to the Russian lines, but he found to his disgust that "the general feeling in the Camp was against escape." This made recruiting a partner—a desirable thing for an escapee to have—nearly out of the question. He resolved to break out alone.

"I saw clearly that it would be fatal to let it be known generally that I intended to have a go," Hill wrote. "It would be very difficult for me to collect enough food of the right sort without someone to help, and without that it would be hopeless. However, by November food parcels began to arrive and I began to collect any tinned food which would be suitable to take with me when I left. I hoped this would be in the spring."

In the meantime, he spent his days much as his fellow captives did: reading, making furniture, walking round the garden. To pass the time, he also practiced conjuring.

THERE IS MAGIC . . . and there is magic. To many of us, "magic" denotes the stage conjurer's art, a piece of theater designed to dazzle and delight. But there is also the magic that is a foundation stone of traditional belief worldwide: displays of supernatural phenomena, often brought about by a spiritual authority such as a witch, wizard, or medium. It is the stage conjurer's task to produce magic of the first kind while giving the illusion of the second. "Any demonstration that appears to contradict our current understanding of science," the psychologist and magician Gustav Kuhn has written, "is generally considered to be magic."

Theatrical magic is benevolent deception, and the audience knows it. Viewers are aware they are being fooled, and if the act is good enough, they do not mind. Jones and Hill would have the far harder task of deceiving their captors while keeping them unaware that deception was taking place. To do so they would need the trappings of the stage: props, costumes, and a rigorously rehearsed script. They would also need keen psychological awareness, for if stage magic is born of mechanical engineering—the trick box, the false-bottomed hat—it depends even more crucially on psychological engineering. The great Robert-Houdin stated the connection elegantly more than a century ago when he said, "A thorough understanding of the human mind is the necessary key to all successful conjuring."

Today, there is a lively branch of scholarship devoted to the psychology of magic, many of whose practitioners are both academic psychologists and working conjurers. "To the psychiatrist, the psychological side of magic is of particular interest, for *it gives him an opportunity to observe the illusory impulses of the sane,*" the U.S. Army psychiatrist Douglas McG. Kelley wrote in 1943.* "From the moment the magician starts his performance, he is continually swaying the 'minds' of his whole audience by one form of misdirection or another, and is really juggling not so much with billiard balls and thimbles as with the 'senses' and perceptions of those before him."

One of the most fundamental mind games a magician plays involves false causation: getting the viewer to impute a cause-and-effect relationship between two things where none exists. As Peter Lamont, also a psychologist-magician, has noted:

According to Robert-Houdin, the conjuror should "induce the audience to attribute the effect produced to any cause rather than the real one." In one of his most famous illusions . . . he suspended his son in the air, and told his audience that this was due to the mysterious powers of ether. This, it should be said, was in the 1840s, when ether was widely regarded as a substance with rather

---

* A skilled amateur magician, Douglas McGlashan Kelley (1912–58) was one of the U.S. Army psychiatrists assigned in the aftermath of World War II to evaluate Nazi defendants' competence to stand trial at Nuremberg for war crimes. He published a nonfiction book based on his experiences, *22 Cells in Nuremberg,* in 1947.

mysterious properties. In other words, it was not quite so implausible then, but whatever his audience thought about ether, it diverted them from thinking, at least temporarily, about wires and other hidden supports.

Conjurors almost always employ some form of pseudo-explanation, even if it is only implicit in the performance. The snapping of fingers, a gesture of the hand, the saying aloud of the magic words,* these are . . . the implied causes of the effects that follow.

For the magician, then, the real trick is to sell the effect (the child suspended in air) while concealing the method (the physical means of support). As Lamont writes: "If you go to the theatre to see Peter Pan, and when he flies above the stage, you ignore the wires, then that is a willing suspension of disbelief. But if you go to see David Copperfield, and see him fly above the stage, you do not ignore the wires. You look for the wires. You do not see them. That is magic. . . . If you look for the wires and see them, then it is ineffective magic. If you do not look for them because the possibility of wires did not cross your mind, then you do not need magic because you must live in a world of endless wonders."

To enact his miracles, the conjurer must establish his authority from the start. He must appear to know all, see all, and possess a level of assurance about the workings of the world that is unattainable by ordinary men. He must have charisma to burn, allowing him to instill and sustain unquestioning devotion—even when the ideas he puts forth run clearly counter to reason. As the German psychologist and magician Max Dessoir wrote incisively in 1885, "Create a belief and the facts will come of themselves."†

What is striking about conjurers' techniques—plumbing the human

---

* As the psychologist and magician Matthew L. Tompkins told me recently, a "misdirection" ploy like any of these "involves much more than simply controlling where a spectator looks—it's about controlling *how the spectator thinks.*"

† In an 1889 article, Dessoir, a skeptical member of the Society for Psychical Research, would coin the term "parapsychology" (German, *Parapsychologie*), which he defined as the study of "the phenomena that step outside the usual process of the inner life." He added: "The word is not nice, yet in my opinion it has the advantage to denote a hitherto unknown fringe area between the average and the pathological states."

psyche, setting up false causation, establishing authority, and making well-rehearsed events seem to happen of their own accord—is that all are equally vital weapons in the arsenal of the confidence man.

DURING THE WINTER and early spring of 1917, Hill "thought of nothing but escape." He made covert inquiries among the few men he thought might be willing to go with him but found no takers. It was clear that the prisoners remained overwhelmingly against the idea of flight. "Anyone who tried," Hill concluded, "would be counted as a rotter by the majority of the officers at Yozgad and would get a very poor reception on arrival in England." In May he began training for a solo escape. Each day he ran a mile before breakfast and walked several more miles round the grounds. In the Hospital House basement he found a stack of loose tiles and each night after dark would walk round the empty basement with forty pounds of them slung over his shoulders. "If I succeeded in getting away from the Camp," he wrote, "my plan was to walk at night carrying about 35 lb of food and hide during the day."

He planned to leave in June. If all went as he hoped, he would climb out through the basement, where he had managed to dislodge a small barred window; slip past the sentries in the dark; and, climbing a walnut tree in the Hospital House garden, scale the 7-foot wall surrounding it. But there are few secrets in a prisoner-of-war camp, and days before his planned exodus Hill was summoned to meet with the most senior British officer interned there.

"I know all your plans," the officer told him. "You don't stand a million to one chance of getting away. Don't you realise that if you escape you will endanger the lives of not only the prisoners of this camp but of all prisoners in Turkey?" Hill was made to give his parole—his word of honor, in the military parlance of the day—that he would not escape. He did so, but during the coming weeks he was aware that his compatriots were watching him closely. "I felt terribly miserable," he recalled. "What seemed to be my only hope in life had gone, and I was now the most unpopular officer in the Camp." Still obsessed with thoughts of flight, he chafed for the next six months.

He distracted himself by making a camera, an extremely useful (and extremely taboo) thing to have in a prison camp. A fellow prisoner had received a package of ¼-plate films and, having no camera, was allowed to keep them. This officer had also managed to smuggle a camera shutter and one half of a double lens into camp; by cryptogram, Hill asked his sister in England to send him developer and hypo, concealed in a package of food.

It fell to Hill to jury-rig a camera that would accommodate those bits and pieces. He made a literal box camera, whose body was a wooden box, part of a fellow officer's food parcel, that had held Cadbury's chocolate. "The lens and shutter were fitted in one end of the box and a light-tight door at the other," Hill wrote. "I made a roller arrangement with frame suitable for a ¼ plate film and fixed this carefully in a position, inside the box, which gave infinity focus for the lens. Being only half a double lens the focus was abnormally long but in spite of this we took some excellent photographs and developed them. Someone took the camera to England after the war ended and I understand that Cadbury & Co put it on show in a shop window in London." This camera—"a masterpiece of ingenuity and patience," Jones called it—was the first of two that Hill would wield at Yozgad. The second would help spring them from the camp.

ON JANUARY 30, 1918, the day he hooked the Commandant, Jones quietly approached Hill. "I asked him what risks he was willing to take to get away from Yozgad," Jones said. "He objected, at once, that he was on parole, and that the feeling of the camp had to be considered."

"I know," I said, "but supposing I can get you off that parole, and fix the camp safely, how far would you go?"

Hill did not answer for a considerable time.

"You're not joking?" he said, at last.

"No," I replied.

"Then I'll tell you." Hill spoke slowly and with emphasis. "To get away from this damned country I'll go . . . all out. I won't be retaken alive." . . .

The man was terribly in earnest. I told him, briefly, how I had been struggling for months to get a hold over the Turks, and how the opportunity had come that very afternoon. I outlined my plans as far as they had been framed. Hill listened eagerly, and in silence.

"It amounts to this," I concluded; "before we openly commit ourselves in any way towards escape, we must obtain proof of the Commandant's complicity and place that proof in the hands of somebody in the camp. That will make the camp safe. I guarantee you nothing but a share in what will look like a practical joke against the Turk. It may go no further than that. And I warn you that if the Turk finds us out, it may be unpleasant."

They shook hands, and the con began. Over the coming months they would need to perfect a plot centering on a hunt for a nonexistent treasure, with clues supplied by nonexistent ghosts. Jones, by agreement, would take primary charge of planning the hoax; Hill would handle the mechanical engineering. And somehow, working under constant surveillance and with limited resources, they would have to make the whole thing utterly irresistible—and utterly plausible.

CHAPTER EIGHT

In Confidence

EVERY CON STARTS with a good story, and Jones would need one so good that it would propel him, Hill, and their captors straight out of camp. Though the structure of confidence games would not be anatomized formally until 1940, Jones intuitively understood the importance of narrative in setting the stage. "I have two small mites of children," * he wrote in 1919.

> They usually demand a "story" of an evening. Since my return they have gradually established a precedent, and it has become a condition for their going to bed. I take them on my knees, their silky hair against my cheeks, and look into the fire for inspiration about "elephants" or "tigers" or "princesses," or whatever may be the subject of immediate interest and then I begin. I don't go very far without a question, and when that is successfully negotiated there are two more questions on the ends of their restless tongues. The linked answers comprise the story. Nobody makes any bones about the credibility of it, because "father tells it." Thousands of other fathers are doing the same every day. Parents yet to be will continue the good work for the generations unborn.
>
> What the parent is for the child, the medium is for "believers." The gentle art . . . is merely a matter of shifting the authorship of the answers from yourself to some Unknown Third, whose authority has become as unquestionable to the "sitter" as the father's is to the child. Once that is achieved the problem in each case is

---

* Jones's son Bevan — "the Little Unknown" — was born in January 1916, during the siege of Kut.

precisely the same. It consists in answering questions in a manner satisfactory to the audience. . . . If you have ever watched a true believer at a sitting you will know exactly what I mean; and if you can describe the palace of an imaginary princess, you can also describe the sixth, or seventh, or the eighth "sphere." But of course you must always be careful to call it a "palace" in the one instance, and a "sphere" in the other.

The story Jones planned to tell his captors, via the Ouija board, was this:

At the start of the war, a certain rich Armenian of Yozgad, fearing he would not survive the Turks, converted his wealth to gold and buried it in a spot known only to him. He did not disclose the location to his family lest they be tortured for it. Instead, he wrote down three clues that together revealed the treasure's whereabouts: The first clue was a compass direction. The second gave the distance to measure. The third told the spot from which to measure. He sealed each clue in a metal container, placed a golden coin inside as an identifying token, and buried the containers in separate places. He chose three friends elsewhere in Turkey whom he expected to survive the war, and disclosed the location of one clue to each. In the event of his death, the friends were to join forces, dig up the clues, find the treasure, and provide for his family.

The Armenian was now dead. Two of the three friends had also died, and with them the location of the first two clues. The third friend was alive and had unearthed his clue, but without the other two it was worthless. The treasure had never been found. However, the Spook would continue, there was one last hope: As spirit mediums, Jones and Hill could raise the specters of the two dead friends, learn the location of Clues 1 and 2, and dig them up. Then, with their captors as chaperones, they would set out across the country, find the living friend who held Clue 3, and the treasure would be the Turks' to share. (In the interest of spiritual purity, Jones and Hill would refuse all profits.) They could divine this friend's whereabouts because they were not only spiritualists who could converse with the dead but also telepathists who could read the minds of the living.

But before the Spook could embark on this story, Jones had three problems to solve: getting Hill accepted as his new spooking partner, securing time and privacy for them to plot every stage of the con, and reinforcing Kiazim's still-shaky commitment to the project.

"It would have been simple enough had Hill taken any prominent part in our séances," Jones said of the first problem, "but all his work had been behind the scenes. He had been responsible for the manifestations, which was a task of an extremely private nature, so the Pimple had no acquaintance with him as a spookist. His sudden appearance as a medium might give rise to suspicion." Happily, all three problems could be dispatched in a single stroke: the mind-reading act.

IF THE LATE nineteenth century was a golden age of spiritualist ardor, it was also the heyday of belief in thought reading, a vogue that lasted from the 1870s through the 1910s. The two ideologies went hand in glove, spiritualism centering on disembodied communication between living and dead, thought reading on disembodied communication between living and living. The technological marvels of the age that had buoyed spiritualism were likewise lending support to the possibility of transmitting thought: If person-to-person discourse via telegraphed messages, radioed voices, and telephonic speech was a reality, then why not direct communication from mind to mind, without the intervening technology? Many investigators of spiritualist phenomena, including the Society for Psychical Research, were busy exploring thought reading as well.

The thought-reading craze is said to have begun in 1873, after an American mentalist, John Randall Brown, astonished patrons of a Chicago tavern by finding, blindfolded, an object secreted in the room. He did so, he assured the crowd, by reading the mind of the man who had hidden it. That man, with the blindfolded Brown holding on to him, had been instructed to walk round the room, concentrating deeply on the object's location but uttering no sound. Time after time, with one audience member after another, Brown ordered his companion to halt at the correct spot.

Brown soon became a sought-after performer, playing to packed houses across the United States. "Naturally, not all demonstrations

were successful, but that only undergirded the . . . perceived genu-
ineness of Brown's powers," a historian of the craze has noted. "After
all, *only a trickster would be successful every time.*"

It was not until 1877 that Brown's method was elucidated. Writing
in *Popular Science Monthly,* the American neurologist George M.
Beard said that the act depended upon "the general fact that mind
may so act on body as to produce involuntary and unconscious muscular motion"—in other words, motor automatism—and upon Brown's
exquisite ability to detect those tiny movements. It was only with
Brown's ascendancy, Beard wrote, that "it [was] demonstrated that
this principle could be utilized for the finding of any object . . . on
which a subject, with whom an operator is in physical connection,
concentrates his mind."

Beard coined the term "muscle-reading" to describe the technique.
Brown's act, he wrote, worked as follows:

> The operator, usually blindfolded, firmly applies the back of the
> hand of the subject . . . against his own forehead, and with his
> other hand presses lightly upon the palm and fingers of the sub-
> ject's hand. In this position he can detect, if sufficiently expert, the
> slightest movement, impulse, tremor, tension, or relaxation, in
> the arm of the subject. He then requests the subject to *concentrate
> his mind* on some locality in the room, or on some hidden ob-
> ject. . . . The operator, blindfolded, marches sometimes very rap-
> idly with the subject up and down the room or rooms, up and
> down stairways, or out-of-doors through the streets, and, when he
> comes near the locality on which the subject is concentrating his
> mind, a slight impulse or movement is communicated to his hand
> by the hand of the subject. This impulse is both involuntary and
> unconscious on the part of the subject. . . . The expert and prac-
> tised operator . . . is, in many cases, as confident as though he had
> received verbal communication from the subject.

As spiritualism had done, thought reading became mass entertainment; by the 1880s it was attracting audiences throughout the United
States and Britain. It, too, found champions among the foremost intel-
lectuals of the day. One distinguished American writer asserted that

the coincidences that pepper the history of ideas could be explained by the unconscious transmission of thought from one mind to another: "If one should question that this is so," he wrote in 1891, "let him look into the cyclopaedia and [consider] once more that curious thing in the history of inventions which has puzzled everyone so much—that is, the frequency with which the same machine or other contrivance has been invented at the same time by several persons in different quarters of the globe. The world was without an electric telegraph for several thousand years; then Professor Henry, the American, Wheatstone in England, Morse on the sea, and a German in Munich, all invented it at the same time. The discovery of certain ways of applying steam was made in two or three countries in the same year. Is it not possible that inventors are constantly and unwittingly stealing each other's ideas whilst they stand thousands of miles asunder?"

The author of that passage, from his article "Mental Telegraphy," is Mark Twain, who had been a believer in mind-to-mind communication since the 1870s. In the article, which appeared in *Harper's* magazine, he confessed that he had held off publishing his conclusions for nearly twenty years for fear that his reputation as a satirist would tarnish his earnest belief "that minds telegraph thoughts to each other." As he explained:

I made this discovery sixteen or seventeen years ago, and gave it a name—"Mental Telegraphy." It is the same thing around the outer edges of which the Psychical [Research] Society of England began to grope . . . four or five years ago, and which they named "Telepathy." * Within the last two or three years they have penetrated toward the heart of the matter, however, and have found out *that mind can act upon mind in a quite detailed and elaborate way over vast stretches of land and water.* And they have succeeded in doing, by their great credit and influence, what I could never have done—they have convinced the world that mental telegraphy is not a jest, but a fact, and that it is a thing not rare, but

---

* "Telepathy," which marries the Greek *tele-,* "far," and *-pathy,* "feeling," was coined in 1882 in a publication of the Society for Psychical Research, which defined it as "cases of impression received at a distance without the normal operation of the recognised sense organs." The word supplanted earlier terms including "thought reading."

exceedingly common. They have done our age a service—and a very great service, I think.*

Happily for Jones and Hill, then, the era was as ripe for sham mind reading as it was for bogus séances. They had begun work on their telepathy act in the autumn of 1917, months before they began collaborating on escape; it had been conceived simply as "a leg-pull for the benefit of the camp wiseacres." Unlike Brown's solo act, which relied on muscle reading, their two-man routine depended on surreptitious verbal communication. Jones recalled its genesis:

Hill knew from his study of conjuring that stage telepathy was carried out by means of a code, and we set to work by trial and error to manufacture a code for our purposes. By the middle of January [1918] it was almost complete, and we had become fairly expert in its use. . . . Hill then announced to a few believers in spooking that he had learned telepathy in Australia and would give lessons to one pupil who was really in earnest. As a preliminary to the lessons, he said, the pupil must undergo a complete fast for 72 hours, to get himself into a proper receptive state. Most of us had had enough of fasting during the last few years so his offer resulted, as we hoped it would, in only one application for lessons in the telepathic art— that one being, of course, from myself. For three days I took no meals in my Mess, and I made a parade of the reason. To all appearances I was fasting religiously. People told me I was getting weaker, and that the whole thing was absurd. Which shows what the imagination can do; because three times a day I fed sumptuously on tinned food (a luxury in Yozgad) and eggs, in the privacy of Hill's room. At the conclusion of the "fast" Hill "tested" me, and announced to the few believers interested that I had attained the necessary receptive state, and that he had accepted me as a pupil.

This was the position when the Commandant was hooked [on January 30], and after some discussion we saw how to use it to the greatest advantage.

---

* The prospect of "mental telegraphy" doubtless appealed to Twain from an economic standpoint, too. A famously improvident businessman, he numbered among his failed investments of the late nineteenth century an actual magnetic telegraph.

• • •

ON THE AFTERNOON of February 2, 1918, three days after Jones's auspicious interview with Kiazim, the prisoners gathered for one of their regular concerts, the homemade entertainments that could feature singing, clog dancing, and, courtesy of Hill, conjuring. This afternoon the Pimple was also in attendance, and as Jones sat blindfolded on the platform, Hill addressed the crowd: "As some of you know, I once underwent a course of telepathy, or thought-reading, in Australia. Within the last fortnight an officer in this camp went through the painful preliminary of a three days' fast, and became my pupil. Possibly because of his previous knowledge of the occult, he has progressed at a surprising rate, and, although he considers himself far from ready for a public exhibition, he has very kindly consented to help me. . . . I ask you to remember that he is only a beginner, and if our show turns out a complete failure you will, I am sure, give him credit for his attempt." Much applause followed.

Hill proceeded to stroll through the room, asking audience members to hold up whatever they had in their pockets. "Quickly," he might admonish Jones, "what have I here?"

"A bit of wood," Jones, with a look of ferocious concentration, would reply. And sure enough, the prisoner was holding up a piece of wood.

"Tell me," Hill continued, "what this is?"

"A pipe," Jones replied. And so it was.

"Now, do you know what this article is?"

"A wick." That, too, was correct.

And so it went, with Jones identifying most of the proffered objects. "A few suspected a code, and said so," he wrote, "but were utterly in the dark as to how such a code could be arranged. Others were simply bewildered. And still others, and among them none more ardently than the Pimple, professed themselves entirely satisfied that here at last was genuine telepathy and nothing less. We learned afterwards that the Pimple left the concert before its close to inform the Commandant of the supernatural marvels he had witnessed."

Mastering the code had taken three months of clandestine practice. "There is nothing harder in mentalism than a two-person code act worked on a verbal exchange," the English mentalist Tony Corinda wrote in 1968. "Both partners must know the code inside out and be able to translate it at a high speed. . . . The code must be up to date and comprehensive. . . . You should be able to send *any word* or *any number*. . . . The code must be indetectable. If the audience know you are using a code it's no good."

Jones and Hill's code worked like this: First, they compiled a list of eighty objects that audience members were apt to have on their per-

			THIS	THING
Yes I want you to tell me	0	A M	Watch	Chain
Thanks Will you say?	¼	B N	Pin	Nail
Thank you Bones [Jones's nickname]	½	C O	Button	Badge
Well I want you to tell us	1	D P	Banknote	Coin
All right Say	2	E Q	Handkerchief	Tie
Quick Come on	3	F R	Glass	Cup
Quicker Come along	4	G S	Cork	Corkscrew
Quickly Come	5	H T	Matchbox	Match
Tell me Good	6	I U	Pipe	Box
Tell us Very good	7	J V	Cigarette	Cigarette paper
Can you tell me? I want to know	8	K W	Pencil	Rubber
Can you tell us? We want to know	9	L X	Letter	Card
Will you tell me?	10		Book	Notebook
Will you tell us?	11		Knife	Scissors
Do you know?	12	Y	Candle	Lamp
Can you say?	20	Z	Fruit	Flower

*The first eighty objects—about one-sixth of the eventual total—
in the telepathy code used by Jones and Hill.*

sons. (When one is dealing with a literal captive audience, that list is manageable, and fairly predictable.) Next, they arranged the eighty words into a table of sixteen rows and five columns. Rows were designated by phrases common to interrogations ("Quick," "Tell us," "I want you to tell me"), columns by simple, identifying nouns and pronouns ("This," "Thing," "Article"). The intersection of row and column identified the mystery object.

WHAT I HAVE HERE	ARTICLE	ONE
Key	Ring	Strap
Screw	Buckle	Belt
Star	Crown	Medal
Purse	Pocket-book	Spectacles
Tie clip	Cap	Scarf
Mug	Bottle	Saucer
File	Tin-opener	Adze
Bit of wood	Stone	Earth
Pipe cleaner	Tobacco	Case
Cigarette roller	Cigarette lighter	Cigarette holder
Fountain pen	Nib	Charcoal
Envelope	Photo	Stamp
Paper	Ink	Ruler
String	Wire	Rope
Oil	Wick	Candlestick
Vegetable	Grass	Leaf

If a prisoner held up a watch, for example, Hill would say to the blindfolded Jones, "I want you to tell me what this is" or "Yes—what is this?" For a fountain pen, he could say either "Can you tell me what I have here?" or "I want to know what I have here." And so on. "I raised many a good laugh by touching a head and saying to Jones, 'Quickly, what have I here,' especially if the head belonged to a colonel," Hill recalled. Unexpected objects could be spelled out by means of the row headings, which also denoted letters of the alphabet; numbers, such as the date on a coin, could likewise be telegraphed.

Over time, the original list grew to nearly 500 objects, requiring additional tables. To signal that an item appeared in Table 2, for instance, Hill would preface his question with the word "Now": "*Now* tell me . . . ," "*Now* I want to know. . . . ." Table 3 was indicated with the preface "Now then." *

The telepathy act was such a hit that it had two unintended consequences. The first was that several prisoners told Hill they were now willing to undergo the three-day fast in order to become his disciples. (Thinking quickly, Hill told them that his limit was one pupil at a time.) The second was that Doc O'Farrell, awed by the exhibition and hearing Hill say that the lack of privacy was impeding Jones's progress, let the two of them use his dispensary for their classroom. "As a *quid pro quo*," Jones said, "we promised that he should be taken on as the next pupil as soon as my education was completed."

A tiny room above the senior officers' woodpile, the dispensary offered a welcome smoke screen. "Here we could meet without fear of interruption," Jones wrote. "Everybody knew we were studying the problems of telepathy, which was a sufficient explanation of our constant hobnobbing, both for the Turks and for our fellow-prisoners. So nobody suspected us of plotting to escape."

On the evening of February 2, 1918, the day he saw their act, the Pimple came for a private séance with Jones. Speaking reverently to the board, which he always addressed as "Sir," he beseeched the Spook to divulge the treasure's whereabouts. Jones seized the opening:

---

* In present-day telepathy acts, the psychologist-magician Matthew L. Tompkins told me, "communications can get bogglingly complex." Magicians and mentalists, he said, "have developed ways of coding that will be undetectable on a written transcript. You can encode information in a cough, a breath, in the tempo of pauses *between* words."

The Spook promised to tell all, but warned us it would take time. It instructed us to get proper mediums and place them in a proper environment. It indicated Hill as the best medium in the camp, but informed us that he was afraid to "spook," and had kept his powers dark.

Next day the Pimple came to me beaming. He reported having approached Hill, who with great reluctance had confessed to being a medium. Hill had not seemed anxious to take part in a séance, but under great pressure had agreed to do so. The Pimple was greatly pleased. He did not know how carefully Hill's reluctance had been rehearsed. He reported to the Commandant that thanks to a hint from the Spook and his own persuasive powers, he had secured the best possible man to help me in my task.

Jones and Hill held their first joint séance on February 6, 1918, in the dispensary. That little room would do for the time being, but their most pressing need was to get themselves sequestered twenty-four hours a day. This would let them plot in far greater safety, for while they feared discovery by their captors, they feared discovery by their compatriots at least as much: Either scenario would mean the ruin of their plans. In addition, if they were isolated before they escaped, it might insulate their countrymen from charges of aiding them.

And so it was that Elias Henry Jones and Cedric Waters Hill determined to have themselves arrested, tried, convicted, and (with Kiazim's full participation) sentenced to solitary confinement for transmitting war news by telepathy.

THEY BEGAN LAYING the groundwork for their arrest at once. At the February 6 séance, the Spook, recognizing a kindred spirit, welcomed Hill to the board. "The glass . . . spelled out its delight at the meeting, and it ignored the Pimple," Jones recalled. "It went on to warn us we were making an improper use of the Ouija. It was wrong to seek gain, wrong and dangerous. . . . Under the best possible conditions the discovery of the treasure would take a long time, possibly many months. And the present conditions were hopeless." Steered by Jones, the glass elaborated:

"You must live together," said the Spook to Hill and myself, "so that your two minds become as one mind and your thoughts are one thought. Also it is most necessary that it be all kept profoundly secret. Above all you must be free from other thought influences; . . . the other prisoners unconsciously project their thoughts between you, thus preventing unity. You ought to be removed elsewhere. Even prison would be better for you than this. . . . Ask them" (*i.e.*, the Commandant and the Pimple) "either to give up all hope of my help in finding the treasure, or do what I say and remove you." And It again suggested we should be clapped into prison. . . .

This was enough for one sitting, so the "force began to go," as the Spiritualists put it, and the Pimple found himself confronted with the delicate task of breaking the news to the mediums. . . . As is usual with all mediums of any standing, Hill and I were always "absolutely ignorant" of what had been said by the Spook until the Pimple saw fit to read it out to us. At times it was a matter of no little difficulty to avoid displaying our knowledge of what had occurred. When, for example, the Pimple had omitted a negative, or in some other simple way altered the whole tenor of the Spook's order, it was extremely tempting to correct him. But that would have been fatal. We learned to endure his mistakes in silence.

Informed by the Pimple that the Spook wanted to cast them into prison, Jones and Hill were horrified. But they acknowledged that it would be perilous to defy the Spook's instructions. In Australia, Hill let slip, he had once contravened orders from his spirit control. He knew far better than to risk such a thing again. Asked by the Pimple what had happened, "Hill could only cover his face with his hands and shudder. It was TOO DREADFUL to be told."

They knew the Pimple would relay the Spook's demand to the Commandant. But Kiazim made no response: He feared reprimand from Constantinople if he jailed Jones and Hill on a spurious charge. The farthest he would go, the Pimple reported, was to move them to Colonels' House, an empty building nearby that was not part of the camp. To give himself plausible deniability for the transfer, Kiazim would offer other prisoners the chance to live there, too, an untenable arrangement.

Eleven days went by, and Kiazim held firm. The Pimple was livid. The Cook was livid. Jones and Hill were livid, all the while feigning relief at the Commandant's willingness to keep them out of prison. On February 17, desperate, they held another séance. They had orchestrated it with care, and if it went as planned, the Spook would give Kiazim a tangible excuse to jail them:

The Spook repeated its suggestion of prison.* Moïse explained that it was impossible, and suggested the Colonels' house, at the same time pointing out that other prisoners might want to go there and that we saw no way of preventing them. . . .

SPOOK. "If I tell you how to do it, will you obey?"

MOïSE. "If it is possible and does not involve too much hardship. Will you please tell us what we are to do?"

SPOOK. "First, in order to conceal from others the real reason of the mediums being placed apart, and to safeguard the Superior, they will be formally arrested."

MOïSE. "My objection to that is the Superior cannot arrest them without excuse."

SPOOK. "Moïse must say he found a letter incriminating them." . . .

MOïSE. "Very good. Please tell us what we are going to do?"

The Spook told the Pimple to select a piece of paper from the blank sheets lying on the table, and examine it closely. "There is a watermark and the words 'English Manufacture' stamped," he observed. The Spook then ordered the three of them to fold the sheet in turn: first the Pimple, then Jones, then Hill. After making the last fold, Hill placed the paper on the table.

MOïSE. "We have done it."

SPOOK. "Next let Moïse hold it on his head." . . .

MOïSE. "In which hand? With or without cap?"

SPOOK. "Left. Without cap."

(Moïse removed his balaclava—an English-made one, no doubt stolen from one of our parcels.)

MOïSE. "I have put it on my head" (holding it there).

* Jones retained verbatim transcripts of many of his 1918 séances, faithfully recorded by the Pimple and later smuggled out of Turkey.

SPOOK. "This is the letter you found, remember."

MoïSE (after a pause, during which the glass moved violently in circles and the mediums grew more and more exhausted). "May I take it off now?"

SPOOK. "Yes."

MoïSE. "May I open it?"

SPOOK. "Have you promised to obey?"

MoïSE. "We all promised whatever we can to obey it."

SPOOK. "Open it."

(Note by Moïse in record: "Both mediums under very high strain.")

MoïSE (in great excitement, seeing the paper was now written on). "May I read it?"

SPOOK. "Yes."

The letter, which bore the identical watermark, had been switched expertly by Hill for the blank sheet.* It read: "Last night at the stated time we received a telepathic message through two fellow-prisoners. It said 'Forces being sent South from Caucasus.' Let me know if this was the exact message sent. If it is correct there is no need to incur further danger of discovery by writing messages. The rest of our arrangements can be made by telepathy. The mediums have been sworn to secrecy and can be absolutely trusted. Put your reply in the usual place."

As the Pimple read those words aloud, Jones and Hill grew terrified. "Can Hill and I withdraw?" Jones asked the board.

"If you withdraw now," the Spook replied, "you are doomed." Both mediums, the Pimple noted, were "cold, giddy, and shivering."

As the Pimple transcribed, the glass continued to move. "The Spook says this is all true," he exclaimed in surprise. "It says this letter is word for word the same as one which has actually been sent."

The mediums looked even more frightened. "That is why we wanted to withdraw!" Jones cried.

"But I thought this letter was merely an invention of the Spook," the Pimple said.

---

* Hill was such an adroit sleight-of-hand artist, Jones said, "that even I, who knew what to expect . . . missed seeing the actual substitution."

"I wish it was," Jones confessed miserably, "for he has given away what we had intended to keep as a deep secret, as it involves others."

"Jones and I got that telepathic message about the Caucasus troops last night," Hill put in. He asked the Pimple not to tell the Commandant that the letter was genuine.

"We were making a strong bid to capture the Commandant's full belief," Jones later explained. "The magic letter, if true, was of extreme importance to the Commandant, for it indicated that amongst his prisoners of war were two mediums capable of sending and receiving messages of military importance. Our agitation, our attempt at withdrawal, our confession to the Pimple and our request that he should hide from the Commandant the fact that the contents were really true—all these were certain to be reported to Kiazim Bey."

The Spook proceeded to tell the Pimple how the Commandant should play his part. He was to summon Jones and Hill to his office for a friendly chat about telepathy, together with several "witnesses"—senior British officers who could vouch, innocently, for their skill as thought readers. What these officers would not have been told was that they were actually attending a trial, and that Kiazim would use their testimony, along with the letter, to convict the pair of telepathic espionage. This would let him sequester them so that their minds would become one . . . the better to find the treasure with.

Should Kiazim fail to enact this plan, the Spook concluded, consequences would be dire. As the Pimple rose to leave, an anguished Jones implored him: "You promise not to tell the Commandant we have really been working this telepathy business with somebody outside the camp, won't you? We fear he will be seriously angry and really punish us. If it wasn't for the Spook's threats we would stop now!"

The Pimple gave his promise and, just as they'd known he would, broke it the moment he left.

DURING THE LAST weeks of February, Jones and Hill gleefully prepared for their trial. They gave several more thought-reading shows to shore up belief among their fellow prisoners. They cultivated the officers who would most readily attest to their telepathic skill, including the susceptible Doc O'Farrell. In case Kiazim needed further persuasion, they covertly borrowed O'Farrell's medical books and boned up on biliary colic (as gallbladder attacks were then known), a malady from which the Commandant had long suffered. They had no idea whether or how they would use this bit of insurance, but it would prove an inspired course of study.

By early March they were ready to be arrested, but no arrest came: Though Kiazim craved the treasure, his avarice was eclipsed by his fear of censure. "Moïse arrived with a long list of questions which the Commandant would like the Spook to answer," Hill recalled. "Must he report the trial to the War Office, and if so what should he say; what would he do if the War Office authorities wanted the mediums more severely punished; and what would he do if they wanted to know where the letter was found and who wrote it? . . . The Spook gave satisfactory answers to all questions and . . . gave the assurance that if it did become necessary to tell the War Office, he would dictate any reports required and the Commandant would have only to sign them." It also threatened severe, sanguinary reprisals if Kiazim did not adopt the plan.

Three séances were required to bolster Kiazim's courage until at last their arrest was scheduled. But the appointed day, March 5, passed like any other. The Pimple came to see them on the sixth, bearing the doleful news that Kiazim planned to back out of the treasure hunt. Hoping the Spook could figure out how to bring the Commandant around, he requested a séance. "We sat down to the spook-board," Jones wrote. "There had been no time for a special consultation, but this was likely to be our last chance and we must use it."

> Moïse wrote down a question without uttering it, and slipped it under the board for the Spook to answer. This was awkward. At previous séances the Spook had shown its power of answering questions in this way.* To-day, however, we were not prepared for the test. But I had managed to get a glimpse of one word as he wrote, and that word was suggestive. It was "pardon."

---

* This was normally accomplished by Hill picking the Pimple's pocket, reading the note, and covertly replacing it.

"No use begging pardon," said the Spook; "obey and BEWARE!"

Then came a long pause, the glass remaining quite motionless. Moïse grew more and more impatient.

"Please answer what to do," he said.

For a long time, the Spook was silent as Jones scoured his mind for a way to salvage their plan. At last the glass began to move.

"What will you do?" the Pimple implored the Spook.

"I can but bring on the old pains," the Spook replied.

"What do you mean, please?" the Pimple asked.

"Vomiting," the Spook declared. "Vomiting! Shivers! Such agony that he will roll about and scream for mercy! He knows well, but I shall choose my own time. Unless orders are obeyed today I forbid my mediums to grant further sittings under penalty of madness to themselves. Good-bye."

"How can I make the Commandant do it?" the Pimple begged. But the Spook had gone.

The Pimple scurried out the door, bearing his transcript of the séance.

"There goes our last chance, old chap," Jones said. "If that doesn't fetch him, we've failed."

The next day, a sentry brought Jones a note.

Lieutenant Jones:

The Commandant should like to talk a little with you about thought-reading and telepathy. Will you ask a few officers to come up with you to the office in order to have a little show?

(Signed) for the Commandant,

The Interpreter—Moïse.

JONES AND HILL reported to Kiazim's office that afternoon with their four chosen comrades. The Commandant shook hands all round and had everyone sit down. "What is telepathy?" he asked Jones, as the Pimple translated. "How is it done?"

"It is not known how it is done any more than it is known how electricity works," Jones replied, "but it is similar to electricity in that there is a sender and a receiver, and thought-waves can be sent by one and picked up by another."

"Is this a medical fact?" Kiazim asked O'Farrell.

"It is a well-known fact like mesmerism," O'Farrell replied in all sincerity.

And so it went, with the four officers vouching for the validity of thought reading and Jones and Hill's prowess as telepathists. Then Kiazim reached into his desk, pulled out a document, and handed it to Jones.

"Lieut. Jones showed marked agitation while reading the note," O'Farrell recorded. "He bit his lip, clenched his hands, and appeared as if he was suffering from extreme excitement, from a medical point of view, and as if he was going into a trance from a psychophysical point of view."

Kiazim asked Jones if the charges in the letter were true. "Jones said he did not deny that he had received and sent telepathic messages, and had received war news by these means," another officer wrote afterward. "The Commandant then asked him who his correspondent was. Jones refused to state. The Commandant then threatened Lieut. Jones with solitary confinement, without his orderly, and on bread and water, unless he told him who his correspondent was. He was given 24 hours to decide whether he would answer or not. Further, he was asked to give his word of honour not to communicate telepathically with anyone. This he said he could not do as he could not control his thoughts."

With that, Jones and Hill (whom Jones had made certain to implicate in his testimony) left Kiazim's office, outwardly raging but inwardly rejoicing. They had just become, in all likelihood, the only people in military history to be convicted of espionage-by-telepathy.

The witnesses were aghast. "I never thought the Commandant had it in him to work out such a trap," O'Farrell said.

TWENTY-FOUR HOURS LATER, Jones, Hill, and the witnesses returned to the Commandant's office.* Kiazim, acting his part splendidly,

---

* Jones had built in the twenty-four-hour grace period to give Hill time to withdraw his parole not to escape, on the grounds that he would no longer be residing in the camp.

"began with a graphic picture of the horrors of a Turkish prison and the monotony of a bread-and-water diet."

Then he told us how much he loved us prisoners, and would we spare him the pain of putting us in jail by giving up the name he wanted? Hill and I were models of firmness in our refusal. Kiazim Bey, with a gesture of hopelessness, indicated he could do no more for us. Then came the sentence. The common jail for the present would remain in abeyance, but until we saw fit to confess we would be confined in a back room of the "Colonels' House"—a large empty building opposite the office. We would be allowed no communication whatever with other prisoners, and no orderly, but we might have our clothes and bedding. We would not be permitted to write or receive any letters. To begin with, our food could be sent in by the nearest prisoners' house. If we remained obdurate, we would later sample a bread-and-water diet. No walks and no privileges of any kind, and the threat of a further court-martial and a severer sentence by Constantinople over our heads!

The senior British officer in attendance made a short speech, diplomatically thanking Kiazim for his leniency, and the witnesses left the office. Once they had gone, Jones, Hill, the Commandant, and the Pimple roared with laughter, congratulating one another on the success of the sham trial—and, in their captors' case, doubtless picturing the treasure that would soon be theirs. "The Commandant thought it the best joke of his life," Hill recalled, "and asked us to repeat the speech of thanks over and over again."

Before long, sentries arrived to march Jones and Hill to their new quarters. Kiazim shook hands with them both. "Remember, my friends," he declared, "you have but to ask for anything you want, and you will get it."

CHAPTER NINE

Villainous OOO

———————

THE MEDIUMS NOW had a large house all to themselves. "Absurd as it may seem, Hill and I felt not only happier, but actually freer in our new prison than we had done in the camp," Jones wrote. "We no longer merely existed. We were partners in a great enterprise. There was something definite for which to work, something which would compensate us for every hardship—our hope of freedom."

Their first task was to get their new quarters arranged: Colonels' House was entirely empty. They were allowed to bring one chair and table each, which they moved from room to room as needed. Their meals would be sent over from Posh Castle. Since they couldn't bring the spook-board into captivity with them (it would have been suspicious for men convicted of telepathy to do so), Hill built a new one.

Before they were sequestered, the mediums had apprised their families of their trial, sentencing, and escape plans in coded letters home. Just as it's crucial for a detective under deep cover inside a criminal organization to have a handler on the outside who knows his true identity, it was vital for the mediums to make sure that their relatives in Britain had at least an inkling of their planned course of action. In a postcard to his father dated March 3, 1918, Jones wrote:

> Received a card from my wife dated 6th January, & one from Tendia, & I received also a letter from dear old Bubbles who is pressing me very hard to commence hard work in law. I ought (and must) arrange useful reading. "Common Law"—a damnably dry uninteresting book—arrived a few days ago. So tell B. I am ready to begin with the warm weather. I am quite well. Love to all at home. Harry.

"Tendia," here masquerading as a personal name, is a Welsh imperative verb meaning "Watch!" or "Take care!," the signal to Sir Henry to look for a code. The first word of the code, "Bubbles," is believed to stand for "Bubbly-jock"—a Scottish colloquialism for a turkey, used here to denote the Turks. (Jones's mother was Scottish and would have known the term.) What Jones reveals about his captors is conveyed by the initial letters of the words that follow, starting with "commence hard work in law." When the initials are amalgamated, they spell the Welsh phrase "Chwilio am aur claddu"—"search for buried gold." Decoded, Jones's message reads, "I have received orders from the Turks to search for buried gold."

The Spook, who was only too happy to speak through Hill's new board, ordered the Turks to purchase a fine new stove and loads of wood for the mediums' comfort. He set the Cook to work chopping the wood, lighting the daily fire, sweeping the mediums' rooms, fetching things from the bazaar, and attending to their myriad wants. The Cook, Jones reported, "was delighted to do it. He even brought us some very pleasing dishes of Turkish food, and two kerosene lamps, with an ample supply of oil. The camp had been without kerosene for a year or more. . . . The new lamps were a real luxury, and our enjoyment of them was not lessened by the Pimple's explanation that the kerosene was really a Turkish Government issue for prisoners, but as its price in the market was fabulous the Commandant did not issue it to the camp. He kept it for pin money."

With the household settled, they could truly begin to plot. Jones knew the general outline of the script, but he and Hill would have to engineer every facet of it to transform an ethereal treasure hunt into a real-world escape. They faced a welter of contingencies: How could the search for a local treasure propel them far from camp? Where should they go if they did get out? How could they ensure their own safety and that of their countrymen? How could they incriminate their captors?

The list of problems was so formidable that they agreed to tackle them mainly one by one. They already knew what the initial steps would be: First, tell their captors the story of the treasure; next, have them hunt for the Armenian's buried clues. To buy themselves time to orchestrate these steps fully, they had a copy of Oliver Lodge's *Ray-*

mond sent over from Britain. On the Spook's orders, the Pimple read it and then translated the whole thing into Turkish for the Commandant.

Hill had already prepared the ground for the clue hunt. In the weeks before their arrest he had constructed two small tin cans, each about 4 inches long by 1½ inches wide, with soldered-on false bottoms. Into each he placed a slip of paper, inscribed, with the aid of an Armenian-French dictionary found in camp, in Armenian script. The first slip gave a compass direction, the second a distance. He wrapped each clue around a Turkish gold lira before sealing it inside the false bottom. He filled the main compartment of each can with ashes. There was no third clue, by design.

To hide the clues, Hill went skiing. During their first winter in camp, several officers had made skis out of long, straight boards pried up from the floors of their houses. (Under cover of darkness, they replaced those floorboards with lesser wood bought at the bazaar.) They persuaded the Commandant to let them ski once a week, under guard, in the hills around town. Thus the Yozgad Ski Club was formed, and Jones and Hill became avid participants.* On one outing, Hill brought his cans along. Eluding the sentries' eyes, he buried them in the hills, about three-quarters of a mile apart, in spots he knew he could find again once the snow was gone.

Now, in mid-March, it was time to reel their captors in further. A week into the mediums' solitary confinement, the Spook announced that they were sufficiently in tune to begin holding séances devoted to the treasure's whereabouts. (The Pimple would note approvingly that Jones and Hill now often uttered precisely the same words at precisely the same time, a clear sign that their minds had become one. He never realized, Jones wrote, "what a lot of practice it took to do it naturally.")

But before the Spook could begin the treasure tale, the mediums had to prepare the psychological ground for its reception. For one thing, they would need to be constantly vigilant against any slip that might betray them. ("No real con man," one student of the art has written, "ever has a day off.") For another, they would have to sustain their captors' unswerving faith while simultaneously glutting them

---

* The club held at least one official point-to-point race, with the camp bookmakers doing a thriving business.

The site of the first clue, buried by Hill.   JONES, THE ROAD TO EN-DOR (1919)

with blarney. To fulfill both mandates, they built two devices into their script that let them control its pace: The Spook would divulge the treasure story only bit by bit—a serialized drama meted out in carefully calibrated doses—and the treasure-seekers would meet an imposing new ghost, a man called OOO.

The first "treasure séance" was held in Colonels' House on March 14, 1918, with the Pimple in rapt attendance. Over four and a half hours, the Spook, piecing together the gossip that suffuses the Beyond, began to unspool the story. "The Spook gave an outline of the history of the treasure which he had found out from various spooks in the spirit world," Hill would write. "No one spook knew the whole story except the spook of the late owner of the treasure, and he was not willing to give any information."

Any spook can spin a story, so it was essential that Jones and Hill establish the veracity of this tale. The revolver hunt had been a tantalizing "convincer." They now had to sell their victims on the entire scenario, and they began with a simple appeal to greed: The Spook casually mentioned the treasure's value—£28,000.* Then, at a later séance, the mediums introduced a potent new concept, "trance-talk."

---

* About £1,950,000, or $2,600,000, today.

If, the Spook explained, he were to place Jones and Hill in a deep trance, then they would be able to see the future. Trance-talk was very difficult, he said—even dangerous—but the mediums had agreed to take the risk. That night (on the Spook's orders in darkness), the Pimple witnessed the rigors of trance-talk firsthand. "For some time," Jones wrote, "there was dead silence."

> Then Hill and I began to grunt, and make strange noises in unison. The noises changed gradually from grunts to groans, and from groans to guttural sounds, thence to some unknown tongue, and finally into English. When we had practised together in private (it took a lot of practice to get grunt-and-groan perfect) we had never been able to proceed very far without laughing. . . . But what is ridiculous in daylight may be intensely eerie in the dark. And so it proved. The unhappy Pimple nearly fainted with fright, but he stuck to his post and his note-taking with a courage that roused our unwilling admiration.

In their dual trance, the mediums saw the future, and it looked like this: A man carrying a letter went through a door and into a garden. As he walked, they described the surrounding flowers and trees. The man passed through the garden and into a house, and the mediums chronicled his progress through the hall, up the stairs, and into a bedroom. The bedroom was elegantly appointed, with a red carpet, ottomans, a large footstool, and a sword hung on one wall. There was a man on the bed, but his face was hidden. The man took the letter, read it, and summoned a woman who had lovely hands. They left the house together, carrying a lantern. Outside, they were joined by a man carrying a pick. "Then," Jones wrote, "everything turned black. There was a pause in the trance-talk for perhaps a minute. Then we cried out that we saw the group again. They had been digging."

> We could see the hole by the lamplight. They were pulling things out of the hole—boxes they looked like! Yes, boxes! The man with the pick raised it above his head and smashed open a box, and— "Gold! Gold! Gold!" (so loud and so suddenly did we shout together that the Pimple leapt to his feet). Then blackness again, and a re-

versal of the opening proceedings—we lapsed first into the unknown tongue, and thence through the guttural sounds to the groans and the little farmyard grunts with which we had begun.

A few minutes went by before Hill spoke. "I am afraid it's no good!" he said. "Nothing is going to happen."

"Something *has* happened," the Pimple replied. "You've both been in a trance. It was terrible!"

"Have we?" Jones asked dazedly. "I feel just as usual, only very, very tired."

The house they had described, as the Pimple well knew, was Kiazim's. (Doc O'Farrell, who had treated him there, had supplied a detailed account.) By the time the trance-talk ended, Jones recalled, the Pimple "was half crazed with excitement and nervous strain. It was 'wonderful,' 'marvellous,' 'undoubted clairvoyance.' He congratulated us 'from the base of his heart.' It was a 'beautiful word-picture.' It was more—a 'word-photograph'—and of a house we had never seen! . . . He believed we were greater spiritualists than Sir Oliver Lodge."

HERE OOO ENTERS, and he is a work of genius. OOO was the ghost of the Armenian treasure owner, and an ardent obstructionist. "OOO closes his thoughts to me," the Spook informed the Pimple soberly during an early séance in Colonels' House. "He has not yet shaken off the hatred of your sphere and refuses to benefit those he hates." And thus, whenever Jones and Hill needed to buy plotting time, withhold information, keep their captors in suspense, or whet their appetite for the treasure anew, OOO, intent on safeguarding his hoard from beyond the grave, would hijack the proceedings.

OOO was what magicians call an "out." An out, the magician-psychologists Peter Lamont and Richard Wiseman have written, "gets the magician out of trouble by offering an alternative route. A classic example is one used when the magician fails to locate a selected card. Admitting failure, he asks the spectator the name of the card. He then looks through the deck for the card, pretending not to see it but actually palming it out secretly. 'No wonder I could not find it,' the magician says, casually reaching for his pocket with the card palmed and apparently removing it from the pocket, 'it's been in my pocket all along!'" Outs, they added, "are also of particular use to the pseudo-psychic."

Jones had created an impromptu out during the Upper House séance at which, blindfolded and lost, he banged the glass in one spot, causing a spectator to cry, "Leave that damned 'D' alone!" With OOO, he forged an out durable enough for every occasion. "Though OOO himself was not much to be feared, being a comparatively young and inexperienced spirit," Jones explained, "a company had now been formed to help him, which contained some of the best known organizers in the spirit-world." (OOO's gang of enforcers included Napoleon Bonaparte.)

At a Colonels' House séance, the Spook revealed what he knew of OOO. "I have found out a lot about him," he reported. "It is difficult to tell you about him, because he and his friends are struggling to control the mediums." The glass began to move spasmodically, a sign that OOO and the Spook were locked in battle. "When the glass begins jerking like that," the Spook explained, "it means I have lost control, and the mediums must stop at once, as OOO is in control."

Interrupted by frequent tussles ("Moïse said afterwards that he could see the whole fight going on, and that it was wonderful to watch"), the Spook began to spin the treasure tale. He told of the doomed OOO, his burial of the gold, and how he had made up "T-H-R-E-E C-L-U-E-S A-L-L A-L-I-K-E." One clue, the Spook revealed, "named the place from which to M-E-A-S-U-R-E, one the D-I-S-T-A-N-C-E, and the third gave the D-I-R-E-C-T-I-O-N." Each clue was wrapped round a piece of gold, sealed "in a S-E-P-A-R-A-T-E R-E-C-E-P-T-A-C-L-E and B-U-R-I-E-D" in a separate spot."

OOO, the Spook continued, had disclosed the location of one clue to each of three trusted friends. The friends' names were—

Just then OOO seized the glass.

"I am BEATEN," cried the Spook. "Oh, Moïse, I can never give the names now!" OOO and his minions, he explained, would block him from disclosing them forever. The Spook asked the Pimple to suggest three pseudonyms instead. The Pimple proposed AAA, YYY, and KKK, and the Spook resumed the tale:

OOO went to AAA secretly, and said to him, "I have hidden a certain thing in a certain place." He described exactly the place where the first clue is hidden. He said to AAA, "If I die, send for YYY, and do what he says." Then he made AAA swear a great oath never to reveal what had been told him. He then went secretly to YYY and told him where the second clue was buried. He said, "If I die, someone will send for you and show you a token. When that happens send for KKK." He gave tokens to both AAA and YYY. Then he went to KKK, and, putting him on oath, he told him where the third clue was buried, and said, "If I die, two persons will send for you. You will know them by their tokens. When this happens all three of you go to my heir, and tell him what I have told you." YYY and KKK are dead. I must stop, as the mediums are getting exhausted.

Without the friends' real names, the Spook told the Pimple, it would be extremely difficult to find the buried clues. However, he would add, there might still be a way. He would elaborate at the next séance, in five days' time.

"The Pimple's only criticism of our Stevensonian treasure story," Jones observed, "had been to marvel at the cleverness of OOO. He had swallowed the yarn whole."

THE QUICK AND dirty hoax known as the short con has very likely been played since the dawn of mankind: Recall Jacob persuading Esau to sell his birthright for a mess of potage. But such ruses became known as "confidence games" only in 1849, after the much-publicized arrest of one William Thompson—aka Samuel Thompson, Samuel Powell, Edward Stevens, et al. Thompson, who operated in New York City, plied his satin-smooth trade in the following manner, as the *New York Herald* recounted that year:

For the last few months a man has been travelling about the city, known as the "Confidence Man"; that is, he would go up to a perfect stranger in the street, and being a man of genteel appearance, would easily command an interview. Upon this interview he would say, after some little conversation, "have you confidence in me to trust me with your watch until to-morrow[?]"; the stranger, at this novel request, supposing him to be some old acquaintance, not at the moment recollected, allows him to take the watch, thus placing "confidence" in the honesty of the stranger. . . . In this way many have been duped, and the last that we recollect was a Mr. Thomas McDonald, of No. 276 Madison Street, who, on the 12th of May last, was met by this "Confidence Man" in William Street, who in the manner as above described, took from him a gold lever watch valued at $110; and yesterday, singularly enough, Mr. McDonald was passing along Liberty Street, when who should he meet but the "Confidence-Man" who had stolen his watch. Officer Swayse, of the Third ward, being near at hand, took the accused into custody on the charge made by Mr. McDonald. . . . On the prisoner being taken before Justice McGrath, he was recognized as an old offender, by the name of Wm. Thompson, and is said to be a graduate of the college at Sing Sing.

Thus "confidence man" entered English parlance. William Thompson's legacy also includes Herman Melville's last novel, *The Confidence-Man*, published on April 1, 1857—the day on which it was set. Its title character was unquestionably modeled on Thompson, who remained "so well known in the 1850s," one scholar observed, "that many readers of *The Confidence-Man* could not have helped but connect him with the novel as they read it."

By 1859, *The Rogue's Lexicon*, compiled by New York City's first police commissioner, George Washington Matsell, could define "confidence man" this way:

A fellow that by means of extraordinary powers of persuasion gains the confidence of his victims to the extent of drawing upon their treasury, almost to an unlimited extent. . . . Every man has his soft spot, and nine times out of ten the soft spot is softened by an idiotic desire to overreach the man that is about to overreach us. This is just the spot on which the Confidence man works. . . . The Confidence man is perfectly aware that he has to deal with a man who expects a result without having worked for it, who gapes, and stands ready to grasp at magnificent returns. The consequence is, that the victim—the confiding man—is always *done.* . . . The Confidence man always carries the trump card.

The sustained gambit known as the long con would not emerge until the end of the nineteenth century, for it depended crucially on the new communications technologies. Rigorously produced works of stagecraft, long cons entailed props, costumes, multiple actors, and fully furnished settings. Like any good play, each had a clearly articulated structure. "All confidence games, big and little, have certain similar underlying principles," David W. Maurer wrote in *The Big Con*, his seminal 1940 study of the form. "All of them progress through certain fundamental stages to an inevitable conclusion; while these stages or steps may vary widely in detail from type to type of game, the principles upon which they are based remain the same and are immediately recognizable."

A linguist at the University of Louisville, Maurer spent years in the company of con men, recording their pungent argot. "Mark" or "chump" denotes a victim or prospective victim. The "roper," or "outsideman," is the con artist who makes the first contact with the mark. His partner, the "insideman," reels the mark in deeper and ultimately makes the score. ("Insidemen," Maurer writes, "are highly specialized workers; they must have a superb knowledge of psychology to keep the mark under perfect control during the days or weeks while he is being fleeced.") The "big store" is the club, poolroom, or office, tricked up for the occasion, to which the unsuspecting mark is brought. The "manager" supplies props and set dressing. The "fixer" greases palms of policemen, politicians, and lawyers as needed.*

The long con is about the "play" in every sense of the word. In his book, a nostalgic ode to an era of gaslight and gaslighting that was already on the wane, Maurer anatomized the play's formal properties:

1. Locating and investigating a well-to-do victim. (*Putting the mark up.*)
2. Gaining the victim's confidence. (*Playing the con for him.*)

---

* In 1974, Maurer filed a $10 million lawsuit charging that elements of *The Sting*, the popular 1973 Hollywood film starring Paul Newman and Robert Redford, had been lifted from *The Big Con*. The suit was settled in 1976 for an undisclosed sum.

3. Steering him to meet the insideman. (*Roping the mark.*)
4. Permitting the insideman to show him how he can make a large amount of money dishonestly. (*Telling him the tale.*)
5. Allowing the victim to make a substantial profit. (*Giving him the convincer.*)
6. Determining exactly how much he will invest. (*Giving him the breakdown.*)
7. Sending him home for this amount of money. (*Putting him on the send.*)
8. Playing him against a big store and fleecing him. (*Taking off the touch.*)
9. Getting him out of the way as quietly as possible. (*Blowing him off.*)
10. Forestalling action by the law. (*Putting in the fix.*)

One classic long con was a ruse known as "the wire," which blossomed with the advent of the telegraph. At a racetrack, the roper picks out a well-heeled mark and makes a play for his friendship. Once he gains the mark's trust, he persuades him to come in on a sure thing—a way to pick the winning horse every time, at any track in the country. This is accomplished, the roper explains, through the cooperation of a crooked Western Union employee, who will share the race results, giving the men just enough time to get a bet down, before transmitting them to bookmakers nationwide. Stage sets for "the wire" included a phony Western Union office, complete with ringing telephones, clattering teletypes, and "employees" hired to lend an air of bustle (the conniving telegrapher is played by the insideman). There is also a fake betting parlor in which the mark is gradually parted from his money.

At the "betting parlor," the mark is allowed to win an escalating series of wagers and grows increasingly aflame with avarice. After some time, the con men persuade him—gently, almost reluctantly—to stake an enormous sum . . . with which they promptly abscond. Betting parlor and telegraph office vanish into the mists like Brigadoon.

"Big-time confidence games," Maurer writes, "are in reality only carefully rehearsed plays in which every member of the cast *except the mark* knows his part perfectly":

[The mark's] every probable reaction has been calculated in advance and the script prepared to meet these reactions. Furthermore, this drama is motivated by some fundamental weakness of the victim—liquor, money, women, or even some harmless personal crotchet. The victim is forced to go along with the play, speaking approximately the lines which are demanded of him; they spring unconsciously to his lips. He has no choice but to go along, because most of the probable objections that he can raise have been charted and logical reactions to them have been provided in the script. Very shortly the victim's feet are quite off the ground. He is living in a play-world which he cannot distinguish from the real world. . . . He is the victim of a confidence game.*

WORKING IN EXTREME isolation, with none of the resources available to civilian con men, Jones and Hill would nonetheless have to mirror this script. In one respect their task was simpler than an ordinary con artist's: They wouldn't need to search for a mark, as their victims had been supplied readymade by the Ottoman government. But in all other ways they were at a deep disadvantage. Their circumscribed conditions made constructing a "big store" impossible, yet they would somehow need to duplicate the work of a "manager," transforming the camp and surrounding countryside into a viable stage set. They had no "convincers" of real value, and they would have to make their props from found objects. And if their con was exposed, with no "fixer" on hand to make offenses disappear, they would face a penalty far more lethal than a term in jail.

By virtue of intellect, intuition, and his civilian training, Jones had already anticipated some of the steps that Maurer would codify decades later. He had worked out his initial pitch, conceived in the spring of 1917 after the Pimple asked whether the Spook could find

---

* The Internet age, in which anyone can be a Nigerian prince, has engendered a degree of renewed nostalgia for the era of handcrafted con artistry. As one scholar, writing in 2018, observed of that bygone time: "All this was in the analog era. Such face-to-face meetings and manipulations—with all their intimate orchestration of gesture, tone, eye contact, breath control, their devious oscillation between reassurance and coercion—are becoming obsolete now that it's so much easier to rip people off by remote control."

treasure. Acting as the "roper," he had spun a bewitching story—the centerpiece of a successful long con. He had gained his marks' trust over many months, through séances, "thought reading," and "trance-talk." He had created a formidable "insideman": the Spook. He had given his victims a "convincer" in the form of the buried revolver. At the sham telepathy trial, he had literally gotten Kiazim to speak "the lines . . . demanded of him."

But many hurdles remained. Foremost was how to persuade their captors to leave Yozgad. If they succeeded, there was the question of how to give them the brush-off. (For this problem, Hill would come up with a solution of spectacular daring.) And through it all was the imperative to protect their countrymen, who risked a strafing once the escape was discovered.

They all knew what strafing could be: By this time reports of the practice at other camps had filtered out to Yozgad. After an escape from Kastamuni in 1917, a notice was posted there that anyone else attempting to flee would be shot. The entire camp was later moved to Changri, farther inland and considered more secure. Conditions there, as Dorina Neave would recount in her history of the Kut siege, made Kastamuni look luxurious in comparison. At Changri, she wrote, about 200 prisoners "were quartered in large empty barracks which obviously had been used recently as promiscuous stabling for farmyard animals. The floor was thick with manure to a depth of several inches. The whole place was dirty, crawling with vermin, and without any means of sanitation. There was not a complete window pane and the rain and wind came through great holes in the roof. . . . The British officers . . . had to stay in bed to try and keep warm. Even hot water placed in glass bottles was found frozen in the beds."

Neave also described the aftermath of an escape from Afion Kara-hissar. The remaining prisoners were herded into the village and sequestered en masse in an Armenian church:

> When the officers and their orderlies were securely locked inside the church, there was hardly room for them to turn round, as all their belongings, including beds and furniture, books and musical instruments bought in the bazaars, were piled in, as well as two dogs and a cat. . . . The front iron gates were closed and a guard

placed inside as well as outside the doors. Every passage bristled with bayonets as soon as the hundred prisoners were herded inside the church. . . . Treated as criminals of the worst type, the officers were not allowed to move out of doors except when attended by an escort of two armed men. They were not allowed any exercise. All communication with the outer world was severed. . . . The want of air was stifling. Within a few days the atmosphere was heavy with the stench of humanity and typhus fever broke out in the overcrowded building. It was a little less than a miracle . . . that only two deaths occurred.

It would not suffice, Jones and Hill knew, merely to involve Kiazim in their escape. To spare their comrades, they would also need documentary proof of his involvement. "Kiazim was not an easy man to trap," Jones wrote. "To date there was nothing he could not explain by a theory of collusion between his subordinates and ourselves. He was perfectly capable of sacrificing the Pimple in order to save his own skin. He could . . . pose as the victim of a plot in which he had had no share. When alone with us he was as frank and open as a man could be. But we had no proof of his share in the plot. . . . There was no hope of getting him to commit himself in the presence of others; yet, by hook or by crook, we must produce independent evidence that he was implicated in the treasure-hunt."

They would need to photograph Kiazim as he dug for the Armenian's buried clues. The photo would have to be taken covertly, but at close enough range—no more than seven paces, they reckoned—so that he would be identifiable. Though Jones's account of the problem is tarnished by the Orientalism, essentialism, and racism that pervade many British memoirs of the period, it is clear that the risk of being caught photographing their captors was real. "Discovery would be dangerous," he wrote, "for we were now very much in the Commandant's power. It was no new idea to the Turkish mind, as we knew from the Pimple, to get rid of a man by shooting him on the plea that he was attempting escape; and in our case the camp was more than likely to believe the excuse. Besides, there are many other Oriental ways of doing away with undesirables, and if Kiazim Bey caught us trying to trap him he would regard us as *extremely* undesirable. Now that we were actually up against the situation it looked much less amusing than it had done from the security of the camp."

Hill's chocolate-box camera, which measured about a foot square, was too big to conceal. Providentially, one of their fellow prisoners had managed to smuggle a collapsible "vest-pocket" Kodak into camp, and before the mediums were remanded to Colonels' House, Hill pinched it. He already had film and chemicals, which had been sent covertly from England; on the pretext of helping the camp censor unpack prisoners' parcels, he had palmed them on arrival.

"Now," he told Jones on their first night in Colonels' House, "let us begin to minimize [the] risk. Watch me!"

"For fifteen minutes I stood over him," Jones wrote, "my eyes on his clever hands, watching for a glimpse of the camera as over and over again he took it out, opened it, sighted it, closed it, and returned it to his pocket. I rarely saw it until it was ready in position, and then only the lens peeped through his fingers, but when I did I told him. It was the first of a series of daily practices."

However well hidden the camera was, it would remain audible. "You'll have to talk like a blooming machine-gun, to drown the click of the shutter," Hill warned Jones. In addition, he said, the clue hunt would need to be held on a sunny day. Overcast skies would demand a long exposure, requiring Jones "to *pose* the blighters" as they dug for the buried clues.

And so, in the last week of March 1918, Jones and Hill settled down in their new quarters to wait for the sun.

CHAPTER TEN

The Treasure Test

THE TURKS WERE anxious to hunt for the first clue, the property of OOO's late friend KKK. But on March 27, it rained, and the Spook explained that on so misty a day the mediums would be unable to discern KKK, filmy and insubstantial as he was. It rained again on the twenty-eighth. The twenty-ninth was also untenable, and on the thirtieth there was hail and sleet. Their captors were growing restless; Kiazim and the Cook were already arguing over the putative treasure. "The Turks were now like children in the Hampton Court maze when a fog has come down," Jones said. "They were properly lost in our labyrinth, and appealed to the Spook to tell them what was happening. That capable and inventive gentleman rose to the occasion."

The mediums decided that they would hunt for Clue 1 on the thirty-first, rain or shine. Without it they could make no progress: The clue hunts were the foundation on which the rest of the hoax would be erected. For the Turks, they were the first big step on the glimmering road to treasure. For the mediums, they would serve as renewed "convincers," designed to cement their captors' faith in the wisdom of the Spook. They would also provide the opportunity to take the photos that would be a life insurance policy for themselves and their comrades. The film in Hill's "borrowed" camera contained three unexposed frames, and he hoped to snap all of them.

In scripting the hunt, the mediums faced a thicket of practical concerns: How could the Spook "speak" during the event, since they wouldn't have the Ouija board along? How could Jones keep the search party still for minutes on end if the day turned cloudy? If Hill did get his photos, how could he develop them in secret? How would the mediums communicate with each other while the hunt was in progress?

As usual, they solved their problems with a ghost. At a previous séance, KKK had kindly offered to lead the Turks on the search for his clue, but he had set conditions. Each condition, suitably mysterious on its surface, had an entirely pragmatic rationale—a "secret object," Jones called it. This object (known only to the mediums) corresponded to the "effect" that a stage magician plans to produce; the surface condition (what their captors were told) was the "method" by which the effect was achieved. KKK's conditions included these:

CONDITION	SECRET OBJECT
1. Only those who are present at the digging up of the clue will be allowed to share in the treasure.*	*To let the mediums photograph Kiazim in the act.*
2. The mediums must be prepared to carry out "the treasure-test of the Head-Hunting Waas."	*A delaying tactic that would let Jones pose the Turks if needed.*
3. The Turks must not speak a single word unless spoken to by the mediums.	*To prevent them from drawing one another's attention to anything striking them as suspicious.*
4. Mediums are to wear black.	*They had been issued black waterproof capes, in which Hill would be able to hide the camera.*
5. Mediums are not to be touched at any time after KKK has appeared.	*So that Hill would not be interfered with when using the camera.*
6. Mediums must hold hands when following KKK.	*To let them signal covertly to each other as needed.*
7. One or both of the mediums may collapse under the strain. If they do, leave them quite alone. Do not touch them, or speak to them, or even think of them without orders. Leave them alone and they will recover.	*To enable Hill to break away from the group at the distance from which he would take the photographs, and to keep the Turks' attention off him.*

* Jones writes: "The Commandant kicked very hard against this condition, because he was afraid of being seen in the company of the mediums, but KKK was adamant and Kiazim finally gave way."

8. All to carry sticks and water bottles. Cook to carry a pick and spade under his coat. Moïse to carry the following articles carefully hidden about his person: scissors, knife, adze, water bottle, matches, fire-wood, rags soaked in kerosene, bread, and a clean white handkerchief.

The articles were mostly camouflage, but some (the bread and water in particular) were intended to form a precedent for the time when the Spook would arrange the mediums' final escape.

9. "Obedience! Obedience! Obedience!"

A general precaution.

At the last séance before the hunt, the Spook prepared the hunters for the mysteries that lay buried beneath the earth. "'The clue,' the Spook warned us, 'is very clever'":

"The casual person on opening it would think he had found nothing and throw it down where he found it. If the finder happened to look further, he would find something to cause him surprise and a puzzle to make him talk. When OOO buried the treasure he hoped if this happened the talk would reach the ears of his heir. Therefore, do not be disappointed when at first you find nothing but an emblem of death. Go on looking carefully. The clue itself will puzzle you, but what one man can invent another man can understand."

As if ordained by the spirits, March 31, 1918, dawned bright and clear. At high noon, per the Spook's instructions, Kiazim, the Cook, and the Pimple met the mediums in the local graveyard. Holding hands, Jones and Hill lapsed into a trance and spied KKK sitting filmily on a tombstone. With their captors in tow, they followed KKK as he led them up a nearby hill. "About half-way up the hill, in order to test the Turks, we both 'collapsed' together," Jones recounted. "Our friends obeyed instructions. They turned their backs on us and sat down, carefully refraining from even a glance in our direction. We groaned, and moaned, and made weird noises to see if they would turn round, but they paid no attention. All was well, so we 'recovered' and went on."

As they approached the place where the first clue was hidden, the sky darkened. "Can't snap 'em in this," Hill whispered to Jones; "keep 'em still." Fortunately, Jones had something that could freeze the group in place while simultaneously masking the sound of the shutter: the Treasure-Test of the Head-Hunting Waas.

Months earlier, Jones had impressed his captors with tales of his adventures among the "Head-Hunting Waas" of Burma. While stationed there (as he let the story be bandied about Yozgad), he had been taken prisoner by the tribe. The Waas had tortured him and threatened him with death. He was saved by the local witch doctor, who, recognizing a kindred spirt, made Jones his protégé and taught him all he knew. Upon the witch doctor's death, Jones was elected chief of the tribe. He later returned to the West alight with magic.

Now, outside Yozgad, it was time for the treasure-test. Reaching the spot where he had buried Clue 1, Hill collapsed to the ground. Jones led the group six paces away and announced that the Spook was demanding the Waa test. (Before setting out on the hunt, he had told his captors that he was now sufficiently in tune with the spirits to have the Spook speak directly through him.) He arrayed the men in ceremonial positions, Kiazim to his right, the Pimple and Cook to his left. As they held very still, Jones lit a ritual fire.

Just then, to his anguish, he heard a click: From his awkward position on the ground, Hill had snapped the first picture too soon. "Watch the fire!" Jones cried as fast as he could. "For your lives do not move an eyelid. Be still and watch the fire for a little bird." Then, at top volume, he swung into the Waas' ritual incantation. It was good for finding treasure:

Mi sydd fachgen ieuanc ffôl
Yn byw yn ôl fy ffansi,
Myfi'n bugeilio'r gwenith gwyn,
Ac arall yn ei fedi. . . . .

The "incantation" was an eighteenth-century Welsh love song, "Bugeilio'r Gwenith Gwyn" ("Watching the White Wheat"). Jones sang verse after verse until Hill got to his feet, the signal that he had taken all three pictures. Jones stopped chanting, pointed to a nearby stone, and cried, "The bird!"

"The bird!" Hill echoed. ("Curiously enough, nobody had noticed the bird except Hill and myself," Jones recalled. "We had both distinctly seen it settle close beside the stone before it disappeared into thin air.") Digging frenziedly in the spot where the bird had alighted, the Cook broke his shovel and had to continue with the adze. At last he withdrew from the earth a slender tin can.

"Spread the clean white handkerchief," the Spook instructed through Jones. "As Moïse was forcing off the lid of the tin with his knife," Jones recalled, "Hill and I drank in the scene. The Commandant's dark eyes were ablaze in a face as pale as death. The Cook, all wet with the sweat of his digging, bending forward with a hand on either knee, looked like savage greed personified. The Pimple could hardly master the excited trembling of his hands. His knife slipped and he cut himself. 'Ha!' said the Spook, 'that is good! Blood is drawn, and now no more need be shed.'" Wrenching the can open, the Pimple poured its contents onto the handkerchief. There was nothing but ashes. "All the light," Jones wrote, "died out of Kiazim's eyes."

"The emblem of death, as promised," the Spook intoned. The Pimple, "on the verge of tears," flung the can down the hill.

"Ha! ha! ha!" cried the Spook. "I *said* a casual person would throw it away! Cook! Are you more careful than Moïse?"

The Cook ran after the can, retrieved it, and spied the false bottom. Mindful of the order of silence, he could only gesticulate wildly:

> The pantomime he went through in trying to convey his discovery to the others was almost too much for our solemnity. He poked a dirty finger alternately into the Commandant's side and into the tin, dancing round him the while so that poor Kiazim, who did not understand what he had found, must have thought the fellow stark, staring mad. The Pimple pranced about beside the Cook, trying vainly to see into the tin. He told us afterwards that he thought the Spook had "materialized" a clue at the last moment and put it into the tin. Hill and I would have given a month's pay for freedom to laugh.

Taking scissors to the bottom, the Pimple cut himself once more. But inside, to their captors' wild joy, were the gold piece and the Armenian clue. "The Commandant shook hands with each of us several times over," Jones wrote. "The Pimple was ecstatic. The Cook gave me the fright of my life by trying to kiss me, which made Hill choke suddenly and turn his back. A little way down the hill a group of Yozgad inhabitants were watching in open-mouthed astonishment. The Spook came to the rescue and ordered us all home."

The only surviving photo of the search for the first clue in Jones and Hill's ghostly treasure hunt. Left to right: Kiazim, Jones, the Pimple, and the Cook.   JONES, THE ROAD TO EN-DOR (1919)

On the walk back to camp, the Spook warned the group that OOO, incensed, would try to murder Jones and Hill that night. For the mediums' safety, no one else was to enter Colonels' House before the next morning, so that OOO couldn't "control" a visitor into killing them. This would give Hill the privacy he needed to develop the photos. Kiazim promptly doubled the guards round their house and canceled his corporal's nightly roll-call visit.

Late that night in Colonels' House, Hill locked himself in a cupboard with his camera and chemicals while Jones paced up and down the room like an expectant father. After some time, Hill emerged, holding a roll of film. On it were three images of the clue hunt. In each, Kiazim was clearly recognizable.

The mediums declared the next day, April 1, ripe for finding the second clue, that of YYY, which Hill had buried about four miles from camp. On the way there, with the Pimple translating, Jones regaled his captors with a description of April Fool's Day, explaining the lively

British tradition of pulling pranks on the unsuspecting. The Turks laughed and laughed at this curious custom.

The hunt went much as before, with the mediums relieved of the need to take pictures. This time, when clue and coin were unearthed, they could not escape the Cook's kisses. Returning to camp, Kiazim doubled their guards once more and sent the mediums a bottle of excellent wine and a flagon of very good raki.

THE SPOOK WAS soon running the camp. It is clear from Jones's memoir that Kiazim had begun attending séances himself. Where once he had consulted the village witches before making administrative decisions, he now turned to the Spook. Hungry for treasure, he didn't trust his subordinates to negotiate with the spirits: He had already slapped the Pimple hard across the face after an early séance at which Moïse, deputized to learn OOO's real name, had failed. "The Turks were now entirely in our hands," Jones wrote. "Their confidence in the Spook was absolute. They had reached the high-water mark of faith."

On April 1, just after the discovery of Clue 2, Kiazim received a cipher telegram from the Turkish War Office. Constantinople had been informed of the mediums' trial and sequestration for telepathy; the telegram ordered him to return them to the general population. For the mediums, that would mean the end of their plans, so the Spook told Kiazim that the telegram was OOO's work. He ordered Kiazim to ignore it, and Kiazim did.

The mediums also exploited the Commandant's faith to improve conditions for their countrymen. The Spook had already helped found the Yozgad Hunt Club, which fast became a cherished institution. In early 1918, a group of British officers had pooled their wages to buy a small pack of Turkish greyhounds. They asked the Commandant for permission to go on twice-weekly outings in the countryside, under guard, at which they could bag foxes and hares. Kiazim, then still fearful of his War Office, had refused. The Spook intervened, promising that he would square everything with Constantinople, and Kiazim assented.

In their memoir, *Four-fifty Miles to Freedom,* Maurice Johnston and Kenneth Yearsley, who were interned at Yozgad, called the club "the most useful of [the] concessions" granted to the prisoners. "Some of the happiest recollections of our captivity," they wrote, "are of those glorious early mornings in the country, far away from the ugly town which was our prison. Here for a few brief hours it was almost possible to forget that we were prisoners of war."

The War Office soon got wind of the club, told Kiazim that such organizations were forbidden, and ordered him to close it down. At a séance in Colonels' House, the board had this to say:

> The Spook said It wanted to save the Commandant from disgrace. He had made a bad mistake in giving permission for a Hunt Club, but he would make a much worse one if he carried out his intention of prohibiting it. Such action would make the camp exceedingly angry with Kiazim Bey, and the thought-waves they generated against him would be of the greatest assistance to OOO and the opposition. *They would "block" the treasure messages!* Further, at present the prisoners were happy and contented. Nobody wanted to escape. But, as sure as Kiazim lived, his one hope of preventing escape (which would disgrace him) lay in keeping his promise. The best way of angering an Englishman was to break your promise to him, and if the breaking of the promise touched his pocket* as well as his comfort, the Englishman became quite madly unreasonable, while the Scotsmen (and the camp was full of them) turned into wild beasts. They could no more stop the prisoners from breaking out than they could stop the sea.

Kiazim ignored the War Office, and the Hunt Club stayed open. Now, in April, the club was holding a testimonial dinner in his honor. "Would the Superior like to make a very popular speech tonight?" the Spook asked the Pimple that day. And thus the Spook dictated the entire text of Kiazim's after-dinner speech, in which he granted the prisoners even more privileges. From their prison-within-a-prison in Colonels' House, Jones and Hill could hear their comrades cheering.

---

* The greyhounds, Jones wrote, had not come cheap.

• • •

JUST BEFORE THEY were remanded to Colonels' House, the mediums had told Doc O'Farrell—without divulging the reason—that if they were ever to request medicine via their captors, he was to insist on bringing it to them personally. Now, needing to pass Hill's photos to a confederate for safekeeping, they asked for quinine. The doctor came, and while he was examining them, Hill slipped a small package into his pocket. In it were the three negatives, a note outlining their escape plot, and records of their séances as transcribed by the Pimple.

From then on O'Farrell would be the mediums' trusted clandestine adviser, aiding their escape in ways they had not yet envisioned. He would also help formulate their contingency plan, something every good con needs to have should things go awry. For Jones and Hill, that plan was to simulate madness on the slender chance that if they could be certified insane, they might be returned to Britain in an official exchange of sick prisoners.

Throughout April 1918 the mediums held séances "night and day." Each sitting could last as long as six hours, as their modus operandi—the mediums moving the glass, the Pimple transcribing the message letter by letter—was painstakingly slow. For sham mediums, though, this method has its advantages. Having the Spook speak directly through Jones was far more fluent, but that fluency carried a threat: The Spook had to respond to questions with the speed of normal speech. At the board, Jones said, "spelling out an answer letter by letter gives us psychics plenty of time to think. When an inconvenient question is asked, an unintelligible reply can easily be given, and while the sitter is trying to puzzle out what it means the mediums can consider what the final reply is to be."

The chief item of séance business now was decipherment, for Kiazim had requested the Spook's help in unraveling the first two clues. In Clue 1, the characters were arranged in an unbroken circle, foiling efforts to pinpoint where the message began and ended. The fact that it was written entirely in Armenian capitals also rendered the available dictionaries of little help. With the Spook's grudging assistance, Clue 1 was revealed to contain two words: "south" and "west," the directions in which to seek the treasure.

Clue 2 was even more cryptic. It contained two Romanized Arabic numerals—the distance to measure—but they were ambiguous. Held one way, the clue read "61"; held the other, "19." "The Spook told the Turks that with the aid of a good compass it would be quite easy to decipher," Jones wrote. "We wanted them to produce a good compass, and when the time arrived we would 'dematerialize' it—for it would be most useful to us. We liked that word 'dematerialize.' It was much nicer than 'steal.'"

But before that time came there was the matter of Clue 3. On that clue—on its very nonexistence—rested the plan to have their captors lead Jones and Hill permanently out of camp. Clue 3 belonged to AAA, the only one of OOO's friends still living, and it would reveal the last piece of the puzzle: the spot from which to set out in pursuit of the treasure.

JONES AND HILL knew that once they escaped, their best chance of avoiding recapture lay in getting out of Turkey altogether. In April, during the frenzy of séances, they began to suggest—obliquely—that to find Clue 3 it might be necessary to leave Yozgad. "Straightforward answers are not indulged in by Spooks," Jones said. "The Commandant had studied *Raymond* and knew this. Spooks enjoy puzzling and teasing people over trifles—Sir Oliver Lodge says so. . . . The simplest answer to the simplest question must be 'wrapped in mystery.' The Turks expected mystery, and they got it."

For the Turks, the urgent imperative was to find AAA and pry Clue 3 from him. To that end, Jones and Hill reinvigorated the idea of trance-talk and its attendant dangers, a seed they had planted earlier that spring. AAA, the Spook had learned, was a businessman who traveled between his home in Constantinople and various towns near the coast—a résumé designed to lead them out of camp in search of him. At a séance in Colonels' House, the mediums first tried to discover AAA's identity by reading his thoughts with the spook-board. "Because his mind must be read by telepathy and he was so far away that his thought-waves would be weak . . . the opposition might succeed in blocking them," the Spook cautioned.

Sure enough, their efforts were of no avail. "We had the greatest difficulty in getting through to Constantinople," Jones reported, "for we were connected up in turn with all sorts of people with whom we did not particularly want to talk. . . . We got Turkish headquarters in Palestine, and German headquarters in France, and learned interesting things about the war, but do what we would we could not get Constantinople. The Spook appealed to us for one last effort. We made it, got Constantinople, got AAA on the other end of the 'thought-wave,' and immediately got jammed."

"It is that damned OOO again," the Pimple cried. "He is getting more powerful since he organized his company."

The other option was trance-talk. This would let the mediums peer into AAA's mind, but it entailed grave danger to all concerned. The risks, the Spook reminded them, included madness and even death, not only for the mediums, but also for the Pimple, should he make the slightest mistake in transcription. But as long as the mediums remained in Yozgad, the Spook said, trance-talk was the only possible way to find Clue 3. There were other methods, he noted in passing, but none would work from inside the camp's confines.

Now that the Spook had dropped the hint, Jones faced the most formidable task of the entire con: persuading the men charged by the Ottoman government with keeping them under lock and key to lead him and Hill along the route to freedom. He would rely, as he had from the start, on the rhetorical skills honed in his career as a magistrate. "I had not spent a dozen years in Government service," he wrote in 1919, "without learning how easy it is for the real point at issue to be obscured."

As a lawyer, Jones had been schooled in the verbal seduction that is the con man's foremost asset. "Advocacy . . . is an art, not a science," the Irish-born barrister Iain Morley has written in *The Devil's Advocate,* his popular guide to courtroom argumentation. "It is not about forcing people to agree with you. An advocate persuades—she makes people want to agree with her—and persuasion takes skill."

Morley's book was written in the twenty-first century, but its tenets have stood at the core of forensic argumentation since antiquity. The most successful persuaders, he writes, combine the skills of a thespian with those of an orchestrator, controlling the order, pace, and weight of evidence as it emerges in court. Above all, they must secure the trust of everyone involved. "The whole system collapses if you cannot be trusted," he writes. "You must be trustworthy to the judge, to the jury, to your colleagues, as *without trust you cannot be persuasive,* and if you are caught out on just one occasion, no one will ever believe you again."

The hectoring impulse, Morley writes, must also be resisted; try subtle solicitude instead. "No one likes being told what to do. But everyone likes assistance. . . . Imagine yourself as a guide. We show the tribunal the way home. We facilitate its journey. We make it easy to follow our route."

Advocates who prove hardest to resist have particular skill with two arrows in the persuader's quiver: the psychological phenomena now known as the "Barnum effect" and "theory of mind." Though they would not be named until well into the twentieth century, both have long been used profitably by masters of influence.

The Barnum effect was named for the great sage of humbuggery P. T. Barnum, who reportedly said that the best circuses "have a little something for everybody." Identified in 1949 and named in 1956, the effect centers on people's responses to "assessments" of their personalities. It works this way: Presented with a set of statements purporting to be an individualized character profile—the "profile" is actually nothing more than a list of vague generalities—people routinely believe that it describes them with singular accuracy. The Barnum effect is perennially exploited by fortune-tellers, who deploy nebulous statements ("You sometimes worry about money"; "At times you wish you had more friends") to secure the trust of their clients . . . and the bounty of their clients' purses.

"The Barnum method," one psychologist observed in the 1950s, "must be placed in a category with such arts as palmistry, graphology, tea leaf reading, and astrology . . . methods which upon examination may be found to be similar to the medic's use of sugar pills."

The American psychologist Bertram Forer, who first described the effect in 1949,* drove its operation home in an introductory psychol-

---

* The Barnum effect is also called the Forer effect.

ogy class. In the guise of administering a personality test, he gave his students a questionnaire. Based on the responses, each student received what was billed as a bespoke personality sketch. In reality, everyone got the same sketch, which included these statements:

> You have a great need for other people to like and admire you.
> You have a tendency to be critical of yourself.
> At times you have serious doubts as to whether you have made the right decision or done the right thing.
> At times you are extroverted, affable, sociable, while at other times you are introverted, wary, reserved.
> Security is one of your major goals in life.

Students were then asked to rate how accurately the sketches reflected their personalities. Their ratings, Forer reported, were consistently high:

> After the papers had been returned . . . students were asked to raise their hands if they felt the test had done a good job. Virtually all hands went up. . . . Then the first sketch item was read and students were asked to indicate by hands whether they had found anything similar on *their* sketches. As all hands rose, the class burst into laughter. It was pointed out to them that the experiment had been performed as an object lesson to demonstrate the tendency to be overly impressed by vague statements *and to endow the diagnostician with an unwarrantedly high degree of insight.* Similarities between the demonstration and the activities of charlatans were pointed out. That the experience had meaning for them was indicated by the fact that at least one-third of the class asked for copies of the sketch so that they might try the trick on their friends.

The Barnum effect has immense utility for the confidence trickster. "Those who have been gulled often say that [the con man] has a mesmerizing, or hypnotic, effect when he's into his pitch," the writer M. Allen Henderson says in *How Con Games Work.* "If he appears to have an uncanny knack for seeing right through you to your innermost desires, don't be too impressed. He is assuming that your innermost desires are approximately the same as those of the rest of the population, and he goes from there, using any little clues or confessions you may blurt out to personalize his appeal."

Jones exploited the effect from his earliest days at the spookboard—most notably in the dramatic affair of Louise. "As it concerns a lady," he wrote of the incident with courtly restraint, "I shall . . . call the officer concerned 'Antony,' which is neither his true name nor his nickname."* The lady in question made her appearance at a séance in Upper House one night when the men, tiring of the regular cast of characters, asked the board to send them someone new. The glass began circling.

"Who are you?" one of them asked. Just then the door opened and "Antony" entered.

"I am Louise," Jones, seated at the board, spelled out. He appears to have picked the name at random but "felt Antony give a little start as he read the message."

"Hello, Tony!" the board immediately replied.

"This is interesting," Antony remarked. ("That," Jones observed, "was give-away No. 2. . . . I now knew that somewhere Tony must have met a Louise.")

Jones also knew that Antony had served in Egypt. Some weeks earlier, describing the scenery there, he had told Jones about a long, tree-lined road that had looked marvelous by moonlight. It struck Jones at the time that what had made the road so marvelous was probably romance. "Remembering this," he wrote, "I ventured to say more about Louise. Nothing could be lost by risking it."

"You remember me, Tony?" the board said.†

Antony was cagey. "I know two Louises," he answered.

"Ah! not the old one, *mon vieux*," the board replied. ("A little reflection," Jones wrote, "shows that, given two Louises, one was quite probably older than the other.")

The response delighted Antony. "Go on," he urged. "Say something."

* "Antony" was in fact Lieutenant Arthur Holyoake, as Holyoake reveals in his own memoir.

† As Jones points out, the Louise séance marked one of the rare occasions on which the board made "contact" with a person still living.

The board said: "Long straight road"; "trees—moonlight."

"Where was that?" Antony asked.

"*You* know, Tony!"

"France?"

"No, no, stupid! Not France! Ah, you have not forgotten, *mon cher*, riding in moonlight, trees and sand, and a straight road—and you and me and the moon."

"Yes, I know, Egypt—Cairo."

"Bravo! You know me. Why did you leave me? I am in trouble." ("Tony must have left her," Jones reasoned, "because he had come to Yozgad without her. But Tony did not notice. He was too interested, and his memory carried him back.")

"You told me to go," Antony replied. "I wanted to help." (Which showed, Jones realized, that he hadn't.)

Antony began another question, "Have you gone ba—" but stopped himself. "No," he said, "I won't ask that—Where are you now?" ("He had already, without knowing it, answered his own question," Jones wrote, "but he must be given time to forget it.")

"Ah, Tony," Louise purred, "you *were* a dear! I did love so your hair." ("This was camouflage, but it pleased Tony.")

There were more sweet nothings from Louise before Antony beseeched her again: "Tell me where you are."

"Oh, dear, Tony, I *told* you I was going back. I went back!"

"By Jove!" Antony said. "That settles it. Back to Paris?"

"I wish you were here," Louise replied.*

"What's your address?" he asked eagerly.

Rather than risk an answer, Jones had his most dyspeptic spook interrupt the proceedings. The glass began moving jerkily. "Look here, young feller!" it admonished Antony. "You get off the pavement. I don't want you butting round here! I'm Silas P. Warner." And so the séance ended.

Afterward, Jones wrote, "Tony . . . declared he had never seen anything so wonderful in his life."

---

* This simple sentence is one of Jones's most inspired examples of what is now called a "Barnum statement": The word "here" is so vacuous that it truly offers "something for everybody."

• • •

THE CON MAN is greatly helped, too, by the skill now known as theory of mind. Theory of mind denotes a cognitive capability that most of us possess: the ability to intuit other people's thoughts, desires, and beliefs—to be, in effect, "inside someone else's head." Theory of mind lets us discern that someone is lying or joking or speaking sarcastically. It helps us play chess and other games of strategy (*if I do X, my opponent will probably do Y*). It is theory of mind on which magicians and mentalists draw, Svengali-like, when they "force" an outcome in their act—making a spectator, who believes he is choosing freely, give a rigorously predetermined response.

"An individual has a theory of mind if he imputes mental states to himself and others," the scholars who named the phenomenon wrote in 1978. "A system of inferences of this kind is properly viewed as a theory because such states are not directly observable, and the system can be used to make predictions about the behavior of others. . . . The mental states [include], for example, *purpose* or *intention,* as well as *knowledge, belief, thinking, doubt, guessing, pretending, liking,* and so forth." Most adults have a robust theory of mind (it develops in childhood, over a period of years), although, strikingly, adults and children on the autism spectrum often have difficulty with this skill.

When someone holds a belief that is obviously false, theory of mind makes us aware of the fact, as the philosopher Daniel C. Dennett has observed: "Very young children watching a Punch and Judy show squeal in anticipatory delight as Punch prepares to throw [a] box over the cliff. Why? Because they know Punch thinks Judy is still in the box. They know better; they saw Judy escape while Punch's back was turned. We take the children's excitement as overwhelmingly good evidence that they understand the situation—they understand that Punch is acting on a mistaken belief."

Theory of mind is also what lets us deceive, for what is deception but the planting of false beliefs in the unwary? When we hear the story of Little Red Riding Hood, we know that the figure in the bed is not Red Riding Hood's grandmother but the wolf: We have learned this from observation, for we have "seen" him eat Grandmother. But we also understand, thanks to theory of mind, that Red Riding Hood will *think* the figure is Grandmother. We know, first, that Grandmother's demise happened out of Red Riding Hood's awareness and, second, that by donning Grandmother's clothes, the wolf has implanted a false belief in the girl.

A keen theory of mind makes a razor-sharp con man. It is what lets him anticipate the potential pitfalls of his scheme, "script" his mark's responses in advance with uncanny accuracy, and instill the mark's belief in a string of patent untruths. Jones's theory-of-mind prowess is on rich display in the Louise séance. He would also wield it masterfully—with the help of a little violent stagecraft—to implant the most crucial false belief of his entire plan: that to secure the treasure, the best course of action would be to venture far from camp.

DESPITE THE RISKS of trance-talk the Spook had listed, the mediums insisted on trying it. "Hill and I objected strongly to the idea of being moved from Yozgad," Jones said:

> We pointed out that the Commandant was our friend . . . and that nowhere else in Turkey could we expect to pass our imprisonment under such pleasant conditions. Therefore we proposed trying the telepathic trance-talk, however dangerous it might be, and expressed ourselves willing to run any risk rather than be moved. . . .
>
> The Pimple, on the other hand, did not at all relish the idea of either insanity or death at the hands of the opposition. . . . So we forgave the Pimple beforehand for any mistakes he might make; then we outvoted him, and refused to contemplate a move until we had tried every possible method in Yozgad.

They had set the stage with care. At night, in darkness, the Pimple joined them in their room on the upper floor of Colonels' House. Holding hands, Jones and Hill slipped into the grunt-and-groan chorus that was the prelude to trance-talk. "Then the Spook announced he was going off to Constantinople (where AAA was for the time being) in order to put AAA under similar control."

The mediums rose and descended the stairs, talking all the while to a specter only they could see. As the Pimple followed, they passed through a doorway and into a room on the ground floor. Just then there came a tremendous explosion—it was OOO, trying to kill them! They yelled to the Pimple to run for his life. "Blind with terror, the poor little fellow rushed out of the house and smashed into the ten-foot wall of the yard, which he vainly sought to climb," Jones wrote. "Then, recovering himself bravely, he came back to our rescue."

The mediums were now on the staircase, crying for help as they battled some terrible force in the darkness. Again and again, each clawed his way to the top of the steps, only to be hurled thunderously to the bottom. "Moïse often told us afterwards that it was the most awe-inspiring incident in all his spooking experience," Jones wrote. "It was so dark on the stairs that he could see nothing, but he realized that we were fighting for our lives. Sometimes our calls for help sounded so agonized he feared we were losing the struggle."

"Agonized" they were indeed, because the mediums "were really suffering most abominably from a desire to laugh":

> The tumult on the stairs was of course prearranged. First Hill dragged me backwards then I dragged him, and we both yelled at the top of our voices, pounded one another in the dark, kicked and stamped and raved to drown the laughter that was rising within us. We were seeking to terrify Moïse into another flight, and hoped he would make a bolt for home, but we failed. We did not know until afterwards that he had left the key of the outer gate in our room upstairs, and was as much a prisoner as ourselves.

The Pimple surprised them then. "Hill was halfway upstairs, holding on to the banisters with both hands and shaking them till they rattled," Jones recalled. "I had him by the ankles and was heaving and hauling in an endeavour to break his grip and give him as bumpy a passage to the bottom as he had just given me. We were both yelling blue murder."

Gathering his courage, the Pimple mounted the stairs in the blackness, stamped his little foot, and cried, *"Shoo—shoo!"* at the marauding ghost. That was too much for Jones and Hill, who fled to their room, where they stifled their laughter beneath the blankets. But they hadn't bargained on the Pimple's being brave enough to follow them there. Resuming his post, he took up his pencil and recorded the strange sounds emanating from the bedclothes. "Cries of souls in torment," he wrote.

After the mediums "came to," the three men crept downstairs to inspect the house by candlelight. In the wake of the "explosion" (in reality Hill banging a heavy trap door in the darkness), the floor was awash in shattered plaster and the walls full of holes—all artfully created by the mediums beforehand with the pick they had requisitioned for the clue hunt.

Trance-talk, it was clear, was far too dangerous. "We protested against leaving Yozgad, and wanted to try again, whatever the danger might be," Jones said. "But Moïse had had enough. He agreed with the Spook that we ought to try another plan . . . and when we would not yield he went off to tell the Commandant that he would resign his position as 'sitter' and give up the treasure unless we agreed to being moved as the Spook suggested. He returned with the news that the Commandant was strongly in favour of Plan 2, because if his mediums were killed all hope of the treasure would be gone. Plan 2 entailed our leaving Yozgad."

THE MEDIUMS PLANNED to do more than simply leave. They had determined that their best chance of escape lay in getting to the Mediterranean, 300 miles to the south. Conducted by Kiazim, the Cook, and the Pimple, as Jones outlined for Hill in early April, they would journey to the coast to find AAA. Once they got there, he continued, he had a scheme for getting hold of a boat, giving the three men the slip, and making their escape by water. They could probably get a good head start, he reckoned, because their captors wouldn't dare call attention to the whole enterprise—at least not right away.

Hill listened to Jones's plan, saying nothing. "Why leave the Turks behind?" he offered at last. "Why not take them with us in the boat? In short, why not kidnap 'em?"

It was Jones who was silent now.

"I believe we two could sandbag three Turks any day," Hill added.

"And it would be some stunt to hand over a complete prison-camp Staff to the authorities in Cyprus."

Jones pondered the scenario. "There's another point," he said. "If they were with us they couldn't raise the alarm."

"That settles it, doesn't it?" Hill asked.

They both agreed that it did.

CHAPTER ELEVEN

The Telechronistic Ray

TO GET TO the sea, they would need to go mad. Jones's plan, in which their captors would serve as unwitting assistants, was to have local doctors certify him and Hill as insane. That would give Kiazim a pretext to escort them to Constantinople. As far as the Turkish War Office would be told, the mediums were being conveyed to a mental ward there for observation. As far as their captors would believe, they would be traveling to a spot near AAA, which would let the mediums read his thoughts and find the treasure before all returned happily to Yozgad. What would *actually* transpire, as only Jones and Hill knew, was that once free of Yozgad they would lure the Turks to the seaside, secure a boat, drug them, bind them, and deliver them neatly wrapped to the British authorities in Cyprus.

"If all went well," Jones wrote, "the effect would be that Hill and I would be on the road with the Pimple, the Cook, and the Commandant, and . . . nobody would know anything about us. Yozgad officials would not worry because we had set out for Constantinople; Constantinople would not worry because they would not know we were coming. . . . To make ourselves as inconspicuous as possible Hill and I would dress in the rough Turkish soldiers' uniform which had been issued to the British orderlies at Yozgad—we each had a suit of it—and discard all badges of rank. There was no reason why anyone in authority should question two British prisoners who looked like miserable and half-starved privates—the sight was too common. We might go anywhere in Turkey with Kiazim Bey, and before we left Yozgad Kiazim Bey would know that his job was to take us to the Mediterranean seaboard."

Though their captors were keen to leave camp, they accepted the idea of a seaside trip grudgingly: After nearly two years at Yozgad, they yearned for the bright lights of Constantinople. So Jones decided to make them crave the sea above all else. His scheme involved an idea that he had discreetly planted during a séance in March: the "telechronistic ray." The ray, the Spook had said, "preserves both the past and the future in the present for anyone who can get into touch with it, and . . . Jones and Hill were developing [that] power." That was all their captors had been told then, but it let Jones revive the idea to great effect.

Now, in April, it was time for the ray to do its seductive work. In Colonels' House, a séance with the Pimple unfolded this way:

SPOOK. "Do you understand wireless, Moïse?"

MOÏSE. "Yes, I do, a little. I have just read something about it." . . . (The Spook had previously instructed him to translate to the Commandant a very technical book on wireless telegraphy which was in the camp library.)

SPOOK. "Now for thought-waves. . . . Thought is similar to wireless waves in some ways. For example, it travels best over water. Mountains interfere. A dry desert is bad. . . . If Yozgad was flat and wet, or an island, it would be much harder for OOO to interfere. . . . Thought-reading at a distance requires conditions which are exactly the opposite of those necessary for clairvoyance. For clairvoyance you need a dry clear day, as in the case of KKK, and height helps. That is one reason why I was always doubtful if I could do all three clues here in Yozgad."

MOÏSE. "Quite true." . . .

SPOOK. "Now let me explain how thought-waves *differ* from wireless waves. . . . Thought-waves are attracted by water, as if gravity kept them down low. They travel close to the surface of the sea. The bigger the expanse of water, the more the main body and force of the wave is centred low down. But land has the opposite effect. It throws the main body of the wave high in the air. See?"

MOÏSE. "Yes, Sir." . . .

SPOOK. "The only thing that will bring it down again is a big expanse of water, and the descent is gradual like the trajectory of a bullet."

"A glance at a map," Jones wrote, "will show whither all this rigma-role was tending. At Yozgad it would be difficult to read AAA's thoughts because the thought-wave . . . would be bumped up by the Taurus mountains and the dryness of the desert to the north of them, and would pass very high over Yozgad. Down at the Mediterranean coast things would be simple, for the wave would pass low down over the surface of the sea."

Next, they had to persuade their captors to procure a boat. Thus Jones introduced a remarkable new device, the "Four Cardinal Point Receiver." The receiver, the Spook explained, "was a secret method of thought-reading not known in our sphere. It had once been known to the ancient Egyptians . . . but the knowledge had been lost." Properly used, it would let the mediums read not only OOO's thoughts but also those of every person, past and present, who had ever lived. This method—"infinitely preferable," Jones observed, "to our cumber-some 'trance-talk' and 'Ouija'"—would let them ascertain the where-abouts *of all the treasure in the world.*

"Asia Minor, every Turk believes, is full of buried treasure," Jones wrote. "The stuff hidden before the recent Armenian massacres would be a fortune in itself, and when one thought of the past—of the Greeks, and Romans, and Persians—why! There was no limit to the wealth that lay within our grasp."

FOR JONES, THE Four Cardinal Point Receiver would serve much the same function as the telegraph in a classic "big store" con—a quasi-miraculous communications medium that could transcend time and space to yield vast riches. What worked in his favor was the fact that such a device sounded far less preposterous in 1918 than it does today.

The nineteenth century had witnessed unprecedented advances in communications technology, with five vital new media—the tele-phone, the phonograph, electric light, radio, and motion pictures—bursting forth in the last quarter of the century alone. "Only since the late nineteenth century," the media historian John Durham Peters said, "have we defined ourselves in terms of our ability to communi-cate with one another."

By the turn of the twentieth century, communications media had advanced to the point where their workings were beyond the ken of laymen. "Electricians were amused at the miraculous powers vested in devices for electrical communication by the technologically naïve," the historian of technology Carolyn Marvin has written. "These powers displayed . . . magical capabilities that to experts were inconceivable for any mode of communication. A popular misconception was that telegraph and telephone messages were written down and physically transported over the wire." Germs, too, were believed to enjoy free and easy passage through the lines. "As late as 1894," Marvin writes, "the editor of a prominent Philadelphia daily newspaper . . . cautioned his readers not to converse by phone with ill persons for fear of contracting contagious diseases."

The more a new medium defied understanding, the more it was seen as something miraculous—even spiritual. An 1889 article in a Pennsylvania newspaper captured sublimely the nexus of magic and modernity at which its subject, a telephone call between New York and Boston, stood:

That Hello! took advantage of its opportunities and travelled. It went down through the desk, down through the floor into the basement of the building, then out into an underground conduit, rushing along under all the turmoil and rush of New York City, then up the Hudson, taking a squint at the Palisades, past Yonkers and Tarrytown and Sleepy Hollow, then out into the land of the wooden nutmegs, to and through New Haven, Hartford, Providence, Newport, on to Boston.

It crossed rivers and mountains, traversed the course of fertile valleys and past busy factories, noisy with the whirr of a thousand machines. It went through lonely forests, past places where they used to burn witches, and scenes familiar to the Pilgrim Fathers. It heard the music of the sea, it saw the homes of the rich and the poor and it caught a glimpse of Bunker Hill monument before it plumped into the city of baked beans and reached its destination in the ear drum of a man seated in a high building there. . . .

In about one millionth of the time it takes to say Jack Robinson, it was there. It had turned a thousand curves, it had climbed up and slid down a hundred hills, and yet it came in at the finish fresh as a daisy on a dewy June morning. It was as if by a miracle the speaker had suddenly stretched his neck from New York to Boston and spoken gently into the listener's ear. It beat all to smash all the old incantations of Merlin and the magi of Munchhausen, Jules Verne, or Haggard. . . . It was the long distance telephone.

Perhaps no other medium was so closely connected with spiritualist ideas as radio, invented in 1895. Communication via telephone and telegraph at least had a visible modus operandi: The wires were there for all to see. But the "wireless" was something truly apart, bound up with nineteenth-century ideas about the ether, the invisible cosmic medium through which an array of filmy intangibles—phantasms and even thoughts—were believed to fly. "As Kafka notes," Peters said, "those who build new media to *eliminate* the spectral element between people only create more ample breeding grounds for the ghosts." In radio's early years, he wrote, audible static was construed by some as communication from spheres beyond our own.

THE SPOOK PROMISED to tell the mediums how to operate the Four Cardinal Point Receiver provided they kept the instructions a deep dark secret. "Get on to the surface of the sea—preferably in a boat," he told them, "so as to be on a level with the main body of the thought-wave":

Go at night when the wave is at its strongest. Take with you, ready prepared, a drink that is stimulating to the nerves—e.g., coffee. Four of you, facing in different directions, drink quickly and in silence. Then lie down, and pillow your heads on vessels of pure water—which will help to concentrate the telechronistic wave. Then count three hundred and thirty-three. Having counted, think of a pleasant memory for five minutes. All this to be done with your eyes open. The counting should be aloud, but in a low murmuring tone, and the process of counting up to three hundred and thirty-three and thinking for five minutes must be repeated three times in all, for three is the mystic number in the system. The ob-

ject so far is to make the mind "receptive." You next think hard of
what you want to discover.

"I am so glad we chose the seaside for our holiday," the Pimple said
after the glass had done its work. "It fits in beautifully."

IN EARLY APRIL, the Pimple told the mediums that a detachment of
prisoners from Changri was being brought to Yozgad, escorted by
their commandant and interpreter. This development was heaven-
sent, as it would let Kiazim strike out in search of treasure while
Changri's commandant took over Yozgad in his stead. The Spook ordered Kiazim to consult with local doctors about a possible stone in
his hepatic duct. Since the mediums, courtesy of Doc O'Farrell, were
intimately familiar with the symptoms, the Spook told him precisely
what he should say. As a result, the doctors authorized three months'
medical leave.

Kiazim, Jones wrote, "was very grateful to the Spook who, in his
opinion, had 'controlled' the Turkish doctors, and he told us that Constantinople would undoubtedly grant him the leave on the strength of
his medical certificate." He would then authorize vacations for the
Cook and the Pimple so that all could go to the seashore together.
"The Cook, especially, was in flames to start at once, and had he been
our Commandant the next day would have seen us galloping for the
coast."

All that remained now was for Jones and Hill to go insane. First,
they too would need to be certified by local doctors; next, the Spook
would have Kiazim tell the War Office that their work as mediums
had driven them mad and they would need to go to Constantinople for
observation. This scenario, too, sounds risible today but was hardly
farfetched in 1918: At the time, mediumship was widely thought to
cause insanity.

"The link between spiritualism and insanity was generally expressed [in the contention] that spiritualism was the cause of insanity," Peter Lamont has written in his book *Extraordinary Beliefs*. "John
Henry Anderson, the conjuror-debunker, publicly claimed that spiritualism was 'a delusion that has driven ten thousand persons mad in

the United States,' and the periodical press spoke of 'lunatic asylums, filled with maniacs on the subject of Spiritualism,' and noted that 'it is a fact, that many of the persons who constitute the circles of the spiritualists . . . are either insane or on the verge of insanity.'"

Even highly credentialed psychiatrists held this view. Writing in 1924, Houdini championed their findings:

Not the least of the evils of Spiritualism is the insanity which it causes. A mental specialist of high standing in Birmingham, England, issued a warning in 1922 quoting numerous cases which came under his observation and were the result of Spiritualistic teaching. An English doctor has estimated the number of such cases at a million. It is a well-established fact that the human reason gives way under the exciting strain of Spiritualism. . . . Not long ago Dr. Curry, Medical Director of the State Insane Asylum of New Jersey, issued a warning concerning the "Ouija-board" in which he said:

"The 'Ouija-board' is especially serious because it is adopted mainly by persons of high-strung neurotic tendency who become victims of actual illusions of sight, hearing and touch at Spiritualistic seances."

He predicted that the insane asylums would be flooded with patients if popular taste did not swing to more wholesome diversions.

In March, 1920, it was reported in the papers that the craze for the Ouija-boards . . . had reached such a pitch in [a] little village . . . across San Francisco Bay, that five people had been driven mad.

The available amount of evidence of this sort is almost unbelievable, but enough has been given to show the extent of the evil.

To prepare to "go mad," Jones and Hill had begun fasting weeks before, subsisting on dry bread and tea. The ascetic diet, the Spook had announced, would "increase clairvoyant powers." The real motive, Jones wrote, was "to give us a 'starved look' which might be ascribed to madness." By April, between the fasting and the marathon séances, they were growing weak, thin, and exhausted. On his

DRIVEN DAFT

By the Ouija Board

Spiritualism Makes Maniacs of Man and Wife.

They Place Their Children in Solitary Confinement,

And Perform Queer Antics With Knives and Other Weapons.

Sad Mental Plight of a Couple of Intelligence.

Officers Find Them Raving Mad and Thirsting For Blood.

They Are Adjudged Insane and Ordered To an Asylum—The Ouija Board Finding Other Victims.

The practice of spiritualism, including the use of Ouija boards, was popularly believed to cause insanity, as these headlines from an 1892 article in the Cincinnati Enquirer *attest. The persistence of this belief would confer enormous advantages on Jones and Hill.*

visits to Colonels' House, O'Farrell schooled them in various symptoms of insanity. Since it would be more convincing if each came down with a different type of madness, it was decided that Jones would have "general paralysis of the insane"* (the period's name for paralytic dementia, a neuropsychiatric disorder caused by syphilis), with delusions that he was a Turk. Hill would suffer from acute religious melancholia.

Their captors had been told that the Spook would control Jones and Hill into acting crazy. That would let Kiazim summon local doctors for an opinion, which would ultimately let him conduct them to the "asylum" in "Constantinople." "Kiazim was greatly pleased with the idea," Jones wrote, "for the doctors' recommendations would relieve him of all responsibility."

They prepared for the doctors' visit as they had for no other stage of the con. For days on end they neither bathed nor shaved. Kiazim now allowed other prisoners to visit them (this, too, was part of the plan), but the mediums affixed a stark notice to the front door of Colonels' House:

"GO AWAY! WE DON'T WANT TO SEE YOU!"

Many comrades forced their way in anyway, and Jones and Hill were deliberately, insufferably rude to all of them. "Our condition dis-

---

* So named because it also entailed muscular degeneration.

tressed them," Jones wrote. "We were unshaven and dirty, our faces pale, drawn, and very thin. The fortnight's starvation had put a wild look into our eyes. But our chief pride and horror was our hair—we had refrained from cutting it for the last two months, and now we did not brush it, so that it stood up round our heads like the quills of the fretful porcupine." It wasn't long, he said, before "the camp thought us crazy."

Then there was their bedroom, a stage set of the most glorious kind. Picture the most egregious teenage boy's room you know, dial up the disorder a hundredfold, and you will start to get the faintest whiff of it. Unswept and unaired for days on end, their room was a maelstrom of dust, dirty laundry, discarded tin cans, torn paper, old food, slop pails, and more. What doctor could take it in and not smell madness? And once the report of the doctors' visit had been sent to the War Office, permission for their transfer to Constantinople seemed assured.

The mediums had also prepared for the abduction by sea: In the hollow handle of his shaving brush, Jones, courtesy of O'Farrell, "carried enough morphia to put a Turkish battalion to sleep." It would be slipped to their captors in the coffee that the ritual of the Four Cardinal Point Receiver demanded. Once they were sound asleep (and after having counted to "three hundred and thirty-three . . . in a low murmuring tone" three times over, they surely would be), the mediums would bind them with ropes and straps they had hidden away for the purpose. By the time the three men awoke, Jones reckoned, the boat would be halfway to Cyprus. They would have fresh water, which the ritual also required. In case the morphia failed, they would have an adze to use as a weapon ("We thought we could carry one adze for chopping firewood without causing any suspicion").

The plan seemed impeccable. Jones and Hill had examined every facet of it "scores of times," anticipating every contingency, exterminating every flaw. Nothing could go wrong now.

Then . . . disaster.

ONCE THE CHANGRI prisoners got to Yozgad, a group of Yozgad prisoners would be sent to Afion Karahissar to make room for them. The mediums' plan—with Kiazim's enthusiastic cooperation—was to travel part of the way with the Afion party, chaperoned by the Commandant, the Cook, and the Pimple. On reaching Angora, the five of them would leave the group, ostensibly to continue on to the hospital in Constantinople. In reality, their captors believed, they would strike out for the seaside and Clue 3. So far, so good.

But shortly before the group set out for Afion—this was before the local doctors came—Jones and Hill made a single strategic error: They told their compatriots that they would be joining the Afion party. "The Spook had told Moïse to let it be known that although we would not take anyone's place, we would be added to the party because the Commandant was anxious to get rid of us," Jones wrote. "Moïse had obeyed the Spook, and it was soon known in the camp that we were leaving Yozgad. We had not imagined any possible harm could come of our friends knowing it." He added, "We paid dearly for our mistake."

Hearing of their impending departure, one British officer was moved to action. (With characteristic discretion, Jones refers to him simply as "X.") A close friend of Jones's, X believed that Kiazim was literally trying to "get rid" of the mediums, now widely considered the camp's black sheep. Fearing that they would be pulled aside and shot on the trek to Afion, he concocted what he thought was a salutary lie: He told Kiazim that Jones and Hill planned to escape during the trek and should thus be forced to remain in camp.

The Pimple brought them the news of X's "betrayal." The Commandant hadn't believed X—that wasn't the problem. "He knows you are too weak to go ten miles," the Pimple assured them. But Kiazim believed that X was being controlled by OOO, and X's story left him terrified of what the spirits had in store. "He thinks this is a warning, not of what *you* intend to do, but what our Spook or perhaps OOO intends to do for you," the Pimple explained. "He fears the Spook or OOO will make you disappear.

"He is troubled, much troubled," the Pimple continued. "Even now he has gone to his witch, to ask her to read the cards. He is a damn fool, and a coward! Why does he not trust the Spook? Everything it has promised the Spook has done, and still he is afraid! He will spoil everything!"

And so he did. The Commandant, Jones wrote, "distrusted us not at all," and still wanted his treasure. But "he was superlatively afraid of the unseen powers, and especially of OOO. . . . What was to prevent OOO from killing not only the two mediums, but the whole batch of treasure-hunters?" Kiazim now refused to leave camp with the Afion group, and he forbade the Cook and the Pimple to go, too. With no one left to escort them to the "hospital," his decision kept the mediums from leaving Yozgad.

They pretended to take the news blithely, but Jones was in despair: The scheme on which he had worked for more than a year was over. There would be no trip to the seaside, no abduction, and no escape over the water. "Hill," he wrote, "came nearer to losing his temper than I have ever seen him. But there was nothing for it. We gave up the kidnapping plan." Their only recourse now was to "go mad" for real.

CHAPTER TWELVE

Certifiable

FROM THE VERY beginning they had had a plan B: feigning insanity in the hope of being repatriated in a sick-prisoner exchange. And so, in mid-April, the plot's second phase began, a con within the con. This hoax would be the most grueling of all, for not only would the mediums have to convince a series of doctors that they were mad, they would also need to be committed to an insane asylum to prove it.

They discussed their prospects during a long night in Colonels' House. The likelihood of two men from the same camp losing their minds simultaneously, Hill pointed out, was minute. He offered to improve Jones's chances by withdrawing from the scheme and letting Jones "go mad" alone.

"I like to think," Jones wrote, "of the depths it revealed in Hill's friendship for me. We were at the gloomiest period of the war—April 1918. The German successes lost nothing in the recounting in Turkish newspapers. To every appearance our imprisonment might last for years. Yet Hill tried hard to sacrifice his last faint hope of liberty for my sake. In the end I reminded him that we had pledged ourselves to stick together, and threatened that if he returned to camp I would fulfil my part of the contract by going back with him."

"Well, Bones," Hill replied, "I'll come. I don't know what special kind of miseries the Turks keep for malingering lunatics, but I promise you that without your permission they'll never find out through me."

To get their captors solidly behind the new plan, the Spook assured them that the treasure hunt was still on. From the hospital in Constantinople, he said, Jones and Hill would be able to read AAA's thoughts—and help them bag all the treasure in the world. Despite the Spook's warnings to keep silent, Kiazim's wife was soon boasting around town about her coming wealth.

There were also mad letters to write. The mediums were confident that they could fool the local doctors. But if permission to go to Constantinople was granted, they would have the daunting task of conning the highly trained nerve specialists there. To hedge their bet, they began a flurry of correspondence — wild, dazzlingly paranoid letters, addressed to some of the highest officials in Turkey. Many centered on their shared "delusion" that a fellow prisoner, Major Edward Baylay, a decorated officer whose Posh Castle mess prepared their food, was trying to kill them.*

"To the Light of the World, the Ruler of the Universe, and Protector of the Poor, the Sword & Breastplate of the True Faith, his most gracious Majesty Abdul Hamid . . . of Turkey," read one, to an Ottoman sultan:†

Greeting: This is the humble petition of two of your Majesty's prisoners of War now at Yozgad in Anatolia. We humbly ask your most gracious protection. We remain here in danger of our lives owing to the plots of the camp against us. They are all in league against us. Baylay is determined to poison us. He tried to drag us into the garden to murder us. He is in league with all the camp against us. We cannot eat the food they send because he puts poison in it. . . . Also the doctor who was our friend until Baylay persuaded him to give us poison instead of medicine. Please protect us. The Commandant is our friend. When Baylay tried to he said no and put us in a nice house please give him a high decoration for his kindness we cannot go out because Baylay will kill us and all the camp hate us who shall in duty bound ever pray for your gracious Majesty.

E. H. Jones.   C. W. Hill.

O'Farrell continued to coach them in their mad roles. "Ye're a pair of unmitigated blackguards," he told them warmly, "an' I'm sorry for the leech that's up against you. There's only one thing needed to beat

---

* Major Edward John Baylay (1881–1969), who fought with Townshend's forces at Ctesiphon and Kut, was awarded the Distinguished Service Order.
† Deposed in 1909, Sultan Abdul Hamid II died in February 1918. Jones and Hill may well have been trying to reinforce the illusion of their own madness by writing in April of that year to a man both deposed and dead.

the best specialist in Berlin or anywhere else, but as you both aim at getting to England you can't do it."

"What is that?" they asked.

"One of ye commit suicide!" the doctor declared, laughing.

"By Jove! That's a good idea!" Jones exclaimed. "We'll *both* try it."

"If ye do it," said O'Farrell, momentarily caught up in the spirit of things, "there's not a doctor in Christendom, let alone Turkey, will believe you're sane!" Then, remembering his vocation, he gave them a stern warning: "A fraction of a minute might make all the difference," Jones recalled, "and convert our sham suicide into the genuine article."

But the mediums would not be deterred. If they were sent to Constantinople, they resolved, they would hang themselves, "within limits," along the way.

AS DIRECTED BY the spook-board, Kiazim summoned local military doctors, and on April 13 a pair of them, Major Osman and Captain Suhbi Fahri, arrived in camp. The week since the collapse of the kidnapping plot had let the mediums further sabotage their room and persons. They had eaten almost nothing for the past three days. On the twelfth they stayed awake all night, "that our eyes might be dull when the doctors came, and we took heavy doses of phenacetin* at frequent intervals, to slow down our pulses." They smoked all day, keeping the windows shut and the stove hot as could be, until the climate indoors was asphyxiating. Just before the doctors arrived, they overturned a bucket of dirty water near the door of their room, and Hill stuffed his pipe full of plug tobacco, which always made him ill, and smoked until "he had the horrible, greeny-yellow hue that is known to those who go down to the sea in ships." The crowning olfactory touch was a bottle of "Elliman's Embrocation," a liquid preparation "for Horses, Dogs, Birds [and] Cattle," splashed liberally over the scene.

---

* An analgesic and fever reducer introduced in 1887. Implicated over the years in cases of cancer and kidney failure, phenacetin was withdrawn from the United States market in 1983.

Led by the Pimple, the doctors climbed the stairs of Colonels' House and opened the bedroom door. They found Jones writing frenziedly on sheet after sheet of paper, flinging each one to the floor as he set to work on the next. Hill, bundled in warm clothing from head to toe, sat motionless beside the roaring stove. Major Osman stood frozen in the doorway, which he did not leave for the duration of the visit. "Captain Suhbi Fahri tiptoed silently round the room, peering into our . . . slop-pails and cag-heaps," Jones wrote, "until he got behind my chair, when I whirled round on him in a frightened fury, and he retreated suddenly to the door again. Neither of them sought to investigate our reflexes—the test we feared most of all—but they contented themselves with a few questions which were put through Moïse in whispers, and translated to us by him." Among the questions were these:

OSMAN. "What are you writing?"
JONES [nervously]. "It is not finished yet." . . .
OSMAN. "What is it?"
JONES. "A plan." . . .
OSMAN. "What plan?"
JONES. "A scheme."
OSMAN. "What scheme?" . . .
JONES. "A scheme for the abolition of England! Go away! You are bothering me." . . .
OSMAN. "Why do you want to do that?"
JONES. "Because the English hate us."
OSMAN. "Your father is English. Does he hate you?"
JONES. "Yes. He has not written to me for a long time. He puts poison in my parcels. He is in league with Major Baylay. It is all Major Baylay's doing."

"I grew more and more excited," Jones recalled, "and burst into a torrent of talk about my good friend Baylay's 'enmity,' waving my arms and raving furiously. The two doctors looked on aghast, and I noticed Captain Suhbi Fahri changed his grip on his silver-headed cane to the thin end. It took them quite a time to quieten me down again. At last I gathered up my scattered manuscript and resumed my writing. Hill had never moved or paid the slightest attention to the pandemonium. They turned to him."

> OSMAN. "Why are you keeping the room so hot? It is a warm day."
> [The Pimple had to repeat the question many times before Hill seemed to hear it. He responded to all questions in a monotone.] . . .
> HILL. "Cold." . . .
> OSMAN. "Why don't you go out?"
> HILL. "Baylay."
> OSMAN. "Why don't you sweep the floor?"
> HILL. "Poison in dust."
> OSMAN. "Why is there poison in the dust?"
> HILL. "Baylay."
> OSMAN. "Is there anything you want?" . . .
> HILL. "Please tell the Commandant to lock the door and you go away."

"The two doctors, followed by Moïse, tiptoed down the stairs," Jones wrote. "We heard the outer gate clang, listened carefully to make sure they had gone, and then let loose the laughter we had bottled up so long. For both the Turkish doctors had clearly been scared out of their wits." The Pimple later returned with two "certificates of lunacy"—"imposing documents, written in a beautiful hand, and each decorated with two enormous seals." On the doctors' recommendation, a sentry was assigned to their room to keep them from committing suicide.

On April 14, the certificates were dispatched to the War Office, together with an explanatory cable from Kiazim, dictated, at his request, by the Spook. "Somewhere amongst the Turkish archives at Constantinople," Jones wrote, "the following telegram reposes":

> For over a year two officer prisoners here have spent much time in study of spiritualism and telepathy, and have shown increasing signs of mental derangement which recently have become very noticeable. I therefore summoned our military doctors Major Osman and Captain Suhbi Fahri who after examination diagnosed

melancholia in the case of Hill and fixed delusion in the case of Jones and advised their despatch to Constantinople for observation and treatment. Doctors warn me these two officers may commit suicide or violence. I respectfully request I may be allowed to send them as soon as possible. . . . If permitted I shall send them with necessary escort under charge of my Interpreter who can watch and look after them en route and give any further information required by the specialists. . . . My report* together with the report of the doctors, follows by post. Submitted for favour of urgent orders.

On April 16, the War Office answered the Spook's wire, granting Kiazim permission to remand Jones and Hill to Haidar Pasha Hospital in the capital. The Pimple brought them the news. "Hurrah!" he cried. "The Spook has controlled Constantinople!"

For the mediums, there was little cause for celebration. They knew that their time in the hospital—where they would be watched day and night for signs of malingering—would be replete with hardship, though they could scarcely have conceived of its depth and duration. But of one thing they were certain: "We were working now," Jones said, "at our last hope."

---

* This, too, was dictated by the Spook, and was, Jones wrote, "of a character so useful to the Constantinople specialists that Kiazim was thanked for it by his superiors at headquarters."

BOOK THREE

DEMONS

CHAPTER THIRTEEN

Two Lunatics, 500 Pounds of Butter, and a Great Deal of Flour

THE MEDIUMS NOW had the onus of completing a double hoax. They had already convinced their captors that they could salvage the treasure hunt by being "mad enough" to be dispatched to Constantinople. They would next have to convince Constantinople that they were "mad enough" to be returned to Britain. If they failed to con Haidar Pasha's experts, they would be sent back to Yozgad—or worse.

Before leaving the camp, they had several urgent items of business. During the second half of April, they held a frenzy of séances at which the Pimple, who would be escorting them to the hospital, received rigorous marching orders. The Spook, he was told, would control the mediums into acting crazy, though they would remain unaware of their mad deeds. The Pimple was ordered to make a scrupulous record of everything they said and did, which he would deliver to the doctors in the capital. "Thus," Jones wrote, "while the Turks thought the Spook was practising on us, making us appear mad, we were really practising our madness on the Turks." O'Farrell made covert daily visits for coaching, and each night the Spook drilled the Pimple mercilessly on what he was to say on reaching Constantinople:

It made a strange picture: Moïse, leaning over the piece of tin that was his Delphic oracle, told his tale as he would tell it at Haidar Pasha. His face used to be lined with anxiety lest he should go wrong and incur the wrath of the Unknown. Hill and I, pale and thin with starvation, and the strain of our long deception, sat motionless . . . with our fingers resting on the glass and every sense strained to detect the slightest error in the Pimple's story or in his tone or manner of telling it. And when the mistakes came (as to begin with they did with some frequency), the glass would bang out the Spook's wrath with every sign of anger and there would follow the trembling apologies and stammered emendations of the unhappy Interpreter. Hill and I had got beyond the stage of wanting to laugh. . . . It was absolutely essential that the Pimple's story should be without flaw. . . .

When at last by dint of ceaseless tuition Moïse had thoroughly grasped the situation, and the nature of the story he was to tell, the Spook held an examination and asked every conceivable question we and O'Farrell thought the Constantinople doctors might set. Moïse passed the test with great credit; and we felt we were ready for the road.

But first there was the matter of OOO's golden coins. Kiazim had kept the two lira they had unearthed with Clues 1 and 2. Wanting to destroy the only things of real value that the clue hunt had produced (and wanting to implicate Kiazim further), the mediums had the Spook request a vise and a hacksaw. When these had been procured from a local goldsmith, the Spook ordered Hill to cut each coin into three segments. Jones and Hill each received a segment, as did the Pimple, the Cook, the Commandant, and the Commandant's wife. Per the Spook's instructions, they wore them round their necks as a sign of fealty. The real reason for the charade, Jones wrote, was "to provide us with an additional proof of Kiazim's confederacy. . . . Should the occasion arise for us to denounce him it would cause him some trouble to explain how we all came to be wearing portions of the same coin if we were not in some sort of league together."

There were also instructions for the comrades they would leave behind. Confiding in Lieutenants Alec Matthews and Edward Price (the officers who had been present the night Sally first appeared), they told them what to do about the nonexistent Clue 3. On reaching Constantinople, the mediums explained, the Spook would tell the Pimple that Clue 3 lay buried on the grounds of Yozgad itself. When the Pimple returned to camp to dig for it, the officers were to tell him that they had come upon the tin can, opened it, and promptly lost the slip of paper with the curious writing on it.

The mediums also needed to protect their compatriots from being strafed once the escape was discovered. They told Matthews and Price that in the event of a strafing—with Jones and Hill by then safely back in Britain—they should pass the negatives of the clue hunt on to Kiazim's superiors. As it turned out, this well-meaning injunction, and the well-meaning response, would have severe unforeseen consequences.

In the days before their departure, Jones and Hill made sure that the small comforts the Spook had arranged would be further enhanced. On April 24, 1918, they held their last séance in Yozgad. In it, the Spook impressed on the Commandant that he could preempt future escapes—and thus spare himself ignominy—by granting the inmates still more privileges. "He kept his promise," Jones wrote, "and after we left Yozgad the camp was better off in the matter of facilities for exercise than it had ever been in our time. Two days a week there was hunting, once a week a picnic to the pine-woods, and, on the remaining four days, walks; also access to the bazaar was easier to obtain."

The mediums would give their countrymen one last gift: They had contrived to rid the camp forever of the Pimple, who was roundly despised for his pilfering from parcels. And so, during their final days at Yozgad, the Spook began massaging the Pimple's ample ego. The Pimple, the glass asserted, was wasting his talents in a backwater like Yozgad. He should remain in Constantinople, where he would make a glorious reputation. The Pimple agreed. He would not fully appreciate what the Spook had in store for him until he got there.

AT 10:00 A.M. on April 26, Yozgad's two best carts, each drawn by two of its finest horses, pulled up at the camp. They would carry the group and their belongings on the five-day, 120-mile ride to Angora, where they would board the train for Constantinople. "The group" included Jones, Hill, the Pimple, and the two sentries deputized to accompany them. "Belongings" included the mediums' clothes and bedding (tied discreetly with the rope they would use to "hang" themselves), the spook-board, Hill's Bible, and 500 pounds of butter. The Pimple had procured it, and insisted on bringing it along: He planned to sell it at a profit in the capital.

The mediums' joy at leaving was tempered by the parts they had to play, and by the knowledge that they would have the pressure of acting those parts unremittingly:

Ever since Major Osman and Captain Suhbi Fahri had certified us insane we had feigned madness whenever any Turk was near, and in the presence of some of the visitors from the camp. We had found no great difficulty in maintaining our roles as occasion arose, and indeed it was rather amusing to be able to heave a brazier of charcoal at a sentry, or try to steal his rifle, without fear of punishment. For the strain of acting was only temporary. We contrived to give the special sentry who was detailed to prevent us doing harm to ourselves or others such a very hot time that he preferred to do his tour of duty outside our room. So for most of the hours of the twenty-four we were alone, and could be rational. But we realized that from the moment we left our sanctuary and started on our journey to Constantinople, our simulation must be kept up night and day. As soon as we reached Haidar Pasha our escort would probably be questioned about our behaviour *en route,* and it was well they should corroborate the Pimple's report of our actions. We agreed there must be no half measures. Alone or together, in sickness or health, to friend and foe, at all times and under all circumstances we must appear mad. O'Farrell warned us that the strain would be terrible, but not even he, doctor as he was, guessed half what it really meant.

Playing his part with fiendish glee, Jones got hopelessly underfoot as he "supervised" the loading of the baggage. After thwacking one of the drivers with a fly swatter and bidding Kiazim "a florid and affectionate farewell," he clambered aboard a cart and began gaily strewing banknotes into the crowd of curious townspeople, crying that he reviled the English and was now a Turk. The Pimple, who had been charged by the Spook with retrieving all money thrown away by Jones, had the unenviable task of wading into the crowd to repossess it.

"The Turks," Jones wrote, "put down my happiness to the fact that I was leaving behind the English who were so intent on murdering me, and going to Stamboul to see the Sultan, and Enver Pasha, and become a great man in the Turkish Government." Hill, meanwhile, apparently oblivious of the hubbub around him, sat on a stone reading his Bible. He had to be hoisted onto the cart. As the little caravan pulled away from Yozgad with its baggage and butter, he sat slumped in a heap of reverent sorrow, "but once, when he glanced at me," Jones said, "I noticed his eyes were sparkling."

THEY DID NOT dare hold séances on the journey. Though their guards spoke no English, the mediums couldn't risk having them see Moïse in the role of recorder, lest they report his collaboration to Constantinople. Instead, as the glass disclosed at one of their last Yozgad séances, the Spook would speak through Jones for the duration of the trip. Jones would signal that he was "under control" by twisting the button of his coat.

On day two of the journey, the drivers asked the men to walk a while, to lighten their load in the mountainous country. As they walked, the Pimple drilled the mediums in French, the second language of many educated Turks, so that they would be able to communicate with their doctors at Haidar Pasha. They proved wretched pupils, and the Pimple chastised them roundly. Suddenly he snapped to attention. He was staring at Jones's coat. "Sir!" he exclaimed.

The spirit was speaking. "The Spook reminded him that both Hill and I were now in a trance and knew nothing of what was being said," Jones wrote. "Moïse was to keep it secret, lest we got frightened." To further support their claim of madness, the Spook continued, he would "control" the mediums into hanging themselves during the trip.

"Mon Dieu!" the Pimple cried.

The Spook reproved him in excellent French and went on to give him rigorous instructions for his role in the hanging, which would take place on the fourth night of the journey. "We decided to put on this show at Mardeen,* which was about halfway to Angora and the

---

* "Mardeen," a historical Ottoman place-name, is believed to denote Denck Ma'arden (also called Danek Madeni), a town southeast of Ankara. The town is known today as Maden, or Keskin.

only large town where we would be staying the night," Hill explained long afterward. "We wanted plenty of publicity and some independent witnesses."

The plan horrified the Pimple. But he had his orders and was compelled to obey.

ONE OF THE most striking things about belief in the Spook was that it transcended religious affiliation. The mediums' fellow prisoners were Christian, the Cook and the Commandant Muslim, and the Pimple an Ottoman Jew, yet Jones and Hill made believers of nearly all of them.* This ecumenical fervor makes sense when one considers that the dreamworld they conjured was in many respects a cult, with the Spook as its leader and the men of Yozgad its followers.

"The term cult is not itself pejorative but simply descriptive," the American psychologist Margaret Thaler Singer, who spent her career studying cults, has written. "A cultic relationship is one in which a person intentionally induces others to become totally or nearly totally dependent on him or her for almost all major life decisions, and inculcates in these followers a belief that he or she had some special talent, gift, or knowledge."

Throughout history, cults have coalesced around a wide spectrum of beliefs. While some are overtly religious, others have centered on political leaders, been devoted to self-improvement, promised eternal life, worshiped alien beings, or held out visions of vast wealth. Singer, who over the years interviewed thousands of active and former cult members, wrote that the United States alone has been home to "at least ten major types of cults, each with its own beliefs, practices, and social mores." Among them are "neo-Christian religious," "Hindu and Eastern religious," "psychology or psychotherapeutic," "flying saucer and other outer-space phenomena," and "spiritualist."

* As expressed in *The Road to En-dor,* Jones's attitude toward Moïse's Jewishness—of a piece with the prevailing ideology of his time, place, and class—makes regrettable reading today. Invoking the Pimple's habit of pilfering and prevarication, Jones calls him "a typical Ottoman Jew." Later in the book, he describes him as having "all the natural intelligence and acumen of the cosmopolitan Jew." Still later, recounting how he used the Spook to manipulate the Pimple by stroking his ego, he writes, "He was not, I suppose, any more or any less ambitious than the average young Jew, but he undoubtedly had a very high opinion of himself."

Despite their surface diversity, Singer found that cults have common structures, functions, and aims. Their organizational structure is one of top-down authoritarianism, with the leader posited as a godlike figure possessed of superhuman knowledge and skill—an image that can be reinforced by means of magicians' tricks. Followers, who come from a range of faith traditions, tend to feel disenfranchised by the larger culture and become transfixed by the group's utopian "false promises and bogus ideology." Cults often spring up in locales that are isolated from ordinary life, and they tend to flourish in times of social unrest, notably wartime.

At its core, every cult is about manipulation. The sham promises it extends, along with its rigid structure and associated rituals, serve its fundamental goal: to beguile followers, gradually and undetectably, into a state of blind obedience. If the cult functions as intended, Singer explains, a member "can be hoodwinked to such a degree that she or he gives up job, family, and the freedom of self-determination." The process by which this is accomplished—a subtle but highly persuasive program of thought control that can take months or even years—is akin to a long con.

"The key to successful thought reform," Singer says, "is to keep the subjects unaware that they are being manipulated and controlled—and especially to keep them unaware that they are being moved along a path of change that will lead them to serve interests that are to their disadvantage. The usual outcome of thought-reform processes is that a person or group gains almost limitless control over the subjects for varying periods of time."

ON APRIL 29, 1918, two years to the day after the fall of Kut, the carts pulled into Mardeen. Jones already knew the town: His echelon had been allowed to rest there for a day on its long trek to Yozgad. "My second entry into Mardeen was happier than the first," he said. "The Spook could get us all the comforts we wanted, and though we still denied ourselves proper food the starvation was nothing, for it was a self-imposed means to an end. In place of a hopeless captivity there lay ahead of us the hope of early freedom. So we bumped joyfully over the cobbled streets and drew up in the market square."

In the square, Hill caught sight of a group of children sifting through garbage for food: Mardeen had been ravaged by wartime inflation and a typhus epidemic. He discreetly nudged Jones, and Jones, propelled by the Spook, began flinging banknotes toward them. "My Turkish being already good enough to enable me to tell each recipient to run like smoke, the Pimple had a desperate ten minutes," he recalled. "He returned from his last chase puffing and blowing, and bundled me back into the cart."

Their next objective was to find the right inn for the night, and the tourist guide has yet to be written that rates accommodations by their suitability for a hanging. There were three inns in Mardeen. At the first, they were shown room after room. None had anything to which they could affix their ropes. "Hill was mooning along with us, reading his Bible as he went and pretending to take no interest in the proceedings," Jones wrote, "but I knew that the mournful look he bestowed on each room as we entered had taken in every detail. I glanced at him and he gave the tiniest shake of the head. I turned on Moïse.

" 'Is this the accommodation you offer me, ME, a friend of the Sultan!' I said in simulated rage, twisting my coat-button as I spoke. 'This is an insult! Take us where we shall find worthy lodging, or you shall suffer!' "

Returning to the courtyard, they found that the sentries, Bekir and Sabit, had already unloaded the baggage, including the butter:

> When the Pimple told them we had refused to stay there, sentries and drivers alike were furious. I added to the hub-bub by dancing about the yard in a frenzy and ordering them to harness up at once. Bekir, his face red with anger, took me roughly by the shoulder and growled at me in Turkish. I pushed him off, and foaming with rage informed him that he was reduced from Lieutenant-Colonel (to which rank I had promoted him that very morning) to a common "nefer" (private) again, and if he didn't load up at once I'd have him shot, I'd report him to the Sultan, I'd tell Enver about him and blow him from the cannon's mouth. The Pimple translated. It was a very pretty little scene, and quite a crowd gathered in the gateway.

The sentries grudgingly packed up, and they made their way to the second inn. It was no better. They moved on to the third, the finest in

Mardeen. It was there, Hill said long afterward, that he nearly came to believe in the Spook himself, for the room they were shown—the only vacancy in the place—seemed to have been ordered up by the spirits. It boasted a high ceiling and, firmly planted in the ceiling, four metal rings that looked, Jones recalled, "strong enough to hold an ox." Hill immediately sat down on the floor to read his Bible. The sentries unpacked and stationed themselves in the room.

There remained the problem of how to reach the rings. Jones reckoned the ceiling to be 11 feet high, and there was nothing on which to stand. He pondered the matter while simultaneously augmenting his madman's credentials:

Opposite the door of our room, on the other side of a small narrow passage, was the coffee-shop of the hotel. It was full of a motley crowd of drovers and shepherds. At my suggestion Bekir, Moïse and I entered it, leaving Hill at his religious duties in the corner and Sabit to watch him. Before Moïse could stop me I had ordered and paid for coffee all round—it cost a shilling a cup! While this was being drunk I went amongst the drovers and asked confidentially if there were any English in the town, and if any of them knew Major Baylay. There were no English in Mardeen, and Baylay was utterly unknown. In my joy at the news I ordered ten cups of coffee for each guest and threw a pile of bank-notes on the counter. Moïse grabbed it, explained to the crowd that I was mad, and amid much sympathetic murmuring and "Allah-Allahing" from the drovers I was hustled back into my own room. In preparation for what was coming later, the hotel habitués had been given a hint of our mental state, and I had seen what we wanted in the coffee-room—a small table.

Before returning to his room, Jones asked the Pimple to have a meal brought in; it was the pretext for getting the table. With the Pimple safely in the coffee room placing the order, Jones and Hill tackled the next problem: how to set their room up for a hanging without the sentries seeing. Pretending he was reading aloud from his Bible, Hill offered a suggestion. Once they had eaten, he said, Jones should invite the sentries and the Pimple across the hall for coffee; in their absence, Hill would rig the nooses. On some pretext, Jones would return "momentarily" to their room, where they would bar the door with the table, climb atop it, and commence the double hanging.

The Pimple returned with the food and the table, and the five men sat down to supper. When they had finished, Jones asked everyone to coffee. Hill, deep in the Bible, ignored him; the others accepted. (The sentries were content to leave Hill on his own, Jones knew, because they considered him harmless.) But when they stepped across the hall, they found the coffee room had closed.

Bekir offered to buy a bottle of cognac instead if Jones gave him the money, and Jones briefly considered getting him and Sabit drunk. But that scenario, he realized, was far too risky: Protocol would demand that the others match the sentries drink for drink, and he, Hill, and the Pimple would need all their wits about them for the hanging to succeed "within limits." For hours they all drank tea in their room as Jones, with the Pimple translating, regaled Bekir and Sabit with tales of Welsh life while inwardly pondering his next move. The attempted hanging, and the Pimple's report of it to Haidar Pasha, was vital to getting them admitted to the hospital.

At ten o'clock, Jones asked the sentries to escort him to the lavatory, signaling to Hill to join him. On the way, with the Pimple out of earshot in the bedroom, he slipped Hill two coins, a Turkish gold lira and an Indian rupee. As he did, he sang a little song:

It's up to you to show them some tricks.
I'll say it's magic, you get them keen,
Then offer to show them one still more wonderful
If they'll stand outside the door while you prepare.

Hill squeezed Jones's arm in acknowledgment. Returning to their room, Hill resumed reading as Jones gradually brought the subject around to magic. "Ask Bekir if he has ever seen magic," he told the Pimple.

Bekir had often heard of magic and djinns, but had never seen any. Yes, he would like very much to see some, but where?

I pointed to Hill, huddled up in his corner, and told them he knew all the magic of the aborigines of Australia. I'd make him show us some, if they wished it. They were delighted at the idea.

But Hill would not oblige. He said magic was "wicked" and he had given it up.

"Shall I force him to do it?" I asked.

Bekir and Sabit nodded. They were very keen already, and knew that Hill usually obeyed me—it was a feature in his insanity that he gave in to me more readily than to anyone else. But tonight he simulated great reluctance. I had to threaten to take his Bible away before he would do as he was told. Finally he stood up, the picture of mournful despondency, and slowly rolled up his sleeves. We lit a second candle and placed it on the table. We moved the table to the spot we wanted it—not directly under the rings but slightly to one side, so that we would swing clear when we stepped off. Then Hill began.

Hill's performance, with the audience barely a yard in front of him, was bewitching. To the sentries' gasps, he made the silver rupee materialize in his palm as if from nowhere. He stunned them further by making gold appear—the Turkish lira. "It is good," Bekir declared after biting the coin and handing it back. "Make more, many more." Hill, wearing a look of deep boredom, began plucking gold lira from the air—here, there, and everywhere—storing each one in his pocket as soon as it appeared. Then, having had enough wickedness, he sat down with his Bible.

"More!" Bekir cried. "Show us more magic."

"Would you like to see the table float about the room?" Hill asked. The sentries eagerly assented.

"Then step outside the door while I speak to the djinns."

The Spook had told the Pimple exactly what to do: He was to stand outside the door and as soon as he saw the light go out beneath it, call to Jones and Hill. Getting no answer, he would rush in to find them dangling. He would lift them up as best he could and cry for help. "Moïse was terrified of what the Spook might do to him if he allowed one of us to get killed," Hill recalled, "and if that happened the treasure seekers would never find the third clue, which would be a greater worry."

Now, as Jones stayed behind to help Hill with his "illusion," the Pimple left the room with the sentries, taking one of the candles with him. The mediums could only pray that he would follow his instructions to the letter. Each man took a rope, which Hill had fashioned into a noose. Climbing onto the table, they affixed the free ends to the rings and slipped the nooses round their necks.

"Ready?" Jones whispered.

"I'm O.K.," Hill replied. They shook hands.

"Take the strain," Jones said. Holding the rope above his head with one hand, he bent his knees. "I could not see Hill, but knew he was doing the same," he wrote. "We did not want an inch of 'drop' if we could avoid it."

Jones blew out their single candle, and they stepped off the table into empty air. The Pimple, chatting with the sentries in the hall, did not see the darkness at first. "To anyone desirous of quitting this mortal coil," Jones wrote, "we can offer one piece of sound advice—don't try strangulation."

Than hanging by the neck nothing more agonising can be imagined. In the hope of finding a comfortable way of placing the noose we had both experimented before leaving Yozgad, but no matter how we placed it we could never bear the pain for more than a fraction of a second. When we stepped off our table in the dark at Mardeen we simply had to bear it, and though we had arranged to grip the rope with one hand so as to take as much weight as possible off the neck until we heard Moïse at the door, the pain was excruciating. . . . I revolved slowly on the end of my rope. My right arm began to give out and the rope bit deeper into my throat. My ears were singing. I wondered . . . if I could hear him try the door in time to get my hand away, if he was ever going to open the door at all. It was impossible to say how long we hung thus, revolving in the dark. I suppose it was about 90 seconds, but it seemed like ten years.

"Hill, Jones, are you ready?" At last the Pimple had seen the signal.

We instantly let go of our ropes and hung solidly by the neck—it was awful.

"Hill, Jones!" The Pimple was shouting now. We could not have answered had we tried.

The door crashed open.

The Pimple hollered, and everyone came running: sentries, staff, shepherds, drovers. What happened next was a haze of shouting and activity, but the mediums remembered being lifted up by the legs, taken down, and laid on their backs—Hill on the bed, Jones on the floor. Buckets of ice water were tossed over them. "The hotel-keeper, in a vain effort to save his mattresses, was tugging at Hill's head so as to bring it over the edge of the bed and let the water fall on the floor," Jones wrote. "Hill opened his eyes and began to cry, as Doc O'Farrell had warned him to do. They continued to pour water over us both, until the floor was an inch deep in it."

O'Farrell had counseled Jones to be loud and abusive when he "came to." Staggering to his feet, he shook his fist, raved about the murderous Major Baylay, castigated the Pimple for thwarting the hanging, and hollered imprecations against the assembled multitude in more than passable Turkish. The result was that the multitude beat him up. Sabit hit him in the back with his rifle butt. Someone smacked him hard over the head with a coil of rope. A man wearing wooden shoes kicked him in the stomach. "An overwhelming nausea came over me, everything swam in a giddy mist," Jones said. "I have never felt so ill in my life, and it was hard to keep at it, even in a whisper. They were going to do something more to me, when Moïse intervened. I was profoundly thankful, but went on raving at my rescuer between gasps."

Jones made a grave mistake then. Twisting his coat button, he addressed the Pimple: "Send us to bed," he said.

"Had the crowd in the room contained anyone who knew English that single sentence was enough to show that Moïse was our confederate," Jones wrote. "The moment the words were out of my mouth I realised what I had done, and could have bitten my tongue out. By sheer good fortune, nobody understood. . . . But the lesson was not entirely lost, and never again was my hatred of physical suffering allowed to gain the upper hand."

The next morning, the mediums righteously denied having tried to hang themselves. The Pimple, as ordered, wrote up a report of the incident and had it signed by several witnesses. (He told Jones and Hill privately that the Spook's "control" of them the night before had been awe-inspiring.) "A telegraphic report was sent to the Commandant at Yozgad," Jones wrote, "and we learned later that Captain Suhbi Fahri and Major Osman were delighted at the correctness of their diagnosis."

They left Mardeen for Angora that afternoon, their escort augmented by a local policeman; when they reached the next police post, another took his place. "We were handed on from police officer to police officer, all the way to railhead," Jones said, "for we were now regarded as dangerous lunatics." On the road that night, they were locked down in a local hotel room with the Pimple, the sentries, both drivers, the policeman, and a knot of deputized villagers all standing guard.

ON MAY 1, they arrived in Angora, where they would have to wait five days for a train. This gave the sentries the chance to procure a 200-pound bag of flour, which, not to be outdone by the Pimple, they planned to resell in Constantinople. On the evening of the sixth, the five men boarded the train. The mediums' mad behavior at the station—Jones antic and raving, Hill morose and praying—was only heightened by the tableau of Bekir, Sabit, and the Pimple loading their tiny third-class compartment with all the luggage, the immense bag of flour, and what the mediums privately called the "BBB": the "bloody box of butter." The five of them arranged themselves atop the provisions, and the train pulled out of Angora for the journey to the capital.*

As the train neared Constantinople, the mediums told the Pimple that since they were now so close to the city, they would make a last attempt to read AAA's thoughts. Holding hands in the compartment, they lapsed gradually into trance-talk and by a miracle got a clear connection. Clue 3, AAA revealed, was buried in the prison camp in the garden of what had been OOO's house, now part of Posh Castle. The Pimple was wild with joy at the news, but the mediums soon interrupted his effusions—OOO had seized control! OOO told them that on his orders one of the Posh Castle inmates might have dug the clue

* On reaching the capital, neither the Pimple nor the sentries had any luck as capitalists. Bekir and Sabit resold the flour for exactly what they had paid for it; the Pimple made a loss of about £50 on the BBB.

up already. Unable to make sense of the strange slip of paper, he had thrown it away.

Resuming control, the Spook told the Pimple not to despair: OOO could well be lying. When Moïse returned to Yozgad, he could check for himself. In any case, the Spook added, if all else failed, there was always the Four Cardinal Point Receiver.

The Spook then made a handsome valedictory speech. In it, he told the Pimple that he, Moïse, was capable of real greatness—even, one day, of leading the entire world—if he would only hew to the straight and narrow. He must live righteously, and from this day forward neither lie nor steal. Bidding the company adieu, the Spook faded out. The Pimple wept, and gave his promise.

After two and a half days the train reached Constantinople, and the Pimple led Jones and Hill to Haidar Pasha, a half mile from the station. Before entering the building, each swallowed his last 20 grams of phenacetin. As the Pimple negotiated the paperwork and Hill soberly read the Bible, Jones, acting on the "delusion" that he had arrived at a hotel, ordered a whisky and soda, and called for the night porter to conduct them to their rooms.

Thus were Elias Henry Jones and Cedric Waters Hill admitted to the mad ward of Haidar Pasha hospital.

CHAPTER FOURTEEN

The Mad Ward

HAIDAR PASHA WAS a military hospital with a ward for nervous disorders. Established in the mid-nineteenth century, it occupied an imposing building in Scutari,* a district of Constantinople on the Asian side of the Bosporus. A 1918 British government report described the hospital as one of the best in Turkey, among the "good modern institutions, staffed by Turkish or [Ottoman] Greek doctors of European training, and for the most part by German or Austrian nurses."

Admitted on the night of May 8, 1918, Jones and Hill were led to the hospital's hammam, the communal Turkish bath. There they were relieved of the food they had brought with them, their clothing (Jones never saw his again), and most of their possessions. Hill managed to hold on to his Bible; Jones retained the handwritten manuscript of what would become his magnum opus, *History of My Persecution by the English.* After they bathed, they were issued hospital uniforms: "a vest, a pair of pants, a weird garment that was neither shirt nor nightgown but half-way between, and Turkish slippers." An orderly conducted them to the "nervous ward," a dimly lighted room containing ten beds.

FAKING INSANITY IS a time-honored con. Odysseus feigned madness in an attempt to avoid serving in the Trojan War. In the First Book of Samuel, David, needing to escape mortal peril in the Philistine city of Gath, did likewise: "He disguised his sanity before them, and acted insanely in their hands, and scribbled on the doors of the gate, and let

* Known today as Üsküdar.

his saliva run down into his beard." The renowned American journalist Nellie Bly did so in 1887 in order to be committed to the Blackwell's Island Lunatic Asylum in New York.* Her resulting exposé of the horrific conditions there was published that year in the *New York World* and afterward in book form.

To simulate madness convincingly is fearsomely difficult, but done well, the ruse can be fearsomely difficult to detect. An eminent Irish alienist (the term by which psychiatrists were known before the twentieth century) described the problem of unmasking of sham madness as "one of the most difficult with which alienists have to deal, one requiring much experience, acumen and sagacity." Adding to the difficulty, as an American doctor observed in 1896, was the fact that "there is no established rule or test by which feigned insanity may be detected."

Suspected of malingering, Jones and Hill would be under constant surveillance. In the mad ward, Jones was assigned to Bed 10, Hill to Bed 8; both beds could be seen clearly from the door. The Ottoman officer between them in Bed 9 was almost certainly a spy planted there to observe them. "It was obvious," Hill wrote, "that traps would be set and we would be watched secretly for a long time before we were accepted as genuine."

They lost no time in playing their parts. From his first moment in the hospital, Jones, under the "delusion" that he was a Turk, worked maniacally on his manuscript, which would eventually fill about thirty large notebooks. (He would soon begin work on a second opus, *Scheme for the Abolition of England.*) Hill prayed aloud constantly and refused all nourishment unless commanded to eat by Jones. As O'Farrell had counseled, they forced themselves to stay awake that first night—they had already gone three days without sleep—to get the "insane look" in their eyes before nerve specialists came to examine them in the morning.

Capt. Edward Mousley, captured at Kut and imprisoned at Kastamuni, was hospitalized in Haidar Pasha's eye ward in the summer of 1918. He recalled his first sight of Jones there:

---

* Blackwell's Island is now Roosevelt Island. The asylum is long gone.

In the middle of the night I saw a ghoulish figure, wearing a large, black mantle and with stark, staring eyes, stalking me from bed to bed. With all the uncanny anticipation of one's every movement that usually happens only in a nightmare he divined my every move, for I also tried to get to the door. . . .

At this an attendant came for him. I breathed freely as he left. I thought what a pity it was after all my experiences to meet my end from a mad fellow-prisoner. . . . Then I got a note written to me from him, a veritable mad document assuring me he hated the English and that he feared I was going to kill him. This arrived just after I had met him in daylight. He wore a black overall, a yard of which he had picked into threads, which his busy fingers did incessantly. His hair was long, he wore a beard, and his white, sunken cheeks gave him a ghastly appearance.

Getting Mousley alone, Jones took him into his confidence. "He was a daring actor but not quite finished," Mousley concluded. "More than once I thought [he] overdid it." If their ruse was discovered, the best Jones and Hill could hope for was to be sent back to Yozgad; far worse would be to be separated and sent to other camps, or to be thrown into one of Turkey's civilian prisons. But there was also danger in acting their roles too well: If they were deemed truly mad, they could be committed to a Turkish insane asylum, with little hope of release.

There was another risk, ever present. "Pretend to be what you are not and the desire to be what you are grows in intensity until it becomes an agony of the mind," Jones wrote. "Your very soul cries out to you to be natural, to be your own 'self' if only for five minutes. Then comes a stage of fear when you wonder if you are not what you seem—if you can ever be yourself again—if this creature that weeps mournfully when it should be gay, or gabbles wildly about its own grandeur, is not the real Hill, the real Jones. You believe you are all right, but you want to try so as to be sure—and yet trial is impossible; it would spoil everything."

Fighting sleep in Bed 10 that first night, Jones was jerked to full wakefulness by the sound of blows in the corridor. As he learned afterward, it was only a roaming patient "being pounded back to bed" by the orderlies. He would hear that sound many times during the next six months.

In the morning, a junior doctor, Ihsan Bey, entered the ward, accompanied by the Pimple. Thanks to Jones and Hill's gleeful groundwork, they would have the Pimple's help during much of their time in the hospital, for he would not be returning permanently to Yozgad. As a last gift to their fellow captives, they had let the Spook persuade him to advance his career by reporting to the authorities in Constantinople and demanding to be sent to the front lines. "The Turkish War Office was so astonished at obtaining a volunteer at this stage in the war that they gave him a commission straight off, granted him a month's leave to wind up his affairs and then clapped him into the officers' training school, where he was fed on skilly* and drilled for eight hours a day," Jones wrote:

> He utilized his first afternoon off duty to come to me in the mad ward . . . where he literally wept out his sufferings into my unsympathetic ear and implored the Spook to get him better treatment. The Spook reminded him he had offered to share the starvation of the mediums and informed him that he was now "doing his bit," and it is fair to the Pimple to record that when he heard the verdict he dried his tears, held his head high, and announced that he was proud to do his duty by our great cause; henceforward, he said, he would endure the torments of bad food, bad lodging and hard physical exercise without a moan. He never complained again, but he sometimes referred with regret to the luxuries of his old post at Yozgad—and we felt the camp was avenged.

Arriving with Ihsan Bey that morning, the Pimple told Jones that the doctor would question him. But first Jones had much to say. "I launched into a very long and confused story of how I had been deceived in the dark into believing that the hospital was a hotel, de-

---

* A thin gruel, the stuff of workhouses and prisons.

manded that the mistake be rectified at once, and that I be taken to the best hotel in Pera as befitted a friend of Enver Pasha. The Yozgad Commandant, I said, would be very angry when he knew what Moïse had done, for I was a person of consequence in Turkey. . . . I would answer no questions until I got to the hotel."

Ihsan calmly assured Jones that everyone who sought an audience with the pasha had to answer questions first.

"Your name," the doctor said, "is Jones, lieutenant of Artillery."

"No," Jones cried, "that's wrong! If that's for Enver Pasha it won't do! My name used to be Jones, but I've changed it. I'm going to be a Turk."

"I see," the doctor replied. "What's your name now?"

"Hassan *oghlou* Ahmed Pasha."

Asked by Ihsan what illnesses he'd had, Jones spun out a list that read like found poetry: "Measles, scarlet fever, whooping cough . . . malaria, ague, dengue fever, black-water fever, enteric, paratyphoid, dysentery." None of those, he knew, was what the doctor was seeking.

"Have you ever had syphilis?" Ihsan asked. The disorder Jones was feigning, general paralysis of the insane, resulted from it.

Jones hung his head in silence, as O'Farrell had instructed.

"Enver Pasha is very particular about this question," the doctor urged.

"When I was about eighteen—" Jones began shamefacedly, but could say no more. Then he exploded. "I don't believe Enver Pasha cares two whoops whether I've had syphilis or not. I am sure you have no right to ask me such a thing! I'll report you for it!"

And so it went—Ihsan gentle, Jones volatile.

"Do you ever smell smells that are not there?" the doctor asked.

"There are plenty of real smells in Turkey without worrying about the ones that are not there," Jones shot back. "Why on earth are you wasting my time with these asinine questions? Let's get to the War Office without any more of this foolery."

Why, Ihsan asked, did he want to go to the War Office?

"I leant forward confidentially and told him I had a plan for finishing the war in a week, and once I got to Enver Pasha I'd blow England sky high. I was working at the scheme now. Hill was my engineer and designer—and very soon everything would be completed. I talked on and on about my new aeroplane that would carry 10,000 men, and the coming invasion of England by air."

"You are mad, my friend," the doctor told him before interview's end. "I'm a specialist, and I know."

"I don't know whether you are a specialist or not," Jones retorted, "but I do know you are a most phenomenal liar. I am no more mad than you are. . . . How dare you say I am mad without even examining me?"

"I've been examining you all along," Ihsan said, laughing. Taking out a reflex hammer, he began his physical examination, tapping Jones's knees and looking intently at his pupils. The doctor seemed puzzled, and Jones knew why: Though he had implied he'd had syphilis, he displayed none of the associated physical signs. Ihsan stepped into the hall and returned with another junior doctor, Talha Bey.

Talha asked Jones kindly whether he had ever received injections.

"I saw what the sly fellow was after, and pretended to walk straight into his trap," Jones wrote. "O'Farrell had coached me very thoroughly."

"Oh, yes!" Jones declared happily. "I've had plenty of injections! You've come to the right man if you want to know about injections. I had a regular course of them once."

"Where did they inject you?" Talha asked.

"In the thigh," Jones said. "First one thigh and then the other. A sort of grey stuff it was."

"Not more than once, surely!" said Talha, feigning surprise.

"Oh yes," Jones said. "Every week for about six weeks, and then a spell off, and then every week for another six weeks, and so on, and then I had to take pills for two years. I know all about injections, you bet."

"Dear me!" Talha said solicitously. "What a curious treatment! What was that for, I wonder?"

At that point, Jones recalled, "I managed to look confused, stammered a little, plucked nervously at the hem of my nightgown." Then he brightened. "Malaria!" he cried triumphantly. "Yes, that was it! Malaria!"

Talha went away satisfied. The regimen Jones had described was a standard treatment for syphilis.

• • •

It was Hill's turn next. Ihsan Bey summoned him from his bed to a nearby table. Hill sat down, still clutching his Bible.

"What is the book you are so interested in?" Ihsan asked him.

"The Bible," Hill replied gloomily.

"Why do you read it so much?"

"Because it's a very good thing. Don't you read the Bible?"

"Sometimes," the doctor replied.

"Who is this man?" Hill asked the Pimple.

"He's a doctor," the Pimple said.

"I don't want to see doctors," Hill said. "There's nothing the matter with me."

"Don't you want to go to England?" Ihsan asked.

"I don't care," Hill said. "I want to convert the whole world. I may as well convert Turkey first."

"Why did you try to hang yourself?" the doctor asked.

"I didn't. It is very wicked to commit suicide."

"Do you ever fast?"

"I want to, but Jones won't let me."

"What do you think of Jones? Do you like him?"

"He's a very peculiar fellow. He's very wicked." And with that, Hill was dismissed. The examination by the senior doctor lay ahead.

In attempting to gull their doctors, Jones and Hill had history on their side, for in 1918 the medical approach to mental illness was at a crossroads. Psychiatry of the period stood poised between two nebulous poles: alienism, with its focus on diseases of the nervous system (a subject only hazily understood), and Freudianism, with its pursuit of an elusive unconscious. But in between, during the last years of the nineteenth century and the first years of the twentieth, the discipline rested on what appeared to be firmer ground, relying on a rigorously worked-out classification scheme to diagnose and treat disorders of the mind.

For centuries, the mentally ill had been considered a species apart—people "alienated" not only from the larger society but also from their own minds. The idea of "mental alienation" is attested as far back as the 1300s; the occupational term "alienist," used to describe someone who treats the alienated, arose in the early 1800s. Before the rise of alienism, insanity had been viewed as a moral failing or as evidence of possession by malign spirits. Alienism, a modern scholar has written, was trumpeted as "the victory of psychiatry over demonology" because it sought to bring the study and treatment of mental illness under the umbrella of medicine.

Alienism was tightly bound up with neurology: Ailments of the mind were considered little different from other disorders of the nervous system, such as epilepsy or Parkinson's disease. As a general rule, disorders thought to result from a lesion in the brain came under the neurologist's purview, while those without lesions were the province of the alienist. But which diseases fell into which category was not always clear: Many ailments now classed as psychological maladies were long believed to stem from organic neurological disease. Until the early twentieth century, for instance, hysterical patients were commonly referred to a neurologist first.

Although alienism advocated humane treatment of the mentally ill, it had little real help to offer. The alienist, as the psychiatrist and social critic Thomas Szasz wrote in 1995, functioned largely "as nanny for troublesome adults," with confinement in insane asylums very nearly the only course of action. There, treatments might include purgatives such as castor oil and, in later years, sedatives including morphia salts (an opiate) and hyoscyamine, "an extremely poisonous alkaloid obtained from the plant henbane," as one modern writer describes it, along with "antimony, mercury, digitalis, ergot and strychnine."

In attempting to diagnose their patients, alienists had a bewildering array of mental disorders from which to choose. A perennial goal of alienism was to organize those disorders into a meaningful classification, along the lines of the kingdom-phylum-class taxonomy used to sort the biological world. But there was little agreement on how to go about it. Should disorders be arranged by etiology? By symptom? Though a classification based on etiology was the paramount aim, so little was known about the cause of mental illnesses that alienists had to settle for a scheme based on symptoms. But even on this they couldn't agree, and until the early twentieth century more than a dozen competing taxonomies were in use throughout Europe and the United States. Very nearly the only category on which the systems concurred was the topmost one: the evocative if unhelpful rubric "Insanity."

Below "Insanity" came a taxonomic free-for-all, a welter of gothic descriptions vying for alienists' diagnostic attention. Among them were epileptic insanity, syphilitic insanity, gouty insanity, hysterical insanity, alcoholic insanity, moral insanity, idiocy, cretinism, erotic paranoia, reasoning mania, querulous insanity with a mania for lawsuits, spasmodic asthma with insanity, and sexual vampire delusion.

Then, in the late 1800s, the German physician and alienist Emil Kraepelin began work on an improved taxonomy, one that construed the study and treatment of mental illness as a discipline separate from neurology. Soon considered definitive, his taxonomy would form a bridge between nineteenth-century alienism and twentieth-century psychiatric science. (Kraepelin's scheme is a forerunner of the standard classification used today, as set forth in the *Diagnostic and Statistical Manual of Mental Disorders*.) For his work, Kraepelin (1856–1926) is often called the father of modern psychiatry.

First published in the 1880s and revised many times before his death, Kraepelin's taxonomy, properly called a nosology,* was born of rigorous empirical study. Where older classifications were organized around patients' *behaviors,* subjectively defined—"hysteria," "idiocy," "dementia," and the like—Kraepelin homed in on the underlying organic *causes* of the illnesses themselves, with each malady characterized by a distinctive constellation of symptoms. Through long clinical observation, he identified two major subtypes of mental illness, which he named dementia praecox ("precocious madness," for its tendency to afflict patients in their early twenties) and manic depression. Those classifications, now known as schizophrenia and bipolar disorder, remain salient today. For these disorders and many others, Kraepelin published detailed longitudinal descriptions, documenting their progress from initial manifestation onward.

Kraepelin's taxonomy had enormous advantages for both doctors

---

* The scientific term for a catalogue or classification of diseases, from the Greek *nosos,* "disease."

and patients. In the past, alienists had tried to allay superficial symptoms, analogous to treating a cough without knowing whether it resulted from tuberculosis, lung cancer, or something else. Now, alienists could begin to focus on treating the illness itself. His scheme helped greatly with diagnosis, its longitudinal maps telling physicians what to look for at any given stage.

It was also pay dirt for malingerers—an instruction manual for faking mental illness. Thanks to Kraepelin, aspiring madmen had precise scripts for a range of roles, with every symptom, from onset to final curtain, set down in black and white. Kraepelin's taxonomy was a standard part of medical education in the late nineteenth and early twentieth centuries, and it is clear from O'Farrell's coaching that he was intimately familiar with it. The hallmarks of general paralysis of the insane, for example (the syphilis-based malady from which Jones was meant to suffer), included rampant egoism, delusional boastfulness, and, in the words of a late nineteenth-century physician, "conspicuous degenerations and decay of the moral attributes."

By the early twentieth century, Freud's psychoanalytic ideas had begun to dominate European psychiatry. But they did not take root in Turkey until the 1930s, a state of affairs that seemed providential for Jones and Hill: It is undoubtedly easier to mimic a codified list of symptoms than to ape the obscure workings of the unconscious. In 1918, Kraepelin's ideas remained deeply influential among Turkish alienists, having been brought to the country a decade earlier by Mazhar Osman Bey, a student of Kraepelin's described today as "the founding father of modern Turkish neuropsychiatry."

Trained in Germany, Osman (1884–1951) originally planned to be an obstetrician. But after a coveted obstetrics post went to another candidate—a pasha's son—he turned toward psychiatry. Colleagues tried to dissuade him: At the time the field entailed low prestige and little recompense. He persevered, publishing hundreds of scientific papers, becoming chairman of the department of psychiatry at Istanbul University, writing the first Turkish-language neuropsychiatry textbooks, and in 1914 helping to found the Turkish Neuropsychiatric Society. By 1918 he was considered "the greatest authority on mental diseases in Eastern Europe," an expert in particular on general paralysis of the insane. Less providentially for Jones and Hill, Mazhar

The doctors of the "mad ward" at Haidar Pasha Hospital. Mazhar Osman Bey, "the greatest authority on mental diseases in Eastern Europe," is seated front row center.   JONES, THE ROAD TO EN-DOR (1919)

Osman Bey was also the senior doctor on the mad ward of Haidar Pasha hospital.

OSMAN SWEPT INTO the ward later that first morning, trailed by a coterie of junior doctors, students, and orderlies. "During our stay in Constantinople we were examined at various times by some two score medical men—Turks, Germans, Austrians, Dutch, Greek, Armenian, and British," Jones wrote. "We were subjected to all sorts of traps and tests and questions. There is no doubt we were often suspected . . . but nobody inspired us with such a fear of detection, or with such a feeling that he knew all about his business, as Mazhar Osman Bey."

A courtly man in his mid-thirties, Osman stopped at Jones's bed. He asked him why he looked so angry, and Jones launched into an indictment of Ihsan Bey. Ihsan, he said, had insisted on holding him in the mad ward despite the obvious fact that he wasn't mad.

"Ihsan Bey does not understand you," Osman said sympathetically. "You must learn to speak Turkish."

"I'll learn it in a month,"* Jones promised the doctor happily. "I'll also learn every other language in the world."

---

* With the aid of a Turkish grammar, and lessons from assorted hospital patients and staff, he did.

Osman withdrew to the hall to confer with his subordinates, and they arrived at the decision Jones most dreaded: They would test his blood and spinal fluid for syphilis.

> I had hoped these tests might be omitted, for they would show beyond doubt that I had no syphilitic infection, and I feared that this might prove the first step in the detection of my simulation. But these men were leaving nothing to chance. They were convinced I had syphilis, and were going to prove it. . . . If I wouldn't admit to having suffered from the disease I must submit to the test.
>
> It was too dangerous to make such an admission, for they might—probably would—carry on with the tests in spite of me, and so prove me a liar.

"I protest," Jones told the junior doctors. "I have never had syphilis."

"Your blood and your spinal fluid will prove who is right," Ihsan said with a grin.

Would they care to make a small wager, Jones asked—perhaps £100,000?* The doctors negotiated the figure down to £100, still a princely sum.

They drew blood from his arm, then turned to his spine. An orderly cleared the needle by blowing into the barrel, then wiped it on his breeches before handing it to one of the medical students. "If it had not been for Hill, I think I would have given in and confessed, for I dreaded infection," Jones said. "I knew enough about needles to be in mortal terror of a dirty one." The orderlies held him facedown. The student stabbed into his back three times before hitting the right spot.

When the results came back they were—no surprise—negative. "I danced with simulated joy, jeered at Ihsan and Talha, called loudly, day after day, for my hundred pounds and demanded to be sent forthwith to Enver Pasha," Jones recalled. What *was* surprising was that the findings didn't expose him as a fraud. "I knew the diagnosis was bound to be upset by the negative results of the Wassermann tests,

---

* Jones's £100,000 wager is equivalent to nearly £7 million, or more than $9 million, today.

and did not feel at all comfortable until they began showing me off to visiting doctors as a *rara avis*," he wrote.*

With Hill, the doctors took a different tack: They left him completely alone. It was, Jones wrote, "a treatment quite as trying to the nerves of the malingerer as what I had been through. He knew quite well that though no one went near him he was under observation every minute."

In MID-MAY a panel of doctors convened at Haidar Pasha to review their cases. They were armed with the findings of the junior and senior doctors; the testimonials from the Yozgad doctors, Kiazim, the Pimple, Bekir, and Sabit; and the report of the attempted suicide at Mardeen. They would also be reinterviewing Jones and Hill: The strategy this time was to interrogate each man separately about the other.

Jones was brought in first, and Osman Bey asked him what he thought of Hill. "I replied," Jones wrote, that "he was my engineer and was designing me an aeroplane to carry 10,000 men, and I would make 3,000 such aeroplanes and would invade England with 30,000,000 men, etc., etc., etc."

Then Hill was summoned. Knowing that their belongings were routinely gone through, Jones had planted a wondrous document among Hill's things. Written in an untidy scrawl, it read:

I, Elias Henry Jones, Master of Arts Assistant Commissioner in the Indian Civil Service Deputy Commissioner of Kyaukse District Upper Burma and Headquarters Assistant Moulmein Lieutenant Indian Army Reserve of Officers in the Volunteer Artillery Battery born at Aberystwyth and educated at Glasgow University and Baliol College Oxford CERTIFY and PROMISE by ALMIGHTY GOD that if you will assist me in my great scheme and do everything I require of you including draw and inventions of MACHINERY I certainly will be converted by you and give up all wickedness

---

* Developed in 1906, the Wassermann test—named for the German bacteriologist August von Wassermann—detected syphilis antibodies in blood and spinal fluid.

as you say as soon as my great scheme is finished and until then you must help me with designs and drawings and inventions of NECESSARY MACHINERY.

Signed, E. H. JONES

Hill, a skilled mechanical draftsman, had proceeded to do a drawing of the machine, a Rube Goldbergian riot of ratchets, pulleys, and counterweights; Jones vowed to use it to uproot England from its moorings. The drawing, too, had been left for the doctors to find.

"Did you do this drawing of a machine for Jones?" one of the doctors asked Hill.

"Yes," he replied, "but there is no sense in it, and it is wicked."

"Why did you do it?"

"Because Jones told me to."

"Why do you do what Jones tells you?"

"Because he is very wicked, and I want to convert him. He has promised to be converted if I do what he wants."

"Do you know what all these people are?" a doctor asked Hill a little later.

"I think they are doctors."

"Do you know what disease you have?"

"I have no disease," Hill said. "There is nothing the matter with me."

A murmur ran through the room.

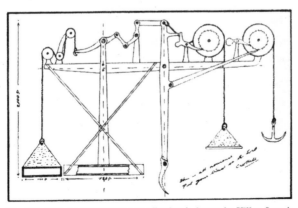

The "Mad Machine" for uprooting England, drawn by Hill to Jones's specifications.   JONES, THE ROAD TO EN-DOR (1919)

• • •

BEFORE ENTERING THE hospital, Jones and Hill had given the Pimple a code. If the doctors thought they were malingering, he was to shake hands with the mediums on saying goodbye each day. If the doctors were undecided, he was to bow. If they believed the pair insane, he was to salute. Day after day, the Pimple had bowed as he took his leave. The day after the panel convened, he looked straight at the mediums and saluted each in turn. Then he decamped to Yozgad to dig for his fortune.

CHAPTER FIFTEEN

Near Death

SO THEY WOULD be going home. It was only a question of when, and they thought they had gleaned the answer. The previous day, after the review of their cases, they had received a visit from a Madame Paulus. Attached to the Dutch embassy in Constantinople, she made it a practice to call on sick prisoners.

"I see you are reading the Bible," she said to Hill in English. "It is a very good book to read."

"Some of the Bible is wrong," Hill said, barely looking up. "I'm going to rewrite it."

"Dear, dear!" Madame Paulus said. She quickly turned to Jones.

"Here are some flowers and chocolate I brought you from the Embassy," she told him.

"Are you sure they are not from the English?" Jones wailed. "Are you certain they are not poisoned?"

Turning back to Hill, she offered him the chocolate.

"It is wicked to eat much," he replied. "I am fasting to-day."

"Oh, dear! dear! When will you eat it?"

"When I have done fasting."

"When will that be?"

"After forty days. Jesus used to fast for forty days."

Growing desperate, she turned back to Jones. "May I write to your relatives?" she asked. "They would like to know how you are."

"No! certainly not!" he cried. "They want to kill me. Don't tell them where I am."

"Oh no! no! No mother ever hated her son. You must give me her address so that I may write. Are you married?"

"Yes. But my wife is the worst of the bunch. She puts poison in my parcels, and I'm going to divorce her, that's what I'm going to do. I'm going to divorce the whole crowd of them, wife, mother, father—every one of them, and be a Turk, for they are all bad, bad, bad!"

Madame Paulus turned to Hill again. "You will be going home soon," she said gently. "Will you like that? All sick prisoners are going home in July."

"I don't care," he replied mournfully.

"Shall I give your mother your love, Mr. Hill?"

"If you like," he said.

"But don't you want to send your love?"

"I don't care."

"Oh, dear, dear me!" she wailed. She went away almost in tears. They felt guilty for days afterward, but they also silently rejoiced. They would be going home in July, six weeks away. They could bear six weeks of shamming, though the risk would be as great as ever. "Our task was 'to keep it up' until the exchange steamer arrived," Jones wrote. "It was a desperate time for both of us. We were watched night and day. We knew that a single mistake would spoil everything."

But May gave way to June, and June to July, and no steamer came. Unable to procure a "safe conduct" from Germany for the voyage, Britain did not want to put ship and passengers at risk. "Had we known that our acting was to be kept up not for six weeks but for six *months,* I think we would have lain down and died," Jones said. "No doubt the British authorities were right to hold back until the safety of the ship was assured, but there was not a prisoner of war in Turkey, sound or sick, who would not have voted cheerfully for running the gauntlet of the whole German Fleet."

IN JULY THE Pimple returned from Yozgad, bearing good news and bad. "The Commandant is being very kind to the camp," he told Jones. "They are enjoying much hunting and freedom." But the Pimple's own lot was not a happy one: On returning to the camp, he had learned the terrible fate of Clue 3. "Everything is going wrong!" he wailed. "The third clue is lost! Price found it—he dug it up in the garden as the Spook said—and he kept the gold lira (he showed it to me), but alas! he dropped the paper of instructions somewhere."

"So he found it?" Jones asked.

"Oh, yes. He found it. In a tin, just like the other clues. He told me it was written in characters that looked like Russian. But he lost it again. I spent days and days looking for it. I spent two days in the carpenter's shop at Posh Castle, searching through the shavings and rubbish. . . . Then the Cook and I looked through all the dust-bins, and went carefully over the rubbish dump under the bridge. But it was gone! Gone!"

Kiazim, too, had been searching. "As soon as the Commandant got my letter telling him the position of the third clue, he decided to dig for it without waiting for me," the Pimple told Jones. "The letter said he was to wait for me, by the Spook's orders, but he sent the Cook to dig at once. The Cook pretended to the prisoners in Posh Castle that he was making a drain, and he dug very hard, but he found nothing."

Jones smiled inwardly at the delight that exhibition must have given O'Farrell, Matthews, and Price. He began twisting his coat button.

"Everything's all right," the Spook intoned. "All is my doing. I am punishing the Commandant."

"What are you punishing him for, Sir?" the Pimple asked.

"For greed and disobedience."

"I know!" the Pimple said. "I suppose you are referring to his digging?"

"Yes," the Spook said. "Tell Jones about it, I'm busy."

Jones swam back to consciousness. "Tell me about yourself," he enjoined the Pimple. On the road to Constantinople, the Spook had promised the Pimple that if he would forsake lying and stealing and "live a righteous and austere life," he could one day become the ruler of the world. The Pimple was busy complying.

"I obey the Spook," he said. "I am living very austerely. I do not even go to the theatre or the cinema. All my leave I have been studying languages as ordered by the Control. I am studying German, Spanish, and Arabic. I know already French and Turkish, also Hebrew and some English. Do you think that is enough?"

"I don't know," Jones replied. "Some of the indigenous American languages might help. I could teach you some Choctaw later on; there's a lot of Choctaw incantations you should learn some day."

"What's Choctaw like?" the Pimple asked.

"Hwch goch a chwech berchill cochion bychain bach." (A Welsh tongue twister meaning "A red sow and six very small red piglets.")

"Mon Dieu!" the Pimple exclaimed. "Now, when do you think we can try the Four Point Receiver?"

THOUGH THEY HAD apparently persuaded the doctors they were mad, Jones and Hill remained under constant suspicion: They were, after all, enemy combatants. The doctors could rescind their findings at any time, and throughout the summer of 1918 they laid further traps. Whenever Hill undertook one of his religious fasts—these could last for days—Osman instructed the orderlies to give him appetite stimulants, and to leave trays heaped with food by his bedside. He forced himself to eat nothing. Talha Bey once offered Jones a bottle of ink: It was, the doctor assured him, an antitoxin that would protect him from the poison he so feared. Jones drank it down, smiled happily, and pronounced it good strong medicine.

Jones's insanity, at least, allowed for such madcap behavior. He once spent weeks hoarding hard-boiled eggs from his hospital lunches. When he had a whole cache, he began gleefully lobbing them, one by one, at the Turk who ran a coffee stall on the hospital grounds, hollering that he had dared serve coffee to the dastardly English. "The man fled across the garden closely followed by Jones hurling eggs as they ran," Hill recalled. "Next day . . . he and Jones became great friends again, Jones patting him on the back and apologizing for misjudging him."

On several occasions Jones managed to slip out of the hospital after dark. One night he donned a fez and made his way to the local railway station, armed with a can of fruit with the label soaked off. Stalking up and down the platform, he waved the can around, announcing loudly that it was a bomb with which he planned to blow up an arriving train of British prisoners. A shouting, whistle-blowing pandemonium ensued. A Turkish soldier rushed up with a bucket of water, grabbed the can, and plunged it inside. Amid the hubbub, Jones melted into the crowd and back to the hospital.

His shenanigans were delicious, but they were also dangerous.

Once, on a nighttime foray from Haidar Pasha, he was nearly shot by a sentry. Caught outside on two other occasions, he began raving that he was on his way to kill Major Baylay. Returned to the hospital, he was drugged with trional* and morphia.

Even routine life on the ward, Jones recalled, entailed constant pressure:

> I had to be ready to "rave" at a moment's notice whenever anyone cared to bring up one of my half-dozen fixed delusions; I had to suspect poison in my food; get up at all times of the night to write the "History of My Persecution by the English" and my "Scheme for the Abolition of England"; form violent hatreds . . . and equally violent friendships; be grandiose; sleep in any odd corner rather than in my bed; run away at intervals; be "sleepless" for a week at a time; invent mad plans and do mad things without end. I refused to answer to my own name and became either "Hassan *oghlou* Ahmed" (Hassan's lad Ahmed) or "Ahmed Hamdi Pasha," as the whim seized me. I wore a most disreputable fez, boasted of being a Turk, cursed the English, and ran away in terror from every Englishman who happened along. All the time I talked nothing but Turkish and to all appearance lived for nothing but to become a Turkish officer. The biggest criminal in Eastern Europe—Enver Pasha—was my "hero," and I fixed a photograph of him above my bed. And every minute of the day or night I had to be ready for a trap, and have an answer pat on my tongue for any question that might be asked. . . . A hard task and a wearing one.

Hill's task was harder still: There were no mad antics to lift his spirits. He had to be seen sitting on his bed, silent and motionless, for hours on end, wearing an expression of unwavering mournfulness. His only respite came in hiding beneath the bedclothes for a few moments at a time. He was obliged to read ceaselessly from his Bible, whose tiny print taxed his eyes so badly he could scarcely see; before his ordeal was over, he had read the entire book through seven times.

---

* A sedative first used in the late nineteenth century.

He had to be prepared to have real tears stream down his face at short notice, which he managed by covertly blowing cigarette smoke into his own eyes. He took no food for days on end, until he was more skeleton than man.

"It was the most wonderful exhibition of endurance, of the mastery of the mind over the body, I have ever seen," Jones said. "Many a time I . . . returned of an evening to the ward, worn out by the unending strain of my own heartbreaking foolery, and ready to throw up the sponge. Always I found Hill resolutely sitting in that same forlorn, woe-begone attitude in which I had left him hours before, and always the sight of him there renewed my waning courage and steadied me to face at least 'one more day of it.'"

Then, in late July, the doctors put the mediums to the severest test of all: They separated them.

GORGING HIMSELF AFTER one of his periodic fasts, Hill developed severe dysentery. He grew crushingly thirsty, was unable to eat, and became so weak he could scarcely walk. Jones was sick, too, with influenza and a fever of 103. Before either had recovered, doctors told them to pack their things. Jones, they said, was being sent at last to see Enver Pasha, and Hill was to go with him. The mediums allowed themselves to hope that they were being sent home: If Jones's hatred of the English had been accepted at face value, the doctors might well describe a trip to England in such veiled terms. But on the appointed day, all that happened was that Jones and Hill were conveyed by train, boat, and cart to the European side of the Bosporus, where they were remanded to another hospital, Gumush Suyu.

By any measure, Gumush Suyu did not reach Haidar Pasha's standard of care, and it had no facilities for psychiatric cases. It looked, at least, as though the mediums would remain there together, but after thirty-six hours Jones was returned to Haidar Pasha. "It amounts to this," he explained: "The bold experimenters at Gumush Suyu were quite ready to practise their prentice theories on Hill, who was harmless and passive under their treatment as befitted his malady, but they had no desire to try their tricks on a lunatic who was active and possibly dangerous, like myself. When I pretended to take a violent dislike to one of the doctors, and tried to buy a knife from the sentry, they thought discretion the better part of valour. This was the sole reason why *I* was a 'case for specialists,' while Hill was not."

Before leaving, Jones quietly offered to renounce their entire scheme so that Hill could receive proper treatment. Hill, by then so debilitated that he "could hardly crawl to the lavatory and back," vowed to carry on. On his own at Gumush Suyu, he learned from a visiting Dutch official that the sick-prisoner exchange would not take place for at least two months, possibly three.

"Judging by the attitude of the doctors, nurse and orderlies towards me, and the fact that Jones and I had been separated, I felt quite sure that we were suspected of malingering," Hill wrote.

> Several times I spotted one of the doctors watching me through the crack of the partly closed door. One of the junior doctors was continually dodging into the ward, a thing he had not done before I came, so I heard the others remark. The orderlies made no attempt to make me eat, and sometimes ate my food when no one else was in the ward and gave me nothing, probably to see if I would complain. The nurse hung about at meal times for no apparent reason. . . . I took no notice of all these things and vowed that although I might give myself away by some unfortunate error, I would die before I would admit to the Turks that I was shamming.

At Haidar Pasha, they told Jones that Hill was dead. It appeared to be a test, but Jones couldn't be sure: He knew how sick Hill had been. He forced himself to stay in character. "It was a good job," he replied, "because Hill was always bothering me to pray with him." But he spent days in inward misery before learning otherwise. Hill would languish at Gumush Suyu for a month, receiving negligible treatment. That he survived at all owes to a fellow patient, Capt. Thomas Walter White.

White was an Australian flier who had been captured near Baghdad. Imprisoned at Afion Karahissar, he was admitted to Gumush Suyu in the summer of 1918 with foot and ankle injuries. He recalled his first sight of Hill there:

I stared in amazement, for I had never seen so woe-begone an object. His unkempt hair grew almost to his shoulders and was lost in an untidy beard. His face was drawn and sunken, his jaw dropped, and his body thin and wasted. A small Bible lay open upon his drawn-up knees and with his pallid face resting in his skinny hands he alternately sobbed and moaned. "What a consummate actor," I thought, with the admiration of an amateur malingerer for a master.*

"Don't speak to him," a fellow patient enjoined White. "He's quite mad. We've all tried to talk to him but he won't talk. He's got religious mania."

Placed in the bed next to Hill's, White could see that he was terribly sick:

At about 2 A.M. I stole to Hill's bed, and finding him sleepless I took his hand and whispered close to his ear that I did not believe that he was mad, but that I could see he was very ill, and that as a fellow Australian I insisted on helping him. Mentioning also that I had a tin of butter, a tin of milk, sugar and a packet of cocoa in my kit, which I received the day I left Afion, I offered to diet him with these foods if he would allow me.

Half expecting an irrational answer, as except for his prayers he had not spoken for months, I was thankful to hear a sane reply. "I have been very ill with dysentery," he whispered, after a pause, "and being neglected am in a pretty bad way. I would be glad of a little of your food, but do not speak to me. We can correspond with notes that can be got rid of in the lavatory."

Whenever Hill stared at him fixedly, White knew that a note awaited, balled up on the floor. Dropping some small object as a pretext for leaning out of bed, he would scoop up the note and read it under the sheets. "I shall ask you to pray with me to-night," one note

---

* White had contrived to enter the hospital as a place from which to escape. In July 1918, while being returned from Gumush Suyu to Afion, he slipped away from his guards, stowed away aboard a Russian merchant ship, and rejoined Allied forces in Bulgaria. His odyssey is recounted in his 1928 memoir, *Guests of the Unspeakable.*

said. "Please curse me heartily and complain to the doctors about it. Ask the Dutch Legation if they visit the hospital again to get me a Bible with larger print. This one is blinding me."

White began covertly feeding his provisions to Hill. He also made him cocoa, which, he said, "gave me the opportunity of doctoring him with opium pills that I had received among the sugar in a parcel. In a few days I had the satisfaction of seeing a little colour come into his wasted cheeks, and the temperature graph above his head ceased to zigzag."

He implored Hill to stop the ceaseless mortification of his own body. "I have made up my mind to persist to the end, if it kills me," Hill wrote in reply. "Maybe I am not so far from being mad already. Watch my eyes when I pray!"

"When he next bent in prayer," White wrote, "I saw what I had not noticed before, that continued silence, sickness, underfeeding and ceaseless deception had so combined to upset his nerves that he could not keep his eyes closed, his eyelids persistently blinking and twitching."

In early August, without warning or explanation, Hill was transferred to Psamatia, a camp in a distant suburb for prisoners discharged from hospitals. He was now little more than a skeleton: Lean and rangy to start with, he had lost more than seventy pounds during his captivity and hospitalization. He was hoisted onto a springless donkey cart, in which he "sat like a ghost" throughout the five-hour journey. The cobbled streets caused him excruciating pain; from time to time, when the donkeys bolted down hills, he was flung into the road. As befit his melancholic persona, "I always looked . . . that I didn't care what happened."

At Psamatia, to which White had also been remanded, they were herded into an empty Armenian religious school with hundreds of British, Indian, Russian, Romanian, and Serbian captives. Their beds, with mattresses of moldering straw, were seething with vermin. Hill's aching bones received another jolt when the rotten boards of his bedstead collapsed and he fell clean through to the floor.

A few days later, Hill was returned without explanation to Gumush

Suyu. There, he was watched unremittingly by the patient newly installed in the next bed, billed as a Russian prisoner but most likely an Ottoman doctor sent to spy on him. On August 17, after a series of false starts including another stop at Psamatia, he was returned to Haidar Pasha. "The general 'messing about' I was put through during the time between leaving and returning . . . was no doubt an attempt to break me down," he wrote. "Owing to the state of health I was in at the time it was almost more than I could take."

On reaching Haidar Pasha, Hill was taken to the hammam, where an attendant shaved off his hair and beard ("more like 'tearing out by the roots,'" he recalled) with a blunt rusty razor. There was another "patient" in the bath, who had clearly been deputized to watch him. Hill—"so emaciated that he could not bear to cross one leg over the other . . . because his shinbones felt so sharp"—was left there, naked on the marble floor, for more than five hours before being deposited in an unfamiliar ward of the hospital.

"The object of the Turks seems to have been to see if they could force a complaint out of Hill or get him to show any interest in his own treatment or his surroundings," Jones wrote. "He was led three times past the ward I was in, probably as a test to see if he would recognize it and come to me for help in his misery. But such was the iron resolution of the man that, though ready to drop from weakness, he managed to appear quite heedless of everything except his Bible."

When Hill was returned to the mad ward at last, shorn and weighing less than a hundred pounds, Jones did not recognize him. Visiting them soon afterward, the Pimple caught sight of Hill and wept.

ALL THAT SUMMER, the Pimple was keen to resume the treasure hunt.

"I am going to punish the Commandant still more," the Spook assured him on one of his visits.

"What for, Sir?"

"For digging without orders and trying to find the treasure before you got back so as to cheat you of your share."

"The devil!" the Pimple said. "I never before realized that that was his object."

"Of course it was," the Spook replied.

"Punish him, Sir!" the Pimple cried. "Punish him hard, the dirty pig! Here am I, suffering at the military school, while he rolls in luxury at Yozgad! Oh, Sir, punish him!"

"I will," said the Spook.

And he did, or so it seemed, for when the Pimple visited again in August, he brought tremendous news.

"There has been a big escape from Yozgad," he reported. "Twenty-six officers have run away. Only a few have been caught so far."

On hearing the news, Jones said afterward, "I could have shouted with joy."

"Neither Kiazim nor the War Office can make out how they got away," the Pimple continued. "But *I* know. The Spook did it! This must be the Spook's attempt to get Kiazim punished."

FOR THE MEDIUMS, the next few months should have been routine: They had only to wait for the doctors to certify them officially for exchange, then maintain their charade until the ship arrived. Yet they found themselves under deeper suspicion than ever. Orderlies watched them even more closely. They were no longer allowed outside to sit in the hospital garden, even with an escort. Turkish patients, once friendly, regarded them icily; whenever Jones entered the ward, all conversation stopped dead. A new patient, an "Armenian," went out of his way to cultivate him. "That evening, by sheer good luck, I saw this man leaving the hospital for a stroll," Jones wrote. *"He was dressed in the uniform of a Turkish doctor!"*

Bathing in the hammam, Jones spied an orderly watching him through a hole in the ceiling. Someone stole all thirty volumes of *The History of My Persecution by the English* before slipping them back among Jones's things the next day. "I wished joy to whomsoever had taken it because it was all unutterable nonsense specially written for the eyes of the Turk," he said. "But the action showed renewed suspicion on somebody's part."

Something had happened—that much was clear—but they had no idea what. On the ward, they heard faint whisperings in Turkish about "a letter from Yozgad." But who could have written such a letter? Not Kiazim: He was in too deep. Not the Pimple: He remained in Constantinople. "What that letter was," Jones said, "we never knew." Only afterward could they piece together what had probably transpired: The letter was the result of a second well-meaning but ill-fated act by a comrade left behind.

The "big escape" of which the Pimple had spoken took place on August 7, 1918. In a meticulously orchestrated enterprise, some two dozen British officers, tunneling out of their respective houses at night, slipped over the garden walls of Yozgad and into the shadows.* In small groups, they made their way over hundreds of miles of arduous country to the Mediterranean, often traveling by night to evade marauding brigands. Many were recaptured, but a handful made it to the coast, where they secured a boat and sailed to Cyprus and liberty.

Kiazim cursed the Spook for not stopping the escape. Then he strafed the camp. All privileges were ended, and all remaining prisoners locked down in their houses. In the cramped, airless conditions—and with the influenza pandemic of 1918 having reached Turkey—many fell ill, and some died. There had been twelve deaths in all since Jones and Hill left Yozgad.

The renewed suspicion of Jones and Hill was collateral damage. Before they left the camp, the mediums had entrusted the clue-hunt negatives to their comrades Matthews and Price, with instructions to use them against Kiazim in the event of a strafing. Those officers knew that this applied only to a strafing that resulted directly from Jones and Hill's escape—one that took place when they were already well out of Turkey. "Never for a moment," Jones wrote, "did we contemplate sacrificing ourselves or our scheme to save our comrades from discomfort *caused by the actions of others*."

But that is what happened. Matthews had escaped with the August 7 group. Price was among the twelve who died. A successor officer, to whom the negatives had been entrusted, misunderstood the instructions, believing they could be used in *any* emergency. After the camp was strafed—and with Jones and Hill in precarious residence at Haidar Pasha—he turned one of the images over to Kiazim's superior, who had been dispatched to Yozgad after the mass breakout.

"The negative showed me standing with my arms raised over the

---

* Their exploits are recounted in *Four-fifty Miles to Freedom,* the 1919 memoir by two of the group, Maurice Andrew Brackenreed Johnston and Kenneth Darlaston Yearsley.

fire in the 'incantation,' and round me the carefully posed and clearly recognizable figures of the Pimple, the Cook and Kiazim Bey," Jones wrote. "Together with this damning photograph the Turkish authorities were given some sort of a summary of our séances. To make . . . doubly sure the investigating official got the negative enlarged. Kiazim was recognised beyond doubt."

Though the Yozgad prisoners secured a reprieve as a result, "the camp," Jones said, "had come very near to blowing us up in the mine we had so laboriously laid for Kiazim Bey." The compromising "letter from Yozgad" appeared to have been written by Kiazim's superior. On learning of Kiazim's collaboration with the mediums, he had written to the War Office; the War Office in turn wrote to Haidar Pasha. But in the end, after this "quite undeserved discomfort and . . . very bad scare," Jones and Hill were officially certified for exchange by Osman himself.

"What Mazhar Osman Bey's final diagnosis was I never discovered," Jones said. "It was written on my medical sheet in technical language, and my small Turkish dictionary did not contain the words used; but I think from the interest shown in me by students and strange doctors, it was something pretty exceptional. I also think that for a long time Mazhar Osman Bey was not a little dubious about it. Indeed I believe that out of the kindness of his heart—for he was a kindly and humane man—he decided to risk his professional reputation rather than do me a possible injustice, and gave me the benefit of the doubt."

Now it was truly a matter of waiting, and of acting their parts through the summer and fall. They would also need to tell the Pimple that they might soon disappear. He visited them in late September to ask when they could resume the treasure hunt, and when he would rule the world. Though he didn't know it, the visit would mark his last communication from the Spook, and that redoubtable spirit made the most of it:

The Spook explained that the strain of being under control for so long had been very severe on the mediums, and he had therefore "controlled" the Haidar Pasha doctors to give us a thorough holiday by sending us to England. The treasure-hunt was temporarily shelved on account of the disobedience and greed of the "double-faced Superior" (Kiazim). But it would not be for long. Very soon we would be back in Constantinople ... with our health re-established, and ready to begin a new series of experiments and discoveries. Until we came Moïse was to continue to be honest, to live austerely, and to do his duty; for this was his training for the glorious future that awaited him.

The Pimple shook hands with me many times over. He walked off at last, his head high, and his eye bright with the vision of his coming omnipotence. As I watched his cocksure little figure strid-ing out of the hospital gates for the last time—the Spook had told him not to come back—I felt inclined to call after him that he had far to go, and that his training would be long—very long—before he could become Ruler of the World. But I did not. I went back to the ward and Hill, and that was the last I saw of the Pimple.

Hill was dispatched homeward first—partly, he later learned, be-cause it was thought he hadn't long to live. ("That," he wrote in his memoir, "was over fifty years ago.") On October 10, he left Haidar Pasha for the two-day journey by boat and train to a transit camp in Smyrna,* where sick prisoners gathered to await repatriation. During his three weeks at the camp, he continued in the role of religious mel-ancholic before boarding the British hospital ship *Kanowna* on No-vember 1.

He hoped Jones would catch up with him, and continued to look for him until the ship pulled out of the harbor. But Jones, still at Haidar Pasha, was the victim of his own success: His paranoid rants had con-vinced the Ottoman authorities that he would commit suicide if he was thrown together with so many Britons, and they initially barred him from making the trip. Allowed to leave some weeks later, he reached Smyrna in time to catch the second exchange ship, sailing a few days after Hill's. As the madmen cleared Turkish waters on their respective vessels, each made a full and miraculous recovery.

---

* Now the Turkish city İzmir.

CHAPTER SIXTEEN

Persuasion

THE FLIMFLAM ODYSSEY of Jones and Hill was a feat of psychological engineering as rigorously planned, labor-intensive, and dangerous as the physical engineering of a tunnel in traditional prison camp escapes. It was remarkable in particular for three things. First, that the mediums were able to cultivate faith across such a broad swath of subjects: their countrymen, their captors, their doctors. Second, that they instilled belief in things that were patently untrue: ghosts, buried treasure, their own madness. Third, that their subjects persisted in those beliefs *in the face of clear evidence to the contrary:* the inadvertent betrayals that nearly gave away the game, the Wassermann tests that came up clean. What made these achievements possible was the mediums' command of the psychological art now known as coercive persuasion, a skill that underpins enterprises from advertising to military brainwashing to political despotism.*

The adman, the con man, the cult leader, the demagogue—all who actively seek to change the minds of others—rely fundamentally on coercive persuasion. In recent years, such mind-changers have come to be known as "influence technicians" (or "compliance professionals"), and all share a common goal: *to preempt critical reasoning on the part of their subjects,* ensuring their compliance with even the most outlandish programs.

---

* The word "brainwashing" gained wide currency in the mid-twentieth century through the work of the American foreign correspondent Edward Hunter. An anti-Communist propagandist, Hunter had worked during World War II for the United States Office of Strategic Services, the precursor of the Central Intelligence Agency. After the war, he reported on the mass Communist indoctrination of Chinese citizens, publishing an influential book, *Brain-Washing in Red China,* in 1951. Sources differ on whether Hunter was in the employ of the CIA at the time of his work.

In an influence technician's hands, coercive persuasion can be wielded in any of three ways. The technician can use force, a tactic on which cults and terrorist organizations often rely. He can directly manipulate his subject's brain using drugs, electroshock, and the like. Or he can change his mark's mind by means of stealth—the perennial choice of the confidence man. All of these measures, known collectively as "weapons of influence," are designed to cast a subject into a state of unquestioning belief, some lulling him so gently that he remains unaware of what is happening.

A technician wanting to instill *false* belief faces an even more challenging task: He has not only to persuade his subject to believe something new but ultimately, in the words of the American psychologist Thomas Gilovich, to *"know what isn't so."* To this end, several weapons of influence prove especially handy. They include the manufacture of confirming "evidence" (think of the con man's "convincer") and, crucially, shifting the burden of proof from the con man to his mark.

Where facts are scarce on the ground, a ripping good yarn is also a powerful weapon. Narrative is inherently seductive, and a propulsive tale can buoy the mark straight into the storyteller's hands: Witness Scheherazade's life-saving gambit of *A Thousand and One Nights* fame. A good story is enthralling and, because the experience of hearing stories harks back to childhood, it is also comfortingly homey. By spinning a tale, an influence technician can exploit the delicious dual meaning of letting his mark be "taken in."

But the technician's most powerful weapon is the unconscious complicity of the mark himself. In this respect, the compliance professional's art is closely allied with the stage magician's. "Magical illusions are possible only through the cooperation of the audience," the magician Robert Bernhard has written. "In fact, the task of the magician is merely to encourage the audience to fool itself." In other words, as the American advice columnist Ann Landers was fond of saying, "No one can take advantage of you without your permission."

THROUGHOUT THEIR WORK, Jones and Hill wielded weapons of influence with prodigious skill. From his earliest days at the spook-board,

Jones established his authority—and the Spook's—through triumphs in repeated tests. He and Hill were impresarios of implied causation, manufacturing confirming "evidence" (buried clues, cathartic cocoa, the staircase tussle with OOO, the double hanging) as the need arose. Their entire scheme was built around riveting narrative, from the foundation story of OOO's buried treasure, to the tale of the lost diamond necklace that lured Kiazim from his hole, to Jones's account of his fearsome sojourn among the "Head-Hunting Waas." The mediums made their captors complicit in their own undoing through constant assurances that they were all in the hunt together. This in turn bought the captors' affirmation of their second-act insanity scheme.

Little by little, as Jones passed tests at the board, the burden of proof shifted: Where he first needed to prove that he wasn't controlling the glass, his countrymen soon had the onus of proving that he *was*. And once a critical mass of captives came to believe in the Spook, it became that much easier to convert the captors. "Belief is the normal response to a statement," Robert Bernhard writes. "Belief is passive; doubt is active."

The very gradualness of the mediums' scheme also worked in their favor: It is well established in psychology that indoctrination by slow, subtle steps is more likely to succeed than a headlong attempt. So, too—counterintuitively—did the imperfections inherent in their homemade plan. "In most human endeavors, mistakes *cost* us," Thomas Gilovich told me recently. "But for mentalists, and for Jones and Hill, minor mistakes are actually a plus. A perfect record leads people to think that 'something's up' and encourages a skeptical mindset; so a *mostly* perfect record is more convincing. I don't know whether Jones and Hill appreciated that fact or used it, but it certainly helped to cover up the rare mistakes they made."*

The mediums were also masters at appearing to argue against their own interests, a favorite tool of influence technicians. A tour de force came in persuading their captors to leave Yozgad. Having impressed the Pimple with the dangers of using telepathic trance-talk to find Clue 3, they went on to object vociferously to the idea of being

---

* For precisely this reason, as the psychologist and magician Mathew L. Tompkins has pointed out, some magicians and mentalists script errors into their routines.

moved ("The Commandant was our friend . . . and . . . nowhere else in Turkey could we expect to pass our imprisonment under such pleasant conditions"). And thus, despite its dangers, they embarked on trance-talk, a carefully staged horror that had the desired effect of making their captors keen to leave the camp.

Hill's knowledge of magic and mentalism was also indispensable, for those skills—what the celebrated mentalist Max Maven has called "the techniques of *verbal control*"—could be deployed at nearly every turn. Mental trickery proved especially valuable in the straitened confines of Yozgad, where the mediums had to stage an elaborate long con without the usual sets, props, and costumes. "It is absolutely necessary for the working mentalist to avoid building a dependency on 'things' with which to accomplish a performance," Maven has observed.* "The late [American mentalist] Theo Annemann once said about our art, 'When you get to the root it is nothing but your personality and wits against that of your watcher, and *a case of telling him to do as he pleases and then letting him do what you want him to do.*'" There are few more impeccable descriptions of the con man's craft.

To give their captors the illusion of free choice, the mediums relied on a time-honored magicians' tactic: equivoque, or the art of forced selection. "Also known as the 'magician's choice,' the word *equivoque* is derived from Latin and means 'ambiguous' or 'to have a double meaning,'" the mentalist James L. Clark has written. "If I have two decks of cards on a table and I ask you to point to one of them, I use whichever deck you pick to arrive ultimately at the one I want to use for my trick. If I want the deck on the left and you point at it, perfect. If, on the other hand, you pick the one on the right, I simply say, 'Great, I'll eliminate that one. . . . No matter what you want as the mentalist, you get it with the magician's choice—and no one ever suspects a thing."

Jones and Hill used equivoque many times. "The best way to get a man to agree to a plan is to make him think it is his own invention," Jones wrote. "This was the system we followed with the Turks." By violently illustrating the dangers of trance-talk, for instance, they forced their captors to clamor to leave Yozgad. Afterward, by intro-

---

* Maven's article is written under his given name, Philip Goldstein.

ducing the Four Cardinal Point Receiver, with its promise of access to all the treasure in the world ("Get on to the surface of the sea . . ."), the mediums forced the idea of securing a boat—the boat in which they planned to make their getaway, with the Turks their prisoners. ("I am so glad we chose the seaside for our holiday," the Pimple had declared afterward. "It fits in beautifully.")

JONES AND HILL did the work of coercive persuasion so well that more than one of their converts remained a believer despite thundering counterevidence. A remarkable example came in their captors' continued faith in the treasure story after the mediums were betrayed by a fellow prisoner, the man Jones called "X." Because of Jones's early masterstroke in creating OOO, their captors were well primed to put the blame on him.

"You see," as a doleful Pimple analyzed the situation, "X is the medium of OOO. . . . Now he is the mouthpiece of OOO in giving a warning. That is what the Commandant thinks. I tell him no doubt X is the medium of OOO; no doubt this message is from OOO, but the object of it is plain! It is evident! Have we not had experience to tell us what it means? Is it not one last despairing effort by OOO to frighten the Commandant, to stop him from sending the mediums to find the treasure? But he will not listen to me."

The most astonishing instance of sustained belief came at Haidar Pasha, in the doctors' continued acceptance of Jones's madness despite the negative Wassermann tests. Jones never did learn what diagnosis his doctors ultimately bestowed on him. But the fact that they made one at all indicates just how neatly he had shifted the burden of proof to them.

The behavior of Jones and Hill's captors (and later their doctors) was consistent with that of subjects of long-term coercive persuasion: Their continued conviction stemmed from an unconscious psychological process known as *confirmation bias*. "When examining evidence relevant to a given belief, people are inclined to see what they expect to see, and conclude what they expect to conclude," Gilovich has written. "Information that is consistent with our pre-existing beliefs is often accepted at face value, whereas evidence that contradicts them is critically scrutinized and discounted. Our beliefs may thus be less responsive than they should to the implications of new information." In other words, "well-supported beliefs and theories have earned a bit of inertia, and should not be easily modified or abandoned because of isolated antagonistic 'facts.'"

Jones witnessed confirmation bias at work when, just before leaving Yozgad, he disclosed his sham spiritualism to O'Farrell, Price, and Matthews:

> To them . . . I made my long-delayed confession that every "message" obtained through my "mediumship" had been of my own invention, and that not only the Turks but also my friends in the camp had been victimized. It was then, for the first time, that I realized how difficult it is to convince a True Believer of the truth. In spite of what I said, these three, who were all my own "converts," tried to force me to admit that there was "something in spiritualism," and that at least *some* of the messages for which I was responsible were "genuine." They quoted the incidents of "Louise" and the . . . [tests] against me, and when I had explained these Matthews turned on me with, "Well, we have got one thing out of it, anyway! We have proved the possibility of telepathy. For I don't believe that the show you two fellows gave at the concert *could* have been a fraud." In reply Hill picked up a small notebook, and handed it to Matthews.
>
> "There's the code we used," he said.

IN THE END, what aided the mediums most of all were the times, for it was only in that liminal era, poised at the nexus of the scientific and the spiritual, that this particular con could have stood a chance. The period saw the resurgence of the Victorian ardor for spiritualism, a movement, itself founded in fakery, that has been called "conjuring in disguise." It was a time when cutting-edge technologies such as the phonograph, radio, and telephone were making disembodied voices audible to an enchanted but largely uncomprehending public, rendering the idea of discourse with the dead an authentic empirical question. It was an age, suspended between alienism and Freudianism, when the observed symptoms of mental disorders had been neatly codified and could thus be well emulated. It was a time when orthodox psychiatry endorsed the belief that mediumship could result in madness. And it was a time of sustained, widespread social upheaval, when many stood ready to grasp at whatever straw might offer succor.

"Con games never remain stationary," David Maurer has observed. "The principle may be old, but the external forms are always changing, for con men know that they must adapt their schemes to the times. This is especially true of the big con." It is clear that Jones and Hill availed themselves of every tool the early twentieth century had to offer, designing a complex, elegant machine that could have been set in motion only at that singular moment.

And yet . . .

Adjusted for contemporary realities, thought reform built on coercive persuasion is a thriving concern today. "Conforming to the dictates of authority figures has always had genuine practical advantages for us," the American psychologist Robert Cialdini has written:

> Early on, these people (for example, parents, teachers) knew more than we did, and we found that taking their advice proved beneficial—partly because of their greater wisdom and partly because they controlled our rewards and punishments. As adults, the same benefits persist for the same reasons, *though the authority figures now appear as employers, judges, and government leaders.* Because their positions speak of superior access to information and power, it makes great sense to comply with the wishes of properly constituted authorities. *It makes so much sense, in fact, that we often do so when it makes no sense at all.*
>
> This paradox is, of course, the same one that attends all major weapons of influence. In this instance, once we realize that obedience to authority is mostly rewarding, it is easy to allow ourselves the convenience of automatic obedience. The simultaneous blessing and bane of such blind obedience is its mechanical character. *We don't have to think; therefore, we don't.*

AFTER THEIR SEPARATE sea voyages from Smyrna, Jones and Hill were reunited in a transit camp in Alexandria. From there, they shipped out for Italy, where they boarded a troop train for Calais and the Channel crossing to England. The Allies concluded their armistice with the Ottoman Empire on October 30, 1918; the armistice with Germany was signed on November 11. In the end, the mediums wound up reaching Britain barely more than two weeks ahead of their fellow captives.

But though their ruse bought them little time, it may well have saved their lives. Had they remained in Yozgad, they could easily have shared the fate of those dozen men, consigned to solitary graves in the hills that ringed the camp. "Amongst the dead," Jones wrote, "were men we loved."

What was more, in a world seemingly devoid of hope, their two-pronged hoax—embracing their career as sham spiritualists and their second calling as counterfeit madmen—sustained them through hunger, privation, loneliness, and pain as perhaps nothing else could. "Freedom was our lodestar," Jones declared. And so, by means of one of the most uncommon confidence games ever played, they followed their lodestar home.

Afterlife

JONES RETURNED TO Mair, Jean, and his son Bevan, the Little Unknown; the couple would go on to have three more children. During the long convalescence that followed his homecoming, he wrote *The Road to En-dor*. The book was intended as a cautionary tale about how easy it is to become a spiritualist charlatan, a species of war profiteer that continued to wring dividends from gold-star families.

"When we reached England Lieutenant Hill and I thought our dealings with spiritualism had served their purpose, but we now hope they may play an even better part," Jones wrote in the preface. "If this book saves one widow from lightly trusting the exponents of a creed that is crass and vulgar . . . or one bereaved mother from . . . the unwholesome excitement of the séance and the trivial babble of a hired trickster . . . then the miseries and sufferings through which we passed in our struggle for freedom will indeed have had a most ample reward."

Jones dedicated the volume to Doc O'Farrell, "an Irish Gentleman who, himself injured, tended the wounded on the desert journey from Sinai into captivity, going on foot that they might ride, without water that they might drink, without rest that their wounds might be eased; and afterwards, with a courage that never faltered through nearly three years of bondage, cheered us in health, nursed us in sickness, and ever found his chief happiness in setting the comfort of a comrade before his own."

While on sick leave, Jones served briefly as a staff member attached to the Middle East Committee led by Lord Curzon, the British foreign secretary. In the early 1920s he went back to his government post in Burma. In 1922, while home on leave, he bought a large house in north Wales and settled his family there before returning to Burma once more. In 1924, at forty, he retired early from the Colonial Service and rejoined his family in Wales. Throughout the years, he and Hill maintained their steadfast friendship, though Hill's long, globe-spanning career with the Royal Air Force gave them few opportunities to meet.

After settling down in Wales, Jones was active in civic affairs. From 1927 to 1933 he served as the editor of *The Welsh Outlook,* a socially progressive Welsh nationalist magazine. In 1933 he was appointed registrar of the University College of North Wales. "His style of working until he was exhausted remained the same," the authors of *En-dor Unveiled,* an electronic supplement to a 2014 edition of Jones's memoir, have written. "He was not at all attracted to university social life, and continued in his spare time to retreat to the wild and lonely countryside with a gun or rod. This was what Mair expected."

From one of those solitary trips, Jones wrote to her: "My dearest dear, I have not yet come to the end of discovering what your love means to me, and I have never deserved this supreme gift of God . . . year after year, through those twenty five years, I have had to say over & over again to myself 'Gosh! what I used to think was love, was only a shadow of it—THIS is the real thing' and it has been growing & growing, ripening, deepening, unfolding in countless ways."

In 1940, the couple's fourth child, eighteen-year-old Arthur, one of the youngest pilots in the RAF Bomber Command, was killed in a plane crash. His death precipitated a decline in Jones's health from which he never recovered. It is clear that he was suffering from some kind of dementia: On occasion, as if recapitulating his "mad" behavior upon leaving Yozgad years before, he would visit the bank, withdraw fistfuls of banknotes, and hand them out to passersby.

Hill came to see him during this time. "Harry was ill and his speech was slurred," *En-dor Unveiled* reports. "Hill didn't say much. Impassive, he stayed about five hours. They sat together on a garden seat at Harry's home, throwing pebbles at a cocoa tin."

In May 1942, Jones bade Mair a last goodbye as he left home to enter the hospital. They had agreed that she was not to see him again: He wanted her to remember him only as he had been. He died of pneumonia there on December 22, 1942, at fifty-nine.

• • •

AFTER A HOMECOMING in Australia, Hill returned to England, where he was recommissioned as a flying officer in the RAF. He served over the years in Palestine, Egypt, Turkey, Malta, and elsewhere, attaining the rank of group captain, equivalent to that of colonel in the army. In 1921, in Egypt, he married a fellow Australian, Jane Lisle Mort; they became parents of a daughter.

In 1930, at the controls of a de Havilland Gipsy Moth, Hill took off from the RAF's Henlow station in Bedfordshire in a race to break the world record for a solo flight from England to Australia. (The record, set by the Australian aviator Bert Hinkler in 1928, stood at just over fifteen days.) Flying from dawn deep into the night, Hill appeared poised to break Hinkler's record. But after twelve days, as he took off from Atambua, West Timor, on the last

Hill on his return to Australia in 1930, after almost breaking the record for an England-to-Australia flight.

NORTHERN TERRITORY LIBRARY

leg of the voyage, his wing clipped a fence. The plane crashed and overturned, suffering smashed wings and fuselage and a broken propeller. Hill was unhurt, but his race was over.

During World War II, Hill commanded all RAF units in Iran. After retiring from active service in 1944, he flew for the Air Transport Auxiliary, ferrying planes between factories, maintenance units, and military airfields. An avid rifle and pistol shot (he was an RAF revolver champion) as well as a skier, photographer, and glider pilot, he was also a member of the Inner Magic Circle, the elite British organization devoted to promoting the performance of magic. Reviewing a private performance of Hill's at the organization's London headquarters in 1929, the group's magazine, *The Magic Circular,* noted approvingly:

Considerable interest was aroused by the appearance of Mr. C. W. Hill, as it transpired that he was one of the [subjects] of that thrilling work, *The Road to En-dor*. It was, we believe, Mr. Hill's first appearance on the CIRCLE stage, but it was soon apparent that he was in the first flight of sleight-of-hand experts.

It did not matter whether he was working with thimbles or cards, his moves and manipulations were all indetectible and distinguished by perfect finish. He also received a round of well-deserved applause for a card feat in the course of which Mr. Hill managed to bring alternately to the top and bottom of the pack, four pairs of cards chosen by different members of the audience.

Hill died on March 5, 1975, at eighty-three, at his home in Berkshire. His own memoir, *The Spook and the Commandant*, was published soon afterward.

Hill's attempt in 1930 to break the record for a solo flight from England to Australia was widely covered in the world press, as in this article from the Sydney, Australia, tabloid Smith's Weekly.

THE PIMPLE SENT three letters to Jones during 1919, and all that is known of his postwar life comes from them. (As Jones wrote that year in *The Road to En-dor*, he had answered none of them.) "I have a lot of news to give, still more to ask," the Pimple, then teaching English and French in Constantinople, wrote in the first letter, dated February 8:

You know that all the officers interned at Yozgad came to Constantinople on their way home. ... I had a chat with many of them, especially with Captain Miller and Major Peel. Miller told me that Hill had made a camera with which you took many photographs of Yozgad. I congratulate Hill for his industry! My talk with Major Peel was more interesting. He looked stiff, and I dare say a little furious with me. He said that the Commt. the Cook, I and two other gentlemen [i.e., Jones and Hill] were looking up for a treasure amounting to £18,000, the arrest of these two officers, the letter, the enquiry, all that was a fraud. The Commandant was acting. He had rehearsed it the day before with the officers. One of the officers told him everything, that Hill has taken a photograph of the Comt. I, the Cook ... sitting round a big fire lighted on great stones at the top of a hill near the camp. I could not understand that. How could they have got such a photograph? ... I cannot make it out. It is not HUMAN: How could they get a photo when there was nobody to take it! It is mysterious.

On February 22, the Pimple wrote again. "I am very anxious about your health and Hill's and it will be for me a great relief when I hear of your perfect health," he said.

You will not believe me if I tell you I am thinking of you both the whole day. I cannot forget our experiment. Instead of thinking of the future, my thoughts are going to the happy past elapsed since March, 1918. Goodness! When you get this letter a whole year will have passed and we were going to be so happy long ago but for the double-faced Superior [Kiazim]. Notwithstanding the promises of help lavished on me by our teacher [the Spook]* nothing seems to

---

* As Jones points out, the Pimple's veiled references were designed to avoid arousing the interest of the Ottoman censors, who continued to vet correspondence with Allied nations.

come of it. Ill luck is going after me. I do not complain because the end will be good. I trust him so much and all's good that ends good! Is it not so?

The Pimple sent his third letter in June. "I am now in the employ of the British here . . . as interpreter," he wrote.

The other day I attended a court-martial, in order to give evidence about the Sup [Kiazim]. Most of the questions ran about *the two officers sent sick to the hospital at Haidar Pasha*.* They showed to me a photo: it represents a hill somewhere near the camp; the Sup. is on the left side; a tall officer is holding his hands up as if he were praying.† I am near him and the old Cook near me. Those four are the only persons in the picture. It puzzles me a lot as I cannot understand who took the photo and admitting it was taken by OOO, how the dickens did he manage to pass it to the camp? . . . Miller, before going to England on his way here, told me that Hill gave it to them with many others. Of course, it is all rubbish but cannot you give an explanation of the riddle? . . .

How is Hill? Is he in England or is he gone to Australia? What are your ideas? Shall we meet again? I hope you have not forgotten what you promised in the train‡ and that nothing wrong has happened since that could irritate the Controller [the Spook] and that we shall be able to resume our studies. . . .

[Signed] Very affectionate, Moïse Eskenazi

What is noteworthy about all three letters, Jones observed, is "not so much . . . the news they contain, as the attitude of mind they reveal. It is an attitude common to many Spiritualists—a refusal to look facts in the face. Until I read them I never could understand how Sir Oliver Lodge and others like him could go on believing in mediums . . . who had already been detected in fraud. But now I see that faith—*even a faith induced by fraud*—is the most gloriously irrational

---

* A deliberately oblique reference to Jones and Hill.

† This was Jones, performing the "incantation" during the first clue hunt.

‡ That the Pimple would one day rule the world.

and invincible phenomenon in all experience, and that, as Hill said, 'True Believers remain True Believers through everything.'"

THE ARMISTICE OF Mudros, which ended the Allies' war with the Ottoman Empire, was concluded on October 30, 1918; hostilities ceased the next day. Afterward, the Yozgad inmate Arthur Holyoake recalled, "The Commandant sent for Col Moore, the Senior British Officer, and read to him through the Interpreter the terms of the Armistice. . . . The Commandant then held out his hand, saying, 'The War is over we are now friends.' Col Moore ignored the proffered hand and replied, 'The War is over. You have lost, we have won. In future you will take your orders from me.'" Kiazim, Holyoake added, burst into tears.

For his involvement in Jones and Hill's scheme, for the mass escape of prisoners from Yozgad in August 1918, and for repeated fiscal malfeasance, Kiazim Bey was indeed court-martialed by the Turkish authorities. The outcome of the court-martial is unknown.

MAZHAR OSMAN BEY, the Haidar Pasha nerve specialist whose certification of Jones and Hill as madmen made their homecoming possible, continued his distinguished career, long reigning, in the words of one historian, as "the leading psychiatrist in the Ottoman Empire."* In 1933 he was named chairman of the psychiatry department at the University of Istanbul; before his death in 1951, at sixty-seven, as the British medical journal *The Lancet* noted in its obituary, "his international repute was recognised by his honorary membership of the Société de Neurologie de Paris, and the American Academy of Neurology."

Jones and Hill, too, came to regard him warmly. "We have no desire to injure, by our story, the deservedly high professional reputation of Mazhar Osman Bey," Jones wrote near the conclusion of *The Road to En-dor*. "We would very much regret such a result, and it would indeed be a poor return for the unfailing courtesy and the gen-

---

* By present-day standards, Osman was not an unalloyed force for progress. An ardent eugenicist, he forced his sisters and his eldest daughter to make propitious marriages to his assistants.

tlemanly consideration that was always shown us by him and indeed by nearly all the doctors of Haidar Pasha Hospital. For to them we were not enemy subjects but patients on the same footing as Turkish officers, to be tested for malingering and treated in exactly the same way as their fellow countrymen. It is only fair to them to say that we attribute our success not so much to our acting as to the manner in which, under O'Farrell's directions, and with the aid of the Spook, our case was presented."

In the years after World War I, as the *Lancet* obituary goes on to say, a marked copy of *The Road to En-dor* was one of Osman's "most prized possessions." In return, Osman sent Jones an autographed copy of one of his earliest publications, the 1910 monograph *Spiritizma Aley-hine*. As Jones, who knew Turkish, would immediately have recognized, its title means "Against Spiritism."

Acknowledgments

A JOURNALISTIC UNDERTAKING is perforce an act of trespass. As I navigated the lush, fascinating, and mysterious terrain that forms the background of *The Confidence Men*, I am deeply grateful to have had the counsel of three learned guides—the historian Yücel Yanıkdağ, the psychologist Thomas Gilovich, and the psychologist and magician Matthew L. Tompkins. All three have read the entire book in manuscript, and their gracious observations, suggestions, and corrections will save me much embarrassment, and perhaps even opprobrium, when this book takes public flight. (Issues of inclusion, emphasis, tone, and interpretation remain my own, of course, as do any residual errors.) Mark Aronoff and Olivier Bonami furnished welcome assistance on matters linguistic.

I am delighted to be working once more with the sparkling crew at Random House (Bennett always was my favorite panelist), who in the strange, atomized, and unprecedented working environment of 2020 have continued to put out books as ably as though they were working under one roof. My dynamic editor, Hilary Redmon, needed no coercive persuasion whatsoever to love the story of Jones and Hill as much as I did. (Special thanks, too, from Mrs. Milligan.) Hilary's associate Molly Turpin has met every contingency with alacrity, grace, and good cheer. Random House's production staff, notably Nancy Delia and Jennifer Backe, has worked its customary magic. The manuscript was copyedited by Sue Warga; Catherine Dorsey prepared the index.

I would be at perpetual loose ends without Katinka Matson, my literary agent from the start of my career to this day. Her straight-from-the-gut response on reading the proposal for *The Confidence Men* was: "Is this for real? These guys are wild!" (I'm happy to report that yes, it is; and yes, they are.) And it was she who noted astutely that the "barbed-wire disease" that threatened to engulf our heroes is the very thing with which so many of us have been grappling this past year. Katinka's colleagues at Brockman, Inc., Michael Healey, Russell Weinberger, Matthew Perez, Thomas Delaney, and Kevin Reilly, also deserve special thanks. And thanks, too—in advance—to Joe Veltre.

This is the first book I have written where I haven't simultaneously been employed at *The New York Times.* I don't miss the pulverizing pressure of daily deadlines one jot, but, oh, how I miss my colleagues! Chief among them are the Obit crew (Bill McDonald, Peter Keepnews, Dan Wakin, Bob McFadden, Amy Padnani, Sam Roberts, Rich Sandomir, Dan Slotnik, our polymathic morgue-meister Jeff Roth, and our farther-flung co-conspirators Neil Genzlinger and Kit Seelye) and the paper's chamber-music-group-in-residence, the Qwerty Ensemble—Dan Wakin (again), Laura Chang, Will Davis, and Aaron Krolik—in which I have the pleasure of serving as cellist. I pine for the day when we can all meet again in situ. As he has for two of my previous books, the brilliant *Times* graphics editor Jonathan Corum has created the maps for this volume.

Last and as always, more thanks, love, and esteem than I can ever properly express are due to the writer, critic, and teacher George Robinson, my boon companion these thirty-five years and more. Weathering lockdown with you has been a very gracious thing indeed.

References

Abbott, Karen. "The Fox Sisters and the Rap on Spiritualism." *Smithsonian*, October 30, 2012. smithsonianmag.com/history/the-fox-sisters-and-the-rap-on-spiritualism-99663697.

Akçam, Taner. *The Young Turks' Crime Against Humanity: The Armenian Genocide and Ethnic Cleansing in the Ottoman Empire*. Princeton, N.J.: Princeton University Press, 2012.

Anthony, Barry. "Evans, Fred (1889–1951)." British Film Institute Screen-Online, screenonline.org.uk/people/id/473302.

Arda, Berna, and Ahmet Acıduman. "Pandemic Influenza 1918–19: Lessons from the 20th Century to the 21st from the History of Medicine Point of View." *Lokman Hekim Journal* 2:3 (2012), 13–21.

Ariotti, Kate. *Captive Anzacs: Australian POWs of the Ottomans During the First World War*. Cambridge: Cambridge University Press, 2018.

Artvinli, Fatih. "More than a Disease: The History of General Paralysis of the Insane in Turkey." *Journal of the History of the Neurosciences* 23:2, 127–139.

Artvinli, Fatih, Şahap Erkoç, and Fulya Kardeş. "Two Branches of the Same Tree: A Brief History of Turkish Neuropsychiatric Society (1914–2016)." *Archives of Neuropsychiatry* 54 (2017), 364–71.

Barker, A[rthur] J[ames]. *The Neglected War: Mesopotamia 1914–1918*. London: Faber & Faber, 1967.

Barnum, P[hineas]T[aylor]. *Humbugs of the World: An Account of Humbugs, Delusions, Impositions, Quackeries, Deceits and Deceivers Generally, in All Ages*. Minneapolis: Filiquarian Publishing, n.d.; originally published 1865.

Beard, George M. "The Physiology of Mind-Reading." *Popular Science Monthly* 10 (February 1877), 459–73.

———. "The Psychology of Spiritism." *North American Review* 129:272 (July 1879), 56–80.

Beer, Gillian. Foreword to Bown et al. (2009), xiii–xv.

Bennet, Darryl, and Neville Parker. "Hill, Cedric Waters (1891–1975)." In John Ritchie, ed., *Australian Dictionary of Biography*, Volume 14, *1940–1980*. Melbourne: Melbourne University Press, 1996. Online via National Centre of Biography, Australian National University, Canberra, adb.anu.edu.au /biography/hill-cedric-waters-10502/text18635.

Bennett, W. Lance, and Martha S. Feldman. *Reconstructing Reality in the Courtroom: Justice and Judgment in American Culture.* New Brunswick, N.J.: Rutgers University Press, 1981.

Bergmann, Johannes Dietrich. "The Original Confidence Man." *American Quarterly* 21:3 (Autumn 1969), 560–77.

Bernhard, Robert Edmund Jr. *The Psychology of Conjuring.* Stanford, Calif.: self-published, 1936.

Blashfield, Roger K. "Pre-Kraepelin Names for Mental Disorders." *Journal of Nervous and Mental Disease* 207:9 (September 2019), 726–30.

Bly, Nellie. *Ten Days in a Mad-House. Or, Nellie Bly's Experience on Blackwell's Island: Feigning Insanity in Order to Reveal Asylum Horrors.* New York: N. L. Munro, 1887.

Bogousslavsky, Julien, and Thierry Moulin, "From Alienism to the Birth of Modern Psychiatry: A Neurological Story?" *European Neurology* 62 (2009), 257–63.

Bonkalo, A[lexander]. "Emil Kraepelin (1856–1926)." *Canadian Medical Association Journal* 74 (May 15, 1956), 835.

Bown, Nicola, Carolyn Burdett, and Pamela Thurschwell, eds. *The Victorian Supernatural.* Cambridge: Cambridge University Press, 2009; originally published 2004.

Braddon, Russell. *The Siege.* New York: Viking Press, 1970; originally published 1969.

Bradmetz, Joël, and Roland Schneider. "Is Little Red Riding Hood Afraid of Her Grandmother? Cognitive vs. Emotional Response to a False Belief." *British Journal of Developmental Psychology* 17 (1999), 501–14.

"A Brief History of Farnborough Aviation Site, Part 1: The Early Days, 1901–1914." Farnborough Air Sciences Trust, airsciences.org.uk/briefings.html.

Bringmann, Wolfgang G., Helmut E. Lück, Rudolf Miller, and Charles E. Early. *A Pictorial History of Psychology.* Chicago: Quintessence Publishing, 1997.

Brown, Patricia Catherine. "In the Hands of the Turk: British, Indian and Dominion Prisoners from the Ranks in the Ottoman Empire, 1914–1918." Master's thesis, University of Leeds School of History, 2012.

Burlingame, H[ardin] J[asper]. *Magician's Handbook: Tricks and Secrets of the World's Greatest Magician, Herrmann the Great.* Chicago: Wilcox & Follett, 1942.

Carpenter, William B. "On the Influence of Suggestion in Modifying and Directing Muscular Movement, Independently of Volition." Lecture to the Royal Institution of Great Britain, March 12, 1852. *Notices of the Meetings of the Royal Institution* 10 (1852), 147–53.

Cato, Conrad. *The Navy in Mesopotamia: 1914 to 1917*. London: Constable & Company, 1917.

Cialdini, Robert B. *Influence: The Psychology of Persuasion*. New York: Collins Business, 2007; originally published 1984.

Clark, James L. *Mind Magic and Mentalism for Dummies*. Chichester: John Wiley & Sons, 2012.

Coon, Dennis, and John O. Mitterer. *Introduction to Psychology: Gateways to Mind and Behavior*, twelfth edition. Belmont, Calif.: Cengage, 2010.

Corinda, [Tony]. *13 Steps to Mentalism*. Cranbury, N.J.: D. Robbins & Company, 1996; originally published 1968.

Cotterell, Paul. *The Railways of Palestine and Israel*. Abingdon: Tourret Publishing, 1984.

Cowley, Robert, ed. *The Great War: Perspectives on the First World War*. New York: Random House, 2003.

Crowley, Patrick. *Kut 1916: The Forgotten British Disaster in Iraq*. Stroud: The History Press, 2016; originally published 2009.

"David W. Maurer Is Dead at 75: An Expert on Underworld Slang." *New York Times*, June 14, 1981, 43, via United Press International.

Deak, John, Heather R. Perry, and Emre Sencer, eds. *The Central Powers in Russia's Great War and Revolution, 1914–22: Enemy Visions and Encounters*. Bloomington, Ind.: Slavica Publishers, 2020.

Dennett, Daniel C. "Beliefs About Beliefs." *Behavioral and Brain Sciences* 1:4 (1978), 568–70.

Dennis, Peter, Jeffrey Grey, Ewan Morris, and Robin Prior, eds., with John Connor. *The Oxford Companion to Australian Military History*. Melbourne: Oxford University Press, 1995.

Dessoir, Max. "Hermann the Magician: Psychology of the Art of Conjuring." Introduction to Burlingame (1942), 7–41. Dessoir's essay originally published in 1885.

———. "Die Parapsychologie." *Sphinx* 7 (June 1889), 341–44.

Dixon, Bryony. "The 'Pimple' Films." British Film Institute ScreenOnline, screenonline.org.uk/film/id/1151483/index.html.

"Dramatic Air Race Ends." *The Age* (Melbourne, Australia), October 20, 1930, 9.

Drewry, William Francis. "Feigned Insanity: Report of Three Cases." *Journal of the American Medical Association* 27:15 (October 10, 1896), 798–801.

Dunnette, Marvin D. "Use of the Sugar Pill by Industrial Psychologists." *American Psychologist* 12 (1957), 223–25.

"Elias Henry Jones." The Home Front Museum, Llandudno, Wales. homefrontmuseum.wordpress.com/tag/elias-henry-jones.

"Elias Henry Jones." *The University of Glasgow Story*, Glasgow, Scotland, universitystory.gla.ac.uk/biography/?id=WH20122&type=P.

En-dor Unveiled: The Story Behind The Road to En-dor. Ebook supplement to the 2014 edition of Jones (1919). London: Hesperus Press, 2014. hesperus press.com/the-road-to-en-dor/downloads/EndorUnveiled.pdf.

Erickson, Edward J. *Ottoman Army Effectiveness in World War I: A Comparative Study.* London: Routledge, 2007.

Escapers All: Being the Personal Narratives of Fifteen Escapers from War-Time Prison Camps 1914–1918. London: John Lane the Bodley Head, 1932.

"Evans, Griffith (1835–1935), Microscopist, Bacteriologist, and Pioneer of Protozoon Pathology." *Dictionary of Welsh Biography.* biography.wales/article /s-EVAN-GRI-1835.

Farschid, Olaf, Manfred Kropp, and Stephan Dähne, eds. *The First World War as Remembered in the Countries of the Eastern Mediterranean.* Würzburg: Ergon Verlag in Kommission, 2006.

Faust, Drew Gilpin. *This Republic of Suffering: Death and the American Civil War.* New York: Vintage Books, 2009; originally published 2008.

Forer, Bertram R. "The Fallacy of Personal Validation: A Classroom Demonstration of Gullibility." *Journal of Abnormal and Social Psychology* 44:1 (1949), 118–23.

Ganson, Lewis, and Dai Vernon. *Dai Vernon's Tribute to Nate Leipzig.* London: Harry Stanley Unique Magic Studio, n.d.

Gardner, Nikolas. *The Siege of Kut-al-Amara: At War in Mesopotamia, 1915–1916.* Bloomington: Indiana University Press, 2014.

Gauchou, Hélène L., Ronald A. Rensink, and Sidney Fels. "Expression of Nonconscious Knowledge via Ideomotor Actions." *Consciousness and Cognition* 21:2 (2012), 976–82.

"The Ghost of Ganargwa: Murder Most Foul!" *Detroit Free Press,* May 5, 1848; originally published in the *Rochester Daily Advertiser.*

Gilovich, Thomas. *How We Know What Isn't So: The Fallibility of Human Reason in Everyday Life.* New York: The Free Press, 1993; originally published 1991.

Gilovich, Thomas, Dacher Keltner, Serena Chen, and Richard E. Nisbett. *Social Psychology,* fifth edition. New York: W. W. Norton & Company, 2018.

Goldstein, Philip T. [aka Max Maven]. *Verbal Control: A Treatise on the Under-Exposed Art of Equivoque.* N.p.: self-published, 1996; originally published 1976.

Grove, Allen W. "Röntgen's Ghosts: Photography, X-Rays, and the Victorian Imagination." *Literature and Medicine* 16:2 (1997), 141–73.

Haines, Michael. "Fertility and Mortality in the United States." Economic History Association, *EH.Net Encyclopedia,* ed. Robert Whaples (March 19, 2008); eh.net/encyclopedia/fertility-and-mortality-in-the-united-states.

Hamilton, Trevor. "Frederic W. H. Myers." *Psi Encyclopedia*; psi-encyclopedia .spr.ac.uk/articles/frederic-wh-myers.

Haw, Camilla M. "John Conolly and the Treatment of Mental Illness in Early Victorian England." *Psychiatric Bulletin* 13:8 (1989), 440–44.

Hayward, Rhodri. "Demonology, Neurology, and Medicine in Edwardian Britain." *Bulletin of the History of Medicine* 78:1 (Spring 2004), 37–58.

"Helena Blavatsky, Russian Spiritualist." *Encyclopedia Britannica*, britannica.com/biography/Helena-Blavatsky.

Helmuth, Laura. "The Disturbing, Shameful History of Childbirth Deaths." *Slate* (Sept. 10, 2013). slate.com/technology/2013/09/death-in-childbirth-doctors-increased-maternal-mortality-in-the-20th-century-are-midwives-better.html.

Henderson, M. Allen. *How Con Games Work*. Secaucus, N.J.: Citadel Press/Carol Publishing, 1997; originally published 1985.

Henson, Louise. "Investigations and Fictions: Charles Dickens and Ghosts." In Bown et al. (2009), 44–63.

Hetherington, H[ector] J[ames] W[right]. *The Life and Letters of Sir Henry Jones, Professor of Moral Philosophy in the University of Glasgow*. London: Hodder & Stoughton, 1924.

Hill, C[edric] W[aters]. *The Spook and the Commandant*. London: William Kimber, 1975.

Holland, Norman N. "The 'Willing Suspension of Disbelief' Revisited." *Centennial Review* 11:1 (1967), 1–23.

Holmes, Marcia. "Edward Hunter and the Origins of 'Brainwashing.'" Birkbeck College Hidden Persuaders Project, bbk.ac.uk/hiddenpersuaders/blog/hunter-origins-of-brainwashing.

Holyoake, Arthur Valentine. *The Road to Yozgad: My War, 1914–1919*, edited by Douglas Bridgewater. Brighton: Menin House, 2013.

Houdini. *A Magician Among the Spirits*. New York: Harper & Brothers, 1924.

Howells, John G., ed. *World History of Psychiatry*. New York: Brunner/Mazel Publishers, 1975.

Hunter, Edward. *Brain-Washing in Red China: The Calculated Destruction of Men's Minds*. New York: Vanguard Press, 1951.

——. *Brainwashing: The Story of Men Who Defied It*. New York: Farrar, Straus & Cudahy, 1956.

Jahoda, Gustav. *The Psychology of Superstition*. New York: Jason Aronson, 1974; originally published 1969.

Johnson, John E. *Full Circle: The Tactics of Air Fighting, 1914–1964*. New York: Ballantine Books, 1964.

Johnston, Maurice Andrew Brackenreed, and Kenneth Darlaston Yearsley. *Four-fifty Miles to Freedom*. Edinburgh: William Blackwood & Sons, 1919.

"Jones, Arthur Bevan." Losses Database, International Bomber Command Centre, losses.internationalbcc.co.uk/loss/214872.

Jones, E[lias] H[enry]. "The Invisible Accomplice." In Klein (1955), 227–38; originally anthologized as "A Game of Bluff" in *Escapers All* (1932), 183–98.

——. *The Road to En-dor: Being an Account of How Two Prisoners of War at Yozgad in Turkey Won Their Way to Freedom.* London: John Lane the Bodley Head, 1919. Paperback, London: Pan Books, 1955. Paperback reprint, with a foreword by Neil Gaiman, London: Hesperus Press, 2014.

"Jones, Elias Henry (1883–1942), Administrator and Author." *Dictionary of Welsh Biography,* biography.wales/article/s2-JONE-HEN-1883.

Jones, Robert F. "Kut." In Cowley (2003), 197–216.

Jones, Sir Henry. *Old Memories.* New York: George H. Doran & Company, 1922.

——. "Will Jones, 1889–1906: A Memoir, Written Early in 1907." In Hetherington (1924), 285–302.

"Jones, Sir Henry (1852–1922), Philosopher." *Dictionary of Welsh Biography.* biography.wales/article/s-JONE-HEN-1852.

Kelley, Douglas M. *22 Cells in Nuremberg: A Psychiatrist Examines the Nazi Criminals.* New York: Greenberg, 1947.

Kelley, Douglas McG. "Mechanisms of Magic and Self-Deception: The Psycho-Logical Basis of Misdirection; an Extensional Non-Aristotelian Method for Prevention of Self-Deception." In Kendig (1943), 53–60.

Kendig, M[arjorie], ed. *Papers from the Second American Congress on General Semantics: Non-Aristotelian Methodology (Applied) for Sanity in Our Time.* Chicago: Institute of General Semantics, 1943.

Keyes, Ralph. *The Quote Verifier: Who Said What, Where, and When.* New York: St. Martin's Griffin, 2006.

Kipling, Rudyard. "En-Dor." In *The Years Between.* London: Methuen & Company, 1919.

Klein, Alexander, ed., *Grand Deception: The World's Most Spectacular and Successful Hoaxes, Impostures, Ruses and Frauds.* Philadelphia: J. B. Lippincott Company, 1955.

Konnikova, Maria. *The Confidence Game: Why We Fall for It . . . Every Time.* New York: Viking, 2016.

Kuhn, Gustav. *Experiencing the Impossible: The Science of Magic.* Cambridge, Mass.: MIT Press, 2019.

Lambert, Carol A. "Trump and Coercive Persuasion: 'He's So Much Like My Abuser!'" *Psychology Today,* November 20, 2016. https://www.psychologytoday.com/us/blog/mind-games/201611/trump-and-coercive-persuasion. Précis at https://carol-lambert.com/blog/2017/01/trump-coercive-persuasion.

Lamont, Peter. *Extraordinary Beliefs: A Historical Approach to a Psychological Problem.* Cambridge: Cambridge University Press, 2013.

Lamont, Peter, and Richard Wiseman. *Magic in Theory: An Introduction to the Theoretical and Psychological Elements of Conjuring.* Hatfield: University of Hertfordshire Press, 2008; originally published 1999.

"The Langham, London." *Cosmopolis: A Magazine on Current Affairs and Culture,* Feb. 6, 2004. cosmopolis.ch/the-langham-london.

Lee, Bandy X. *The Dangerous Case of Donald Trump: 37 Psychiatrists and Mental Health Experts Assess a President,* updated edition. New York: Thomas Dunne Books/St. Martin's Press, 2019; originally published 2017.

Leipzig, Nate. "Thirty-Six Years as a Magician." *The Sphinx: An Independent Magazine for Magicians* 38:11 (January 1939), 208–9.

Lodge, Sir Oliver J. *Raymond: Or, Life and Death.* New York: George H. Doran Company, 1916.

McCain, John, with Mark Salter. *Hard Call: Great Decisions and the Extraordinary People Who Made Them.* New York: Hachette Book Group, 2007.

McRobbie, Linda Rodriguez. "The Strange and Mysterious History of the Ouija Board." *Smithsonian,* October 27, 2013. smithsonianmag.com/history/the -strange-and-mysterious-history-of-the-ouija-board-5860627.

Marvin, Carolyn. *When Old Technologies Were New: Thinking About Electric Communication in the Late Nineteenth Century.* Oxford: Oxford University Press, 1988.

Matsell, George W. *Vocabulum: Or, The Rogue's Lexicon.* New York: George W. Matsell/National Police Gazette, 1859.

Maurer, David W. *The Big Con: The Story of the Confidence Man.* New York: Anchor Books, 1999; originally published 1940.

Meehl, Paul E. "Wanted—A Good Cookbook." *American Psychologist* 11:6 (1956), 263–72.

Melville, Herman. *The Confidence-Man: His Masquerade.* New York: Dix, Edwards & Company, 1857.

Millar, Ronald. *Death of an Army: The Siege of Kut, 1915–1916.* Boston: Houghton Mifflin Company, 1970.

Miller, Morton G. "The Problem of Drug Abuse: Alienation and the 'Alienist.'" *Military Medicine* 134:8 (August 1969), 577–84.

Miller, Scott A. *Theory of Mind: Beyond the Preschool Years.* New York: Psychology Press, 2012.

Moreman, Christopher M., ed. *The Spiritualist Movement: Speaking with the Dead in America and Around the World,* 3 vols. Santa Barbara, Calif.: Praeger, 2013.

Morgan, Kenneth O. *Rebirth of a Nation: Wales, 1880–1980.* New York: Oxford University Press, 1981.

Morley, Iain. *The Devil's Advocate: A Spry Polemic on How to Be Seriously Good in Court,* third edition. London: Sweet & Maxwell, 2015.

Mortality Statistics of the Seventh Census of the United States, 1850. House of Representatives Executive Document 98, 33rd Congress, 2nd session. Washington: A.O.P. Nicholson Printer, 1855.

Mousley, E[dward] O[potiki]. *The Secrets of a Kuttite: An Authentic Story of Kut, Adventures in Captivity and Stamboul Intrigue,* second edition. Uckfield: The Naval & Military Press, 2005; originally published 1922.

Muirhead, John H. *Sir Henry Jones, 1852–1922.* London: Proceedings of the British Academy, 1922.

Nadis, Fred. *Wonder Shows: Performing Science, Magic, and Religion in America.* New Brunswick, N.J.: Rutgers University Press, 2005.

Natale, Simone. "A Cosmology of Invisible Fluids." *Canadian Journal of Communication* 36 (2011), 263–75.

——. *Supernatural Entertainments: Victorian Spiritualism and the Rise of Modern Media Culture.* University Park: Pennsylvania State University Press, 2016.

Neave, Dorina L. *Remembering Kut.* London: Arthur Baker, 1937.

"Obituary: Mazar Osman Uzman." *The Lancet,* September 29, 1951, 599.

O'Brien, Geoffrey. "A Nation of Grifters, Fixers, and Marks: David Maurer's *The Big Con*." *Social Research: An International Quarterly* 85:4 (Winter 2018), 727–38.

Orbach, Barak, and Lindsey Huang. "Con Men and Their Enablers: The Anatomy of Confidence Games." *Social Research: An International Quarterly* 85:4 (Winter 2018), 795–822.

"Ouida." *Encyclopedia Britannica.* britannica.com/biography/Ouida.

Peters, John Durham. *Speaking into the Air: A History of the Idea of Communication.* Chicago: University of Chicago Press, 2000; originally published 1999.

Pimple, Kenneth D. "Ghosts, Spirits, and Scholars: The Origins of Modern Spiritualism." In Walker (1995), 75–89.

"Pioneering Flights—To and from Australia." *A Fleeting Peace: Golden Age Aviation in the British Empire.* http://ata.afleetingpeace.org/index.php /pioneering-flights/10-pioneering-flights/120-pioneering-flights-england australia.

Premack, David, and Guy Woodruff, "Does the Chimpanzee Have a Theory of Mind?" *The Behavioral and Brain Sciences* 4 (1978), 515–26.

Prisoners of War in Turkey: Regulations and Notes for the Help of Relatives and Friends. London: Prisoners in Turkey Committee, August 1918.

Report on the Treatment of British Prisoners of War in Turkey. London: His Majesty's Stationery Office, November 1918.

Roberts, David. *Bangor University, 1884–2009.* Cardiff: University of Wales Press, 2009.

Said, Edward W. *Orientalism.* New York: Vintage, 1979; originally published 1978.

Salgirli, Sanem Güvenç. "Eugenics for the Doctors: Medicine and Social Control in 1930s Turkey." *Journal of the History of Medicine and Allied Sciences* 66:3 (July 2011), 281–312.

Sandes, E[dward] W[arren] C[aulfeild]. *In Kut and Captivity with the Sixth Indian Division.* London: John Murray, 1919.

——. *Tales of Turkey.* London: John Murray, 1924.

Sante, Luc. Introduction to Maurer (1999).

Schein, Edgar H. "The Chinese Indoctrination Program for Prisoners of War: A Study of Attempted 'Brainwashing.'" *Psychiatry* 19:2 (1956), 149–72.

Sconce, Jeffrey. *Haunted Media: Electronic Presence from Telegraphy to Television.* Durham, N.C.: Duke University Press, 2000.

Senn, N[icholas]. "Military Surgery in Turkey." *Journal of the American Medical Association* 29:12 (September 18, 1897), 563–68.

Sheffield, Gary. Introduction to Crowley (2016).

Singer, Margaret Thaler. *Cults in Our Midst,* revised edition. San Francisco: Jossey-Bass, 2003; originally published 1995.

"Sir Oliver Joseph Lodge, British Physicist." *Encyclopedia Britannica,* britannica.com/biography/Oliver-Joseph-Lodge.

Skinner, B[urrhus] F[rederic]. "Has Gertrude Stein a Secret?" *Atlantic Monthly* 153 (January 1934), 50–57.

Solomons, Leon M., and Gertrude Stein. "Normal Motor Automatism." *Psychological Review* 3:5 (1896), 492–512.

Spackman, W[illiam] C[ollis]. *Captured at Kut: Prisoner of the Turks. The Great War Diaries of Colonel WC Spackman,* edited by Tony Spackman. Barnsley: Pen & Sword Military, 2008.

"Spiritualism Exposed: Margaret [*sic*] Fox Kane Confesses That She and Her Sister Were Frauds." *St. Louis Post-Dispatch,* November 4, 1888, 24; originally published in the *New York World.*

Stein, Gertrude. "Cultivated Motor Automatism: A Study of Character in Its Relation to Attention." *Psychological Review* 5:3 (1898), 295–306.

Sten, Christopher W. "The Dialogue of Crisis in 'The Confidence-Man': Melville's 'New Novel.'" *Studies in the Novel* 6:2 (Summer 1974), 165–85.

Steuer, Kenneth. "First World War Central Power Prison Camps." University of Western Michigan, 2013. http://scholarworks.wmich.edu/history_pubs/1.

Stevens, Sara. "Diagnosing Syphilis with the Wassermann Test." STD Resource Center, 2015. stdaware.com/stds/syphilis/treatment/wassermann-test.

Suny, Ronald Grigor. *"They Can Live in the Desert but Nowhere Else": A History of the Armenian Genocide.* Princeton, N.J.: Princeton University Press, 2015.

Szasz, Thomas. "The Origin of Psychiatry: The Alienist as Nanny for Trouble-some Adults." *History of Psychiatry* 6:21 (1995), 1–19.

Taylor, Kathleen. *Brain Washing: The Science of Thought Control.* Oxford: Oxford University Press, 2017; originally published 2004.

Tucker, Spencer C., and Priscilla Roberts, eds. *World War I: Encyclopedia,* 5 vols. Santa Barbara, Calif.: ABC-CLIO, 2005.

Türesay, Özgür. "Between Science and Religion: Spiritism in the Ottoman Empire (1850s–1910s)." *Studia Islamica* 113 (2018), 166–200.

Twain, Mark. "Mental Telegraphy: A Manuscript with a History." *Harper's New Monthly Magazine* (December 1891), 95–104.

The Uses of Elliman's Embrocation for Horses, Dogs, Birds, Cattle. Slough: Elliman, Sons & Company, 1898.

Vischer, A[dolf] L[ukas]. *Barbed Wire Disease: A Psychological Study of the Prisoner of War.* London: John Bales, Sons & Danielsson, 1919. Published in German in 1918 as *Die Stacheldraht-Krankheit.*

Volkan, Vamik D. "Turkey." In Howells (1975), 383–99.

Walker, Barbara, ed. *Out of the Ordinary: Folklore and the Supernatural.* Logan: Utah State University Press, 1995.

Waxman, Olivia B. "*Ouija: Origin of Evil* and the True History of the Ouija Board." *Time*, October 21, 2016. time.com/4529861/ouija-board-history -origin-of-evil.

Weisberg, Barbara. *Talking to the Dead: Kate and Maggie Fox and the Rise of Spiritualism.* New York: HarperCollins Publishers, 2005; originally published 2004.

Whaley, Barton. "Toward a General Theory of Deception." *Journal of Strategic Studies* 5:1 (1982), 178–92.

White, T[homas] W[alter]. *Guests of the Unspeakable: The Odyssey of an Australian Airman—Being a Record of Captivity and Escape in Turkey.* Crows Nest: Little Hills Press, 1990; originally published 1928.

Wiley, Barry H. *The Thought Reader Craze: Victorian Science at the Enchanted Boundary.* Jefferson, N.C.: McFarland & Company, 2012.

Williams, Eric. Introduction to Jones (1955).

——. *The Wooden Horse.* London: Collins, 1949.

Wilson, Philip K. "Conflict and Cooperation of Science and Spiritualism in Late Nineteenth- and Early Twentieth-Century Anglo-American Writings." In Moreman (2013), 2:145–58.

Wixted, E[dward] P. "Hinkler, Herbert John (Bert) (1892–1933)." In Bede Nairn and Geoffrey Searle, eds., *Australian Dictionary of Biography,* Volume 9, *1891–1939.* Melbourne: Melbourne University Press, 1983. Online via National Centre of Biography, Australian National University, Canberra, adb .anu.edu.au/biography/hinkler-herbert-john-bert-6680.

Wright, T[homas] L[ee]. "Some Prominent Features Common to Drunkenness and General Paralysis of the Insane." *Journal of the American Medical Association* 14:25 (June 21, 1890), 884–87.

Yanıkdağ, Yücel. "Flirting with the Enemy: Ottoman Prisoners of War and Russian Women During the Great War." In Deak et al. (2020) [= Yanıkdağ (2020a)].

——. *Healing the Nation: Prisoners of War, Medicine and Nationalism in Turkey, 1914–1939.* Edinburgh: Edinburgh University Press, 2014; originally published 2013.

——. "Ottoman and Allied Prisoners of War and Civil Internees." Book chapter, in preparation, 2020 [= Yanıkdağ (2020b)].

——. "Ottoman Psychiatry in the Great War." In Farschid et al. (2006), 163–78.

——. "Prisoners of War (Ottoman Empire/Middle East)." *International Encyclopedia of the First World War* (n.d.), encyclopedia.1914-1918-online.net/article/prisoners_of_war_ottoman_empiremiddle_east.

Yergin, Daniel. *The Prize: The Epic Quest for Oil, Money and Power.* New York: Free Press, 2008; originally published 1991.

Zacks, Richard. "The 19th-Century Start-Ups That Cost Mark Twain His Fortune." *Time,* April 19, 2016; time.com/4297572/mark-twain-bad-business.

Notes

AUTHOR'S NOTE

xiii **conflating a diverse range of ethnic identities:** As the modern Turkish historian Yücel Yanıkdağ (personal communication) observes, the Ottoman Empire's diverse ethnic and religious groups have been "Turkified" even by some present-day Turkish writers. Such writers, Yanıkdağ says, "will refer to the Ottoman peoples (especially soldiers) as Turkish only. It is as if other ethnicities did not exist." He adds: "To me, this is retroactive nationalist interpretation that denies other people their imperial and ethnic identities."

xiv **"romanticized misrepresentations":** Kate Ariotti, *Captive Anzacs: Australian POWs of the Ottomans During the First World War* (Cambridge: Cambridge University Press, 2018), 34. For the seminal presentation of the idea of Orientalism, see Edward W. Said, *Orientalism* (New York: Vintage, 1979; originally published 1978). Said writes (2–3): "Orientalism is a style of thought based upon [a] . . . distinction made between 'the Orient' and (most of the time) 'the Occident.' Thus a very large mass of writers, among whom are poets, novelists, philosophers, political theorists, economists, and imperial administrators, have accepted the basic distinction between East and West as the starting point for elaborate theories, epics, novels, social descriptions, and political accounts concerning the Orient, its people, customs, 'mind,' destiny, and so on."

INTRODUCTION

xv **Jones's 1919 memoir:** E[lias] H[enry] Jones, *The Road to En-dor: Being an Account of How Two Prisoners of War at Yozgad in Turkey Won Their Way to Freedom* (London: John Lane the Bodley Head, 1919). Jones's title is a nod to "En-Dor," Rudyard Kipling's bitter poem of 1919. In it, Kipling, who had lost a son in World War I, decries the cohort of "spiritualists" who preyed on the families of war dead: "The road to En-dor is easy to tread / For Mother or yearning Wife. / There, it is sure, we shall meet our Dead / As they were even in life." Kipling's title invokes the biblical Witch of Endor, from the First Book of Samuel, whom Saul asks to conjure Samuel's spirit. The poem can be found in Kipling's volume *The Years Between* (London: Methuen & Company, 1919).

xvi **"clay in the potter's hands":** Jones (1919), 70.

xvi ***The Spook and the Commandant:*** C[edric]W[aters] Hill, *The Spook and the Commandant* (London: William Kimber, 1975).

xvi **one of the only known examples:** See, e.g., Barak Orbach and Lindsey Huang, "Con Men and Their Enablers: The Anatomy of Confidence Games," *Social Research: An International Quarterly* 85:4 (Winter 2018), 795–96, whose extensive typological list of con games (including get-rich-quick schemes, gold-brick scams, gold-digging, pyramid schemes, and Ponzi schemes) contains none that can by any stretch of the imagination be considered salubrious.

xvi **political demagogues:** See, e.g., Carol A. Lambert, "Trump and Coercive Persuasion: 'He's So Much Like My Abuser!,'" *Psychology Today,* Nov. 20, 2016, https://www.psychologytoday.com/us/blog/mind-games /201611/trump-and-coercive-persuasion, and Bandy X. Lee, *The Dangerous Case of Donald Trump: 37 Psychiatrists and Mental Health Experts Assess a President*, updated edition (New York: Thomas Dunne Books/St. Martin's Press, 2019; originally published 2017).

xvi **"For a brief period":** Jones (1919), 271.

PROLOGUE: A WRAITH AT THE TOP OF THE STAIRS

3 **huddled in the passageway:** E[dward] W[arren] C[aulfeild] Sandes, *Tales of Turkey* (London: John Murray, 1924), 110.

3 **flickering candlelight:** Sandes (1924), 110.

3 **wrapped in blankets:** Jones (1919), 22.

3 **others wore pajamas:** Ibid.

3 **very nearly the only clothing:** Major Edward Warren Caulfeild Sandes, interned at Yozgad with Jones and Hill, writes, "On arrival in Yozgad many of us had little besides what we stood up in." E.W.C. Sandes, *In Kut and Captivity with the Sixth Indian Division* (London: John Murray, 1919), 408.

3 **on which scores of men:** See, e.g., Eric Williams, introduction to E. H. Jones, *The Road to Endor*, paperback edition (London: Pan Books, 1955), 7.

3 **sentries locked them in:** Arthur Valentine Holyoake, *The Road to Yozgad: My War, 1914–1919*, edited by Douglas Bridgewater (Brighton:

Menin House, 2013), 147. Holyoake reports that as of September 1916 prisoners were being locked into their houses at 7:00 P.M. Sandes (1919), 428, speaks of being locked in, circa December 1916, "at about 8.30 P.M."

3 **disused packing crates:** Jones (1919), 19.

3 **a sheet of polished iron:** Jones (1919), 21.

3 **randomly affixed:** Jones (1919), 19, 21.

3 **a jar of potted meat:** Holyoake (2013), 166.

3 **"spooking":** Jones (1919), esp. 17.

3 **made from a discarded door:** Sandes (1919), 408.

3 **"In spite of the outward":** Jones (1919), 146.

4 **pairs of officers had taken turns:** Jones (1919), 19ff.

4 **"Mere movement":** Jones (1919), 21.

4 **winter night in early 1917:** "Spooking" began at Yozgad in February 1917; "Sally" emerged some three weeks later. Jones (1919), 17, 21–22.

4 **only four remained:** Jones (1919), 20.

4 **They agreed to give:** Jones (1919), 21–22.

4 **"For the last time":** Jones (1919), 22.

4 **"If I could do to the Turks":** Jones (1919), 64; italics added.

5 **his left thumb:** Jones (1919), 43.

CHAPTER ONE: FOR KING AND COUNTRY

9 **More than 4,000 feet:** Sandes (1919), 390.

9 **earmarked for incorrigibles:** Maj. Edward Sandes, interned at Yozgad with Jones and Hill, would write, "Yozgad was reserved, more or less, as a camp for the 'die-hards' and suspected escapers among the officer-prisoners—in fact, it was a 'strafe' camp, and its rules were unusually severe at first." Sandes (1924), 135.

9 **150 miles south:** Sandes (1924), 95.

9 **300 miles north:** Ibid.

9 **five days' journey:** *Report on the Treatment of British Prisoners of War in Turkey* (London: His Majesty's Stationery Office, November 1918), 15.

9 **considered escape-proof:** Williams (1955), 5.

9 **believed to number:** Sandes (1924), 148.

9 **"A solitary traveller":** Sandes (1924), 149.

9 **had been known to beg:** Sandes (1924), 151. The historian Yücel Yanıkdağ (personal communication) notes that in some cases the brigands, who were mostly deserters from the Ottoman Army, collaborated with escaped Allied prisoners.

9 **and even execution:** E[lias] H[enry] Jones, "The Invisible Accomplice," in Alexander Klein, ed., *Grand Deception: The World's Most Spectacular*

and Successful Hoaxes, Impostures, Ruses and Frauds (Philadelphia: J. B. Lippincott Company, 1955), 231. Jones's essay, which reprises the story of his hoax in brief, was originally anthologized as "A Game of Bluff" in *Escapers All: Being the Personal Narratives of Fifteen Escapers from War-Time Prison Camps 1914–1918* (London: John Lane the Bodley Head, 1932).

9 **known as strafing:** See, e.g., Sandes (1924), 135.

9 **who in 1943 escaped:** Eric Williams, *The Wooden Horse* (London: Collins, 1949). Williams's book is sometimes described as a novel, but it is a fact-based account of his wartime experience, with some names altered and some details lightly fictionalized.

9 **FN As the modern historian:** Yücel Yanıkdağ, "Flirting with the Enemy: Ottoman Prisoners of War and Russian Women During the Great War," in John Deak, Heather R. Perry, and Emre Sencer, eds., *The Central Powers in Russia's Great War and Revolution, 1914–22: Enemy Visions and Encounters* (Bloomington, Ind.: Slavica Publishers, 2020), 223, 227, 229 [= Yanıkdağ (2020a)].

10 **"The exhausting . . . march":** Williams (1955), 7.

10 **the forgotten theater:** See, e.g., Patrick Crowley, *Kut 1916: The Forgotten British Disaster in Iraq* (Stroud: The History Press, 2016); Gary Sheffield, introduction to Crowley (2016), 7; A. J. Barker, *The Neglected War: Mesopotamia 1914–1918* (London: Faber & Faber, 1967); Nikolas Gardner, *The Siege of Kut-al-Amara: At War in Mesopotamia, 1915–1916* (Bloomington: Indiana University Press, 2014).

10 **four principal arenas:** Kenneth Steuer, "First World War Central Power Prison Camps," Western Michigan University (2013), 8; http://scholarworks.wmich.edu/history_pubs/1.

10 **entered the war in the autumn of 1914:** Steuer (2013), 8.

11 **In 1913, the First Lord of the Admiralty:** Crowley (2016), 15.

11 **Oil burned hotter:** John McCain with Mark Salter, *Hard Call: Great Decisions and the Extraordinary People Who Made Them* (New York: Hachette Book Group, 2007), 90.

11 **FN The Anglo-Persian Oil Company:** See, e.g., Daniel Yergin, *The Prize: The Epic Quest for Oil, Money & Power* (New York: Free Press, 2008; originally published 1991), 131ff., 145ff.

12 **"The British attitude and policy":** Yücel Yanıkdağ, "Prisoners of War (Ottoman Empire/Middle East)," *International Encyclopedia of the First World War* (n.d.), 6, encyclopedia.1914-1918-online.net/article/prisoners_of_war_ottoman_empiremiddle_east.

12 **"From the Ottoman perspective":** Ibid.

12 **"the British [viewed] the Ottoman Empire":** Ibid.

12 **"blunderland":** Quoted in Crowley (2016), 163.

12 **a siege of 147 days:** See, e.g., Russell Braddon, *The Siege* (New York: Viking Press, 1970), 13.

12 **33,000 British casualties:** Braddon (1970), 250.

12 **"arguably . . . Britain's worst military defeat":** Crowley (2016), 14.

12 **More than 12,000 men:** Yanıkdağ (n.d.), 6, reports that "of the 13,672 prisoners, 1,136 sick and wounded were immediately exchanged for Ottomans in British hands." See also *Report on the Treatment of British Prisoners of War in Turkey,* 5.

12 **"Harry is home":** H[ector] J[ames] W[right] Hetherington, ed., *The Life and Letters of Sir Henry Jones, Professor of Moral Philosophy in the University of Glasgow* (London: Hodder & Stoughton, 1924), 141.

12 **FN Of the 8 million to 9 million:** All figures per Yücel Yanıkdağ, "Ottoman and Allied Prisoners of War and Civil Internees," book chapter, in preparation (2020) [= Yanıkdağ (2020b)].

13 **familiarly known:** Biographical information on Jones and the Jones family per Hetherington (1924); *En-dor Unveiled,* 9ff.; "Jones, Elias Henry (1883–1942), Administrator and Author," *Dictionary of Welsh Biography,* biography.wales/article/s2-JONE-HEN-1883; and "Jones, Sir Henry (1852–1922), Philosopher," *Dictionary of Welsh Biography,* biography.wales/article/s-JONE-HEN-1852.

13 **who had left school at twelve:** Sir Henry Jones, *Old Memories* (New York: George H. Doran & Company, 1922), 35.

13 **"his father's double":** Hetherington (1924), 102.

13 **a chair once held:** John H. Muirhead, *Sir Henry Jones, 1852–1922* (London: Proceedings of the British Academy, 1922), 1.

13 **he studied psychology:** Jones (1919), 19.

13 **along with Greek, Latin:** "Elias Henry Jones," *The University of Glasgow Story,* Glasgow, Scotland, universitystory.gla.ac.uk/biography/?id=WH20122&type=P.

13 **earning a master's degree:** "Jones, Elias Henry (1883–1942), Administrator and Author," *Dictionary of Welsh Biography.*

13 **he worked as a magistrate:** Jones (1919), 33.

13 **described by their father:** Sir Henry Jones, "Will Jones, 1889–1906: A Memoir, Written Early in 1907." In Hetherington (1924), 291, 296.

13 **died in 1906 from appendicitis:** William Henry Jones death certificate, May 27, 1906, National Records of Scotland, scotlandspeople.gov.uk.

13 **in 1910, his sister Jeanie:** Jeanie Walker Jones death certificate, June 9, 1910, National Records of Scotland, scotlandspeople.gov.uk.

14 **Harry became addicted:** *En-dor Unveiled,* 10.

14 **"When I wrote to you":** Ibid.

14 **Mair Olwen Evans:** "Jones, Elias Henry (1883–1942), Administrator and Author," *Dictionary of Welsh Biography.*

14 **"He is well and strong":** Hetherington (1924), 207.

14 **Hal is winning the people:** Hetherington (1924), 205.

14 **In 1913, at twenty-nine:** *En-dor Unveiled*, 10.

14 **the eminent Welsh bacteriologist:** "Evans, Griffith (1835–1935), Microscopist, Bacteriologist, and Pioneer of Protozoon Pathology," *Dictionary of Welsh Biography*, biography.wales/article/s-EVAN-GRI-1835.

14 **when they were both thirteen:** *En-dor Unveiled*, 9.

14 **"I have loved you":** Ibid.

14 **Photographs of the couple:** *En-dor Unveiled*, 11–12.

14 **their first child, Jean:** *En-dor Unveiled*, 11.

15 **Jones obtained a leave of absence:** Hetherington (1924), 124.

15 **in April 1915 enlisted:** *En-dor Unveiled*, 90.

15 **pregnant with their second child:** *En-dor Unveiled*, 12.

15 **since the autumn of 1914:** Crowley (2016), 298.

15 **occupying Basra:** W. C. Spackman, *Captured at Kut: Prisoner of the Turks. The Great War Diaries of Colonel WC Spackman*, edited by Tony Spackman (Barnsley: Pen & Sword Military, 2008), 194.

15 **it took Kurna:** Crowley (2016), 17.

15 **who assumed command:** Crowley (2016), 298.

15 **it captured Amarah that spring:** Crowley (2016), 19–21.

15 **Shipping out from Rangoon:** *En-dor Unveiled*, 13.

15 **joined Townshend's troops at Amarah:** Ibid.

15 **site of the biblical Eden:** Dorina L. Neave, *Remembering Kut* (London: Arthur Baker, 1937), 11.

15 **Furnished with imprecise maps:** Crowley (2016), 270.

15 **the average summer temperature in London:** london-weather.eu /article.55.html.

15 **130 degrees in the shade:** Neave (1937), 10.

15 **"If this is the Garden of Eden":** Neave (1937), 11.

15 **the British had few shallow-draft ships:** Neave (1937), 23–24.

16 **"of a clinging":** Neave (1937), 11.

16 **smeared their bodies with crude oil:** Braddon (1970), 186.

16 **promoted to corporal:** *En-dor Unveiled*, 14.

16 **daily Arabic lessons:** Quoted in *En-dor Unveiled*, 89.

16 **"The life suits me":** Quoted in *En-dor Unveiled*, 96; underscoring in original.

16 **a battle of September 27–28:** Crowley (2016), 299.

16 **two miles long and a mile wide:** Crowley (2016), 38.

16 **town of about 7,000:** Crowley (2016), 39.

16 **"a veritable East End"**: Quoted in Crowley (2016), 38.

16 **By mid-November, Jones was stationed**: *En-dor Unveiled*, 15.

16 **helping erect gun emplacements**: Ibid.

16 **a second lieutenant**: Ibid.

17 **"I'm still one of you"**: Braddon (1970), 141.

17 **filching a wing**: Ibid.

17 **to shore up his dugout**: Braddon (1970), 128.

17 **it was considered too risky**: E. O. Mousley, *The Secrets of a Kuttite: An Authentic Story of Kut, Adventures in Captivity and Stamboul Intrigue*, second edition (Uckfield: The Naval & Military Press, 2005; originally published 1922), 143.

17 **seven and a half months pregnant**: *En-dor Unveiled*, 108.

18 **If the good God grant us**: *En-dor Unveiled*, 106; underscoring in original.

18 **By late November 1915**: Crowley (2016), 33.

18 **some 14,000 troops**: Ibid.

18 **On November 26**: Crowley (2016), 34.

18 **on the twenty-eighth**: Crowley (2016), 35.

18 **nearly 50 percent casualties**: Ibid.

18 **They would be out**: Braddon (1970), 142.

CHAPTER TWO: BESIEGED

19 **roofed with galvanized iron**: Spackman (2008), 60.

19 **Some 30 miles of trenches**: Crowley (2016), 44.

19 **like being buried alive**: Mousley (2005), 62.

19 **By December 7**: Crowley (2016), 49.

19 **some 12,000 British and Indian troops**: See, e.g., Gardner (2014), 66, which gives the following approximate figures for the size of the besieged garrison: British officers, 300; British other ranks, 2,850; Indians (including officers), 8,250; camp followers, 3,500, for a total of 14,900. (Gardner's total does not include Arab townspeople.) Ronald Millar, *Death of an Army: The Siege of Kut, 1915–1916* (Boston: Houghton Mifflin & Company, 1970), 70, reports the garrison (again excluding townspeople) as comprising 11,607 combatants and 3,530 noncombatants, for a total of 15,137. As Patricia Catherine Brown points out in "In the Hands of the Turk: British, Indian and Dominion Prisoners from the Ranks in the Ottoman Empire, 1914–1918" (master's thesis, University of Leeds School of History, 2012), 20, "The confusion of war ensures that it is impossible to calculate how many men are taken prisoner in war." She puts the figure for those ultimately taken prisoner at Kut at 13,500 (13).

19 **about 6,000 remaining townspeople:** Crowley (2016), 47.

19 **some 3,000 camp followers:** Crowley (2016), 100.

19 **forty-three big guns:** Crowley (2016), 280.

19 **small arms sometimes superior:** Sandes (1919), 155, writes, "Hand grenades at first were very scarce in Kut, and here the Turks had a great advantage over us," and says, "Many of the Turks had good telescopic sights on their rifles, while we had none" (167).

19 **thirty British casualties:** Crowley (2016), 51.

19 **As Jones would recall:** Neave (1937), 67.

19 **at Townshend's first line:** *En-dor Unveiled*, 19.

19 **slugs and scorpions:** Neave (1937), 66.

19 **crash of palm trees:** Mousley (2005), 3.

19 **the *crack-crack* of sniper rifles:** Mousley (2005), 57.

20 ***brrp-brrp-brrp*:** Sandes (1919), 198.

20 ***krump-kr-rump-sh-sh-sh-sh*:** Mousley (2005), 77.

20 **sounded like hail:** Mousley (2005), 39.

20 **screams of the starlings:** Mousley (2005), 57.

20 **howling of jackals:** Ibid.

20 **By December 23:** Crowley (2016), 56.

20 **Townshend's men remained hopeful:** Crowley (2016), 49ff.

20 **"a pound of meat":** Braddon (1970), 131.

20 **Plans were under way:** Crowley (2016), 53.

20 **soon after New Year's:** Sandes (1919), 167.

20 **Just after 5:00 A.M.:** Crowley (2016), 56.

20 **began a ferocious assault:** For accounts of the Christmastime assault, see, e.g., Crowley (2016), 56ff.; Mousley (2005), 39ff.; Neave (1937), 41ff.

20 **few proper hand grenades:** Sandes (1919), 155.

20 **shrapnel bullets and old jam tins:** Ibid.

20 **more than 300 casualties:** Crowley (2016), 59.

20 **The Ottoman figure:** Crowley (2016), 59, puts the estimate between 907 and more than 2,000.

20 **the best way to rout the British:** Ibid.

20 **By January 10:** Crowley (2016), 89.

21 **Later that month:** Ibid.

21 **In late January:** Ibid.

21 **"For dinner we had":** Mousley (2005), 101.

21 **Mule stew was pronounced:** Sandes (1919), 192.

21 **"was really first class":** Sandes (1919), 197.

22 **Mrs. Milligan:** Braddon (1970), 125.

22 **bought on the way back from Ctesiphon:** Braddon (1970), 117.

22 **Mrs. Milligan quickly cleared out:** Braddon (1970), 198.

22 **scurvy and beri-beri:** Spackman (2008), 71.

22 **tetanus:** Neave (1937), 63.

22 **cholera:** Mousley (2005), 151.

22 **dysentery, colic, jaundice:** Sandes (1919), 234.

22 **malaria, and tuberculosis:** Spackman (2009), 81.

22 **"would make a London surgeon":** Sandes (1919), 236.

22 **beg to be sent back:** Braddon (1970), 182.

22 **Morale was sinking:** Crowley (2016), 54.

22 **British casualties:** Ibid.

22 **bury their dead in the palm grove:** Braddon (1970), 211.

22 **Auctions were held:** Braddon (1970), 211; Sandes (1919), 234.

22 **"We got accustomed":** Mousley (2005), 32.

22 **assembled at Ali-al-Gharbi:** Crowley (2016), 62.

22 **numbering 19,000:** Spencer C. Tucker and Priscilla Roberts, eds., *World War I: Encyclopedia* (Santa Barbara, Calif.: ABC-CLIO, 2005), 538.

22 **could scarcely remember a time:** See, e.g., Mousley (2005), 127.

22 **sank up to their withers:** Braddon (1970), 170.

22 **men to their waists:** Neave (1937), 64.

22 **"No one who has not experienced":** Quoted in ibid.

22 **lacked adequate land and water transport:** Crowley (2016), 68.

22 **under the influence of lightning:** Braddon (1970), 241.

23 **the first attempt to relieve:** Crowley (2016), 86.

23 **some 8,000 casualties:** Sandes (1919), 175.

23 **still 25 miles away:** Crowley (2016), 87.

23 **On February 13:** Sandes (1919), 189.

23 **a strange, pulsating whining:** Ibid.

23 **The box around them:** Mousley (2005), 60, makes a similar point.

23 **"demon bird":** Ibid.

23 **Flown by a German pilot:** Mousley (2005), 62.

23 **each night at dusk:** Braddon (1970), 193.

23 **showered the already wounded:** Crowley (2016), 129.

23 **By the end of the month:** Crowley (2016), 112.

23 **the first week of March:** Crowley (2016), 115.

23 **"We know we have got":** Quoted in Sandes (1919), 201.

23 **After the tinned milk:** Sandes (1919), 187–88.

23 **finally the tea:** Crowley (2016), 127.

23 **Roast sparrows:** Sandes (1919), 192.

23 **Hedgehog fried in axle grease:** Braddon (1970), 240.

23 **Stray dogs:** Crowley (2016), 150.

23 **Mrs. Milligan returned:** Braddon (1970), 240.

23 **"the way she had found herself":** Ibid.

23 **as she taught her children:** Ibid.

23 **"officers and men":** Quoted in Crowley (2016), 150.

24 **One day in mid-April:** Mousley (2005), 139.

24 **causing violent enteritis:** Braddon (1970), 222.

24 **severe abdominal pains:** Mousley (2005), 127.

24 **Men died:** Braddon (1970), 238.

24 **Townshend forbade the eating:** Ibid.

24 **begun to eat their head ropes:** Braddon (1970), 240; Mousley (2005), 97.

24 **In March:** Crowley (2016), 115.

24 **3,474 British casualties:** Crowley (2016), 124.

24 **3,100 on the Ottoman side:** Ibid.

24 **on April 17:** Crowley (2016), 153.

24 **On the twenty-second:** Crowley (2016), 158. This battle took place at Sannaiyat.

24 **mud up to their armpits:** Crowley (2016), 158.

24 **a steel-clad vessel:** Conrad Cato, *The Navy in Mesopotamia: 1914 to 1917* (London: Constable & Company, 1917), 91.

24 **250 tons of food:** Cato (1917), 92.

24 **an enemy cable:** Cato (1917), 98.

24 **a bid by Townshend to pay:** Crowley (2016), 162.

24 **"4 oz of flour or biscuit":** Spackman (2008), 81.

24 **Fifteen to twenty men:** Crowley (2016), 163.

24 **The gunners ate Mrs. Milligan:** Robert F. Jones, "Kut," in Robert Cowley, ed., *The Great War: Perspectives on the First World War* (New York: Random House, 2003), 215.

24 **on April 29, 1916:** Crowley (2016), 164–65.

24 **The Union Jack:** Braddon (1970), 255.

24 **the white flag:** Ibid.

25 **nearly 9,000 Ottoman casualties:** Edward J. Erickson, *Ottoman Army Effectiveness in World War I: A Comparative Study* (London: Routledge, 2007), 86.

25 **a total of 33,000:** Braddon (1970), 250.

25 **23,000 in the relief force alone:** Ibid.

25 **almost 900 casualties:** Millar (1970), 263.

25 **the last of their tobacco:** Mousley (2005), 153.

25 **some officers pondered:** Ibid.

25 **"Kut was in the hands":** Sandes (1919), 255.

CHAPTER THREE: DESTINATION UNKNOWN

26 **one British officer recounted:** Sandes (1919), 272.

26 **many lacked boots:** Yanıkdağ (2020b), 12.

26 **Expecting to be body-searched:** Sandes (1924), 16.

26 **no search was forthcoming:** Ibid.

26 **On the morning of April 29:** Neave (1937), 97.

26 **Trapped afterward:** Ibid.

26 **by squeezing his sovereigns:** Ibid.

26 **The prisoners had eaten:** Mousley (2005), 158.

26 **including Jones:** *En-dor Unveiled,* 31.

27 **"Like the other belligerents":** Yanıkdağ (n.d.), 8.

27 **A barren, dusty patch:** Neave (1937), 100.

27 **a half-dozen prisoner-of-war camps:** The officers' camps, per Braddon (1970), 310, were Yozgad, Kastamuni, Kedos, Afion Karahissar, and Broussa.

27 **a heap in the dust:** Sandes (1919), 269.

27 **Roundish, hard as stone:** For accounts of the Turkish army biscuit, an item described by nearly every British memoirist of the Kut siege, see, e.g., Mousley (2005), 164; *Report on the Treatment of British Prisoners of War in Turkey,* 6; Sandes (1919), 269–71; Sandes (1924), 13–14; Spackman (2008), 86.

27 **the biscuits were, along with bulgur:** Yanıkdağ (2020), 12.

27 **unfit for any dog:** See, e.g., Sandes (1919), 271.

27 **"Unfortunately," a British officer said:** Spackman (2008), 86.

27 **"A man turned green":** Mousley (2005), 164.

27 **some 300 men died:** Spackman (2008), 87.

27 **along with ailments:** Brown (2012), 66–67.

27 **prisoners bartered:** Braddon (1970), 261.

27 **On May 4:** *En-dor Unveiled,* 31.

27 **nearly a hundred British officers:** Sandes (1919), 293; Sandes (1924), 14.

27 **jeered and drew their fingers:** Sandes (1924), 14.

28 **"as in a Roman triumph":** Sandes (1919), 284.

28 **On May 11:** Sandes (1919), 288.

28 **called at the American consulate:** Sandes (1919), 288–89.

28 **Two of Jones's lira:** Jones (1919), 265.

28 **Under the terms:** Sandes (1919), 401.

28 **able to buy food:** E.g., Sandes (1919), 286.

28 **FN The British did likewise:** Yanıkdağ, personal communication.

29 **On May 12:** Sandes (1919), 289.

29 **from Berlin to Baghdad:** Sandes (1924), 64.

29 **"At the moment":** Braddon (1970), 277.

29 **with little water:** Sandes (1924), 18.

29 **On May 15:** Sandes (1919), 295.

29 **Arab guards on horseback:** Sandes (1919), 293–94; 296.

29 **"We had not marched":** Sandes (1919), 296–97.

29 **would herd the donkeys:** Braddon (1970), 288.

29 **after a day's desert march:** Sandes (1924), 6.

29 **From time to time:** See, e.g., Mousley (2005), 164.

30 **They reached Tikrit:** Spackman (2008), 97.

30 **in a day and a half:** Sandes (1919), 298.

30 **arriving on May 25:** Sandes (1919), 308.

30 **That afternoon:** Sandes (1919), 319.

30 **he addressed the captives:** Ibid.

30 **"as Precious and Honoured Guests":** Quoted in ibid.

30 **the officers remarked:** Sandes (1919), 319.

30 **They left Mosul:** Sandes (1919), 321.

30 **four-wheeled carts:** Ibid.

30 **one hour in every four:** Ibid.

30 **tongues swollen:** Mousley (2005), 171–72.

30 **By June 1:** Sandes (1919), 324.

30 **the genocide of 1915:** For an overview of this vast, fraught, complex subject, whose treatment encompasses an immense literature, see, e.g., Taner Akçam, *The Young Turks' Crime Against Humanity: The Armenian Genocide and Ethnic Cleansing in the Ottoman Empire* (Princeton, N.J.: Princeton University Press, 2012) and Ronald Grigor Suny, *"They Can Live in the Desert but Nowhere Else": A History of the Armenian Genocide* (Princeton, N.J.: Princeton University Press, 2015).

30 **officers saw the remains:** Sandes (1919), 324.

30 **reached Raas-al-Ain:** Sandes (1919), 332.

30 **FN As Yanıkdağ points out:** Yanıkdağ (n.d.), 5.

30 **FN At the start of the twentieth century:** Akçam (2012), esp. ix–xxxiii; Suny (2015), esp. ix–xxi.

31 **they had marched continuously:** Ibid.

31 **There had been 370 miles:** Ibid.

31 **On June 10:** Sandes (1919), 335.

31 **The senior officers:** Ibid.

31 **Crossing the Euphrates:** Ibid.

31 **met with the U.S. consul:** Sandes (1919), 340.

31 **the first word their families had:** *En-dor Unveiled*, 36.

31 **On June 13:** Sandes (1919), 341–42.

31 **ride every other hour:** Sandes (1919), 347.

31 **on June 14:** Ibid.

31 **worn boots and ravaged feet:** See, e.g., Sandes (1919), 297–98.

31 **got out and walked:** Sandes (1919), 347.

31 **drops of hundreds of feet:** Sandes (1919), 348.

31 **The descent of a caravan:** Sandes (1924), 62; italics in original.

31 **reached Posanté:** Sandes (1919), 354.

31 **on June 17:** Ibid.

31 **On the eighteenth:** Sandes (1919), 363.

32 **at Eskichehr:** Sandes (1924), 76.

32 **made to walk:** See, e.g., Braddon (1970), 259; Sandes (1919), 311.

32 **flogged ever onward:** Neave (1937), 121.

32 **"a scene from Dante's 'Inferno'":** Quoted in Neave (1937), 211.

32 **no precise casualty figures:** Yanıkdağ (n.d.), 7–8.

32 **It is nearly impossible:** Ibid.

32 **"It is documented":** Ibid.

32 **FN "the journey to the interior":** Yanıkdağ (2020), 4.

33 **he passed the remainder of the war:** Braddon (1970), 302.

33 **"an English country vicarage":** Barker (1967), 283.

33 **Arriving in Angora:** Sandes (1919), 374.

33 **postcards of four lines:** *En-dor Unveiled*, 38.

33 **to avoid overtaxing:** *Report on the Treatment of British Prisoners of War in Turkey*, 18. The imposition of length restrictions on prisoners' letters, Yanıkdağ (personal communication) notes, "was the case internationally for the most part. Ottomans in Russia complained of the same thing."

33 **I am in excellent health:** Postcard reproduced in *En-dor Unveiled*, 117.

33 **"we were then travel-worn":** Jones (1919), 279.

34 **the prison camp at Broussa:** Neave (1937), 200.

34 **the most isolated camps:** Crowley (2016), 220.

CHAPTER FOUR: A HUNDRED SPRINGS

35 **On June 25:** Sandes (1919), 382.

35 **wild, rocky, gorge-filled country:** Sandes (1919), 382ff.

35 **"The only thing that kept us going":** Undated letter, circa September 1916, from E. H. Jones to Sir Henry Jones; quoted in *En-dor Unveiled*, 126.

35 **"his depression increased":** Neave (1937), 202.

35 **About a hundred British officers:** Neave (1937), 203.

35 **The Turkish Government has announced:** *Report on the Treatment of British Prisoners of War in Turkey*, 14.

36 **On June 30:** Sandes (1919), 288.

36 **many ill:** Sandes (1924), 82.

36 **a population of about 20,000:** *Report on the Treatment of British Prisoners of War in Turkey*, 15.

36 **"for all the world":** Sandes (1924), 94.

36 **whitewashed houses with red tile roofs:** Sandes (1919), 390.

36 **two of these houses:** Sandes (1919), 390.

36 **"Ottomans did not use":** Yanıkdağ (n.d.), 9.

36 **the murder of their Armenian owners:** Sandes (1919), 392.

37 **"Soon after our arrival":** Ibid.

37 **high stone walls:** Maurice Andrew Brackenreed Johnston and Kenneth Darlaston Yearsley, *Four-fifty Miles to Freedom* (Edinburgh: William Blackwood & Sons, 1919), 55.

37 **elderly local gendarmes:** Sandes (1919), 397.

37 **from about 1870:** Ibid.

37 **more than fifty officers:** Holyoake (2013), 142.

37 **just over 42 square feet:** Sandes (1919), 391.

37 **thin-walled, barren of furniture:** Sandes (1919), 391, 408.

37 **on July 16:** Holyoake (2013), 142.

37 **"The conditions under which":** Holyoake (2013), 144–45.

37 **which also included:** Holyoake (2013), 127ff.

37 **had to pay rent:** Sandes (1919), 414.

37 **Jones recalled the tab:** *En-dor Unveiled,* 124.

37 **"Far less prepared for war":** Yanıkdağ (2020), 13–14.

38 **feared they would attempt escape:** Sandes (1919), 400.

38 **terrified of censure:** Sandes (1924), 8, 102, 71–72.

38 **An Ottoman artillery officer:** Sandes (1919), 394.

38 **do largely as he pleased:** Sandes (1919), 395.

39 **"As a specimen":** Sandes (1924), 101–2.

39 **"Caged and helpless":** Sandes (1924), 86.

39 **lie on their mattresses:** Sandes (1924), 85.

39 **served in Lower House:** Sandes (1919), 398.

39 **who paid kickbacks:** Sandes (1924), 101.

39 **Passable at the start:** Sandes (1919), 398.

39 **meals deteriorated:** Sandes (1919), 398–99.

39 **no salary since Baghdad:** Sandes (1919), 401.

39 **if they did not pay:** Sandes (1919), 408.

39 **"Eat less":** Sandes (1919), 401.

40 **"In the middle of September":** Sandes (1919), 416.

40 **neither English nor French:** Neave (1937), 203.

40 **Moïse Eskenazi:** Jones (1919), 362.

40 **called "the Pimple":** Jones (1919), 63.

40 **The interpreter was:** Sandes (1919), 396.

40 **FN silent-film character Pimple:** Bryony Dixon, "The 'Pimple' Films," British Film Institute ScreenOnline, screenonline.org.uk/film/id/1151483/index.html. I am indebted to George Robinson for this reference.

40 **FN the well-known stage comic:** Barry Anthony, "Evans, Fred (1889–

1951)," British Film Institute ScreenOnline, screenonline.org.uk/people /id/473302.

40 **FN said to have rivaled Chaplin's:** Ibid.

41 **"You have completed":** Sandes (1924), 88–89; italics in original.

41 **in late July:** Sandes (1919), 406.

42 **The mulazim swaggered:** Sandes (1924), 89–90; italics in original.

42 **"Never shall I forget":** Sandes (1924), 90–91.

42 **allowed to stroll:** Sandes (1919), 406–7.

42 **In early August:** Holyoake (2013), 146.

43 **Ali had been charging them:** Sandes (1919), 409.

43 **kitchens with wood-burning stoves:** Sandes (1919), 391, 408.

43 **"not work which officer-prisoners":** Sandes (1919), 408.

43 **constructed serviceable ovens:** Ibid.

43 **"There was no end":** Jones (1919), 141–42.

43 **"aptly described the wood":** Sandes (1919), 414. In his memoir, Sandes renders the original French phrase ungrammatically as "Régie *Ottoman Turquie.*"

43 **tools bought from the bazaar:** Sandes (1919), 414.

43 **the houses rang:** Ibid.

43 **who arrived at Yozgad in July:** *En-dor Unveiled,* 51.

43 **nailing legs to a disused door:** Hill (1975), 53.

44 **"I . . . bought half a dozen planks":** Sandes (1924), 27–28.

44 **several more empty houses:** Holyoake (2013), 144–45; Sandes (1919), 423–24, 435–36.

44 **where Hill would live:** *En-dor Unveiled,* 51. The various memoirists of Yozgad do not explain the origin of the house's name.

44 **"a good-tempered cross":** Jones (1919), 26n.

44 **the U.S. embassy began sending:** Sandes (1919), 415.

44 **which over time grew:** Sandes (1919), 415.

44 **In September:** Sandes (1919), 414.

44 **at a lower rate:** Ibid.

44 **"We dragged out":** Sandes (1919), 438.

44 **"For a time," Sandes wrote:** Sandes (1924), 154.

45 **twice-weekly nighttime lecture series:** Sandes (1919), 414–15.

45 **By the light of oil lamps:** Sandes (1919), 415.

45 **a haze of tobacco smoke:** Ibid.

45 **Topics included:** Holyoake (2013), 151; Sandes (1919), 415.

45 **"On the whole":** Sandes (1919), 415.

45 **in subjects ranging from:** Jones (1919), 142.

45 **"We became a minor University":** Ibid.

45 **In October:** Sandes (1919), 416.

45 **Their sticks were fashioned:** Ibid.

45 **the ball was anything:** Ibid.

45 **a tiny dispensary:** Jones (1919), 105.

45 **bought a small violin:** Sandes (1924), 128.

45 **Playing from memory:** Sandes (1919), 428–29.

45 **the only place large enough:** Jones (1919), 143.

46 **three violins, a flute, and a guitar:** Sandes (1919), 435.

46 **"printed in French":** Holyoake (2013), 153–54.

46 **painted with aniline dye:** Holyoake (2013), 154.

46 **pinned-together blankets:** Ibid.

46 **spools of cotton:** Ibid.

46 **The footlights were candles:** Ibid.

46 **manned by a row of orderlies:** Holyoake (2013), 161.

46 **"Don Sandeso's Famous Orchestra":** Sandes (1924), 139.

46 **Sandes, tucked into a corner:** Holyoake (2013), 161.

46 **whose roles included:** Sandes (1924), 138–39.

46 **scraps of fabric:** Holyoake (2013), 161.

46 **Wigs were made:** Ibid.

46 **it lampooned their captors:** Holyoake (2013), 155.

46 **the Turks got wind:** Ibid.

47 **"If any of them had seen":** Sandes (1924), 139.

47 **On December 16:** Holyoake (2013), 155.

47 **after evening roll call:** Ibid.

47 **the Upper House landing:** Sandes (1924), 142.

47 **To their surprise:** Holyoake (2013), 155.

47 **"Their surprise changed":** Holyoake (2013), 155–56.

47 **who had conceived the show:** Sandes (1924), 138.

47 **"looked the most repulsive type":** Holyoake (2013), 161.

47 **habit of pilfering food and clothing:** Sandes (1924), 141–42.

47 **"There was much noise":** Sandes (1924), 142.

47 **"It was only another *rehearsal*":** Ibid.; italics in original.

47 **"When is the final performance?":** Sandes (1924), 143.

47 **"We are very sorry, Mr. Moïse":** Ibid.; italics in original.

47 **"A thousand pities!":** Ibid.

47 **counted each day:** Sandes (1919), 397.

48 **locked in each night:** Holyoake (2013), 147; Sandes (1919), 428.

48 **rains began in December:** Holyoake (2013), 161.

48 **buckets, basins, and jugs:** Holyoake (2013), 161–62.

48 **a Red Cross inspector:** Holyoake (2013), 155.

48 **"Let us hope":** Ibid.

48 **a single four-line postcard:** Sandes (1919), 400.

48 **both sides of a single sheet:** Holyoake (2013), 150.

48 **dated from July 22:** Holyoake (2013), 169.

48 **six or even eight months:** Sandes (1919), 403.

48 **"It was obvious":** Neave (1937), 204.

48 **The autumn after they arrived:** Sandes (1919), 423.

48 **a popular officer:** Ibid.

48 **captured in the Sinai:** Jones (1919), vi.

48 **a round-the-clock volunteer team:** Sandes (1919), 423.

48 **died in late November:** Holyoake (2013), 153.

48 **"This was the first death":** Ibid.

48 **the captives increasingly courted:** Steuer (2013), 40.

48 **"barbed-wire disease":** A. L. Vischer, *Barbed Wire Disease: A Psychological Study of the Prisoner of War* (London: John Bales, Sons & Danielsson, 1919). The work was first published in German in 1918.

48 **it is characterized by:** See, e.g., Yücel Yanıkdağ, "Ottoman Psychiatry in the Great War," in Olaf Farschid, Manfred Kropp, and Stephan Dähne, eds., *The First World War as Remembered in the Countries of the Eastern Mediterranean* (Würzburg: Ergon Verlag in Kommission, 2006), 171.

48 **"The last days":** Sandes (1919), 429.

49 **in February 1917:** Jones (1919), 17.

49 **"I did not know":** Ibid.

49 **"prove the open sesame":** Ibid.

CHAPTER FIVE: SPOOKED

53 **Jones was dismayed:** Jones (1919), 17.

53 **held their first séance:** Jones (1919), 18.

53 **"We took it up":** Jones (1955), 228.

53 **"Talking boards":** Linda Rodriguez McRobbie, "The Strange and Mysterious History of the Ouija Board," *Smithsonian*, Oct. 27, 2013, smithsonianmag.com/history/the-strange-and-mysterious-history-of-the-ouija-board-5860627.

53 **a series of audible raps:** See, e.g., McRobbie (2013); Kenneth D. Pimple, "Ghosts, Spirits, and Scholars: The Origins of Modern Spiritualism," in Barbara Walker, ed., *Out of the Ordinary: Folklore and the Supernatural* (Logan: Utah State University Press, 1995), 84.

53 **In 1886:** McRobbie (2013).

53 **in northern Ohio:** Olivia B. Waxman, "*Ouija: Origin of Evil* and the True History of the Ouija Board," *Time*, Oct. 21, 2016, time.com/4529861/ouija-board-history-origin-of-evil.

53 **no spiritualist, but a shrewd businessman:** McRobbie (2013).

54 **with four investors:** Ibid.

54 **Elijah Bond, a patent lawyer:** Ibid.

54 **The next year Bond was awarded:** Ibid.

54 **"toy or game ... which I designate":** United States Patent 446,054, United States Patent and Trademark Office.

54 **"The objects of the invention":** United States Patent 446,054.

54 **of allowing the fingers:** Waxman (2016).

54 **"The Ouija is, without doubt":** *Pittsburg Dispatch*, February 1, 1891, 12.

54 **FN The origin of the word "Ouija":** McRobbie (2013); "Ouida," *Encyclopedia Britannica,* britannica.com/biography/Ouida; "The Langham, London," *Cosmopolis: A Magazine on Current Affairs and Culture*, Feb. 6, 2004, cosmopolis.ch/the-langham-london.

55 **By 1892, Kennard was operating:** McRobbie (2013).

56 **his aunt's postcard gave:** Jones (1919), 19.

56 **with the hem of his coat:** Ibid.

56 **For fifteen minutes:** Ibid.

56 **Others took turns:** Ibid.

56 **"Ask it some question":** Ibid.

56 **Seemingly of its own accord:** Jones (1919), 19–20.

56 **"B!" everyone cried:** Jones (1919), 20.

56 **"R!" the prisoners chorused:** Ibid.

56 **a large enameled tray:** Ibid.

56 **one he had built:** Jones (1919), 21.

56 **added the raised wooden ring:** Ibid.

56 **"One more shot, Bones":** Ibid.

57 **"I glanced at him":** Ibid.

57 **"One more shot," Jones echoed:** Jones (1919), 22.

57 **"GOOD EVENING, SALLY!":** Ibid.

57 **"Sally had quite a lot":** Ibid.

57 **Jones intended to come clean:** Ibid.

57 **having memorized the positions:** Ibid.

57 **a vigorous poshing:** Jones (1919), 26.

57 **"an arch leg-puller":** Hill (1975), 68.

57 **With the exception:** Jones (1919), 62.

58 **Price and Matthews wrote down:** Jones (1919), 26–27.

58 **began to view their skepticism:** Jones (1919), 32ff.

58 **"I decided one evening":** Condensed from Sandes (1924), 110–11; italics in original.

58 **"that experience changed me":** Sandes (1924), 111.

58 **motor automatism:** Leon M. Solomons and Gertrude Stein, "Normal Motor Automatism," *Psychological Review* 3:5 (1896): 492–512.

58 **ideomotor action:** Hélène L. Gauchou, Ronald A. Rensink, and Sidney Fels, "Expression of Nonconscious Knowledge via Ideomotor Actions," *Consciousness and Cognition* 21:2 (2012), 976.

58 **It was first described:** William B. Carpenter, "On the Influence of Suggestion in Modifying and Directing Muscular Movement, Independently of Volition," Lecture to the Royal Institution of Great Britain, March 12, 1852, *Notices of the Meetings of the Royal Institution* 10 (1852), 147–53.

58 **"muscular movement, independent":** Carpenter (1852), 147.

59 **"The state in question":** Ibid.; italics in original.

59 **was studied experimentally:** Solomons and Stein (1896); Gertrude Stein, "Cultivated Motor Automatism: A Study of Character in Its Relation to Attention," *Psychological Review* 5:3 (1898): 295–306.

59 **her first published writing:** B. F. Skinner, "Has Gertrude Stein a Secret?," *Atlantic Monthly* 153 (January 1934), 50.

59 **"This long time":** Solomons and Stein (1896), 506.

59 **it resembles nothing so much:** Skinner (1934) appears to have been the first to make this connection in print.

59 **"the Psychical Research Society of Yozgad":** Jones (1919), 35.

59 **"The closest inspection":** Ibid.

60 **"As for me":** Ibid.

60 **held over several nights:** Jones (1919), 37.

60 **"Given any one letter":** Jones (1919), 38–39.

60 **barely perceptible nicks:** Jones (1919), 35.

60 **"a sixty-horse-power":** Jones (1919), 40.

60 **"Who are you?":** Jones (1919), 37.

60 **"The glass began to move about":** Ibid.; italics added.

61 **Jones lost his bearings:** Jones (1919), 37–38.

61 **"It's getting wearisome":** Jones (1919), 38.

61 **The problem would have been:** Jones (1919), 38–39.

62 **replying "No" to every question:** Jones (1919), 39.

62 **"thought and thought and thought":** Ibid.

62 **"I do not think my friends":** Ibid.

62 **"You birds satisfied?":** Ibid.

62 **"the gentle art":** Jones (1919), 33.

63 **"placed ghostly apparitions":** Simone Natale, *Supernatural Entertainments: Victorian Spiritualism and the Rise of Modern Media Culture* (University Park: Pennsylvania State University Press, 2016), 3.

63 **begun in 1848:** See, e.g., Barbara Weisberg, *Talking to the Dead: Kate and Maggie Fox and the Rise of Spiritualism* (New York: HarperCollins Publishers, 2005; originally published 2004), 1.

63 **the Fox sisters:** Weisberg (2005), 1; 280 n. 3.

63 **The knocks, they asserted:** Weisberg (2005), 2ff.

63 **the ghost of a peddler:** Weisberg (2005), 20.

63 **$100 to $150 a night:** "Spiritualism Exposed: Margaret [*sic*] Fox Kane Confesses That She and Her Sister Were Frauds," *St. Louis Post-Dispatch* (Nov. 4, 1888), 24; originally published in the *New York World*.

63 **would become international celebrities:** Weisberg (2005), 120.

63 **"The excitement in reference":** e.g., "The Ghost of Ganargwa: Murder Most Foul!," *Detroit Free Press*, May 5, 1848; italics in original. First published in the *Rochester Daily Advertiser*.

64 **"Rochester rappings":** Weisberg (2005), 287 n. 3.

64 **"In Buffalo":** P. T. Barnum, *Humbugs of the World: An Account of Humbugs, Delusions, Impositions, Quackeries, Deceits and Deceivers Generally, in All Ages* (Minneapolis: Filiquarian Publishing, n.d.; originally published 1865), 53.

64 **"Why modern spiritism chose":** George M. Beard, "The Psychology of Spiritism," *North American Review* 129:272 (July 1879), 71–72.

64 **FN In 1888, Maggie Fox acknowledged:** Weisberg (2005), 239ff., 255ff.

64 **FN Barnum, who is erroneously described:** Weisberg (2005), 290, writes that the misapprehension appears to have arisen because the sisters stayed in Barnum's Hotel, owned by a cousin of P. T. Barnum, during their run in New York City.

64 **FN publicly offered $500:** Barnum (n.d.), 69.

65 **2 million new adherents:** Karen Abbott, "The Fox Sisters and the Rap on Spiritualism," *Smithsonian*, Oct. 30, 2012, smithsonianmag.com/history/the-fox-sisters-and-the-rap-on-spiritualism-99663697.

65 **séances in the White House:** Drew Gilpin Faust, *This Republic of Suffering: Death and the American Civil War* (New York: Vintage Books, 2009; originally published 2008), 181.

65 **"some of which":** Ibid.

65 **made its way to Britain:** Louise Henson, "Investigations and Fictions: Charles Dickens and Ghosts," in Nicola Bown, Carolyn Burdett, and Pamela Thurschwell, eds., *The Victorian Supernatural* (Cambridge: Cambridge University Press, 2009; originally published 2004), 54.

65 *The Medium and Daybreak*: Natale (2016), 26.

65 *The Spiritual Telegraph*: John Durham Peters, *Speaking into the Air: A History of the Idea of Communication* (Chicago: University of Chicago Press, 2000; originally published 1999), 95.

65 *The Banner of Light*: Barnum (n.d.), 74.

65 **"usually skeptical, sometimes credulous":** Gillian Beer, foreword to Bown et al. (2009), xv.

65 **FN the infant mortality rate:** Michael Haines, "Fertility and Mortality in the United States." Economic History Association, *EH.Net Encyclope-*

dia, ed. Robert Whaples (March 19, 2008), eh.net/encyclopedia/fertility
-and-mortality-in-the-united-states.

65 **FN dying during pregnancy or childbirth:** At the turn of the twentieth century, more than 600 women died in pregnancy or childbirth for
every 100,000 live births; today, the figure is about 15 per 100,000. Laura
Helmuth, "The Disturbing, Shameful History of Childbirth Deaths,"
Slate (Sept. 10, 2013); slate.com/technology/2013/09/death-in-childbirth
-doctors-increased-maternal-mortality-in-the-20th-century-are-midwives
-better.html.

65 **FN killed thousands of Americans:** *Mortality Statistics of the Seventh
Census of the United States, 1850,* House of Representatives Executive
Document 98, 33rd Congress, 2nd session (Washington: A.O.P. Nicholson Printer, 1855), 17–18.

66 **8 million spiritualists:** Abbott (2012).

66 **"via the European and Levantine":** Özgür Türesay, "Between Science
and Religion: Spiritism in the Ottoman Empire (1850s–1910s)," *Studia
Islamica* 113 (2018), 166.

66 **"a very popular topic":** Ibid.

66 **"Many spiritualist mediums":** Natale (2016), 2.

66 **"The average medium works":** Houdini, *A Magician Among the Spirits*
(New York: Harper & Brothers, 1924), 190.

66 **FN In magicians' parlance:** Matthew L. Tompkins, personal communication.

67 **a vibrant star in the constellation:** See, e.g., Natale (2016), 9, 66.

67 **tightly bound with ropes:** Peter Lamont, *Extraordinary Beliefs: A Historical Approach to a Psychological Problem* (Cambridge: Cambridge
University Press, 2013), 134.

67 **"Throughout this period":** Fred Nadis, *Wonder Shows: Performing Science, Magic, and Religion in America* (New Brunswick, N.J.: Rutgers University Press, 2005), 120.

67 **by then an alcoholic:** Weisberg (2005), 209, 218.

67 **Like most perplexing things:** "Spiritualism Exposed" (1888).

68 **Among the reasons:** Weisberg (2005), 261.

68 **Susceptibility to an array:** See, e.g., Gustav Jahoda, *The Psychology of
Superstition* (New York: Jason Aronson, 1974; originally published 1969),
129; Maria Konnikova, *The Confidence Game: Why We Fall for It . . .
Every Time* (New York: Viking, 2016), 9; Jeffrey Sconce, *Haunted Media:
Electronic Presence from Telegraphy to Television* (Durham, N.C.: Duke
University Press, 2000), 74; Margaret Thaler Singer, *Cults in Our Midst,*
revised edition (San Francisco: Jossey-Bass, 2003; originally published
1995), 29.

68 **eminent men of science:** See, e.g., Philip K. Wilson, "Conflict and Coop-

eration of Science and Spiritualism in Late Nineteenth- and Early Twentieth-Century Anglo-American Writings," in Christopher M. Moreman, ed., *The Spiritualist Movement: Speaking with the Dead in America and Around the World*, 3 vols. (Santa Barbara, Calif.: Praeger, 2013), 2:148.

68 **whose youngest son, Raymond:** Sir Oliver J. Lodge, *Raymond: Or, Life and Death* (New York: George H. Doran Company, 1916), 3.

68 **a widely influential book:** Sconce (2000), 74.

68 **"Death is real and grievous":** Lodge (1916), 6.

69 **"science was to a degree":** Allen W. Grove, "Röntgen's Ghosts: Photography, X-Rays, and the Victorian Imagination," *Literature and Medicine* 16:2 (1997), 141.

69 **"That direct telepathic intercourse":** Lodge (1916), 339–40.

69 **"A few years ago":** Jones (1919), 33.

69 **Subjects of debate included:** Holyoake (2013), 154.

69 **FN Through his work on electromagnetism:** "Sir Oliver Joseph Lodge, British Physicist," *Encyclopedia Britannica*, britannica.com/biography /Oliver-Joseph-Lodge.

70 **"we tried Capt. Dinwiddy":** Holyoake (2013), 166.

70 **Jones built a toboggan:** Holyoake (2013), 163.

70 **"It was a hair raising journey":** Ibid.

70 **"Never were birds":** Sandes (1919), 436.

70 **"Dorothy that's always":** Jones (1919), 51; italics in original.

70 **"Silas had a nasty habit":** Jones (1919), 55.

70 **"In matters of belief":** Jones (1919), 41.

71 **"a rag, with no definite aim":** Jones (1919), 31.

71 **in the spring of 1917:** Jones (1919), 63.

CHAPTER SIX: THE USES OF ENCHANTMENT

72 **"the five-foot-nothing":** Jones (1919), 63.

72 **"You are a student":** Ibid.

72 **He wondered whether:** Jones (1919), 64.

72 **"I want you to answer":** Ibid.

72 **"I walked back":** Jones (1919), 64.

72 **his list of questions:** Jones (1919), 66.

72 **"The answers created":** Jones (1919), 68.

73 **war news bulletins:** Jones (1955), 229.

73 **the ultimate seizure of Kut:** Sandes (1919), 432.

73 **the fall of Baghdad:** Ibid.

73 **In August 1916:** Holyoake (2013), 150.

73 **Jones once sent:** Jones's postcard is quoted in Sandes (1919), 410.

73 **Now Darllenwch:** quoted in Sandes (1919), 410. Eno's was an antacid, Antipon a weight-loss tonic, Formamint a throat remedy, Euthymol a toothpaste.

73 **FN "One thing which makes":** Houdini (1924), 223.

74 **Have sent parcels:** quoted in Sandes (1919), 411. Virol was a malt extract said to promote health.

74 **"Scotland *England*":** e.g., *En-dor Unveiled*, 124, 129; italics added.

74 **whose text was entirely blank:** *En-dor Unveiled*, 43.

74 **"Sir Henry Jones, 184, Kings-road":** Ibid.

74 **high government connections:** *En-dor Unveiled*, 9.

74 **it was Mair:** *En-dor Unveiled*, 43 n. 9.

74 **a long list of items:** *Prisoners of War in Turkey: Regulations and Notes for the Help of Relatives and Friends* (London: Prisoners in Turkey Committee, August 1918), 14.

75 **I remember one occasion:** Sandes (1924), 102–3; italics in original.

75 **"The news that somebody's":** Jones (1919), 17–18.

76 **"of Zeppelin raids":** Braddon (1970), 306.

76 **In early May 1917:** Jones (1919), 68.

76 **"*news obtained by officers*":** Ibid.; italics added.

76 **One summer night:** Holyoake (2013), 168.

76 **hundreds and hundreds of rounds:** Ibid.

76 **Could the gunfire be from the Russians:** Ibid.

76 **"to scare away the devil":** Sandes (1919), 438.

76 **"That's a poor trick":** Jones (1919), 68–70; italics in original. As Yücel Yanıkdağ points out (personal communication), by "witches," Moïse most likely meant "fortune-tellers."

77 **"a limb of Satan":** Jones (1919), 137.

77 **He would not find it:** Jones (1919), 74ff.

77 **Toward the end of May:** Jones (1919), 71.

77 **originally known as the Schoolhouse:** Ibid.

77 **thirteen senior officers:** Ibid.

77 **Visiting between houses:** Jones (1919), 75; Sandes (1919), 428.

77 **a homemade board of their own:** Hill (1975), 71.

77 **The Doc came up to me:** Jones (1919), 33–34.

78 **Millicent the Innocent:** Jones (1919), 46.

78 **whom Jones knew only by sight:** Ibid.

78 **In the bedrooms:** Hill (1975), 73–74.

79 **showering the spook room:** Hill (1975), 76–77.

79 **Jones paid a visit:** Jones (1919), 46.

79 **some 20 feet above the ground:** Hill (1975), 76.

79 **a small enclosed lavatory:** Ibid.

79 **a tiny ventilation window:** Ibid.

79 **a footprint:** Jones (1919), 46.

79 **wiped away the footprint:** Ibid.

79 **In August:** Jones (1919), 73.

79 **The little man glanced furtively:** Jones (1919), 74–75.

80 **Jones also suspected:** Jones (1919), 74.

80 **provided the Pimple could get permission:** Jones (1919), 75.

80 **"I was filled":** Jones (1919), 90; italics in original.

80 **"*I intended to implicate*":** Jones (1919), 89; italics in original.

81 **"the convincer":** M. Allen Henderson, *How Con Games Work* (Secaucus, N.J.: Citadel Press/Carol Publishing, 1997; originally published 1985), 69.

81 **A standard convincer might involve:** Henderson (1997), 69; David W. Maurer, *The Big Con: The Story of the Confidence Man* (New York: Anchor Books, 1999; originally published 1940), x.

81 **rusted Smith & Wesson:** Jones (1919), 76.

81 **it had probably belonged:** Jones (1919), 74.

81 **useless as a weapon:** Jones (1919), 76.

81 **"The magpie instinct":** Jones (1919), 74.

81 **reburied it in the garden:** Jones (1919), 76–77.

81 **wanted to make the Pimple:** Jones (1919), 77.

81 **This time—*and this time only*:** Jones (1919), 77–78.

81 **"My double part":** Jones (1919), 78.

81 **The glass decreed:** Ibid.

81 **"The Treasure is by Arms":** Jones (1919), 79.

81 **obliged to find the arms:** Ibid.

82 **wood shavings, a length of cord:** Ibid.

82 **to bring a companion:** Ibid.

82 **arrive wearing bayonets:** Ibid.

82 **On the afternoon:** Jones (1919), 78.

82 **the unsheathed bayonets:** Jones (1919), 79.

82 **"Do you think":** Ibid.

82 **to enjoy the joke:** Jones (1919), 78.

82 **the Cook bound them:** Jones (1919), 80.

82 **"South!" he shouted:** Jones (1919), 81.

82 **among the cabbages:** Ibid.

82 **"What has happened?":** condensed from Jones (1919), 81ff.

82 **lit a ceremonial fire:** Jones (1919), 82.

82 **"Something is here":** Ibid.

82 **as a group of prisoners:** Jones (1919), 82.

82 "It was a good faint": Jones (1919), 83.

83 "big enough to hide": Ibid.

83 "What happened?": condensed from Jones (1919), 84–85.

83 The prisoners were delighted: Jones (1919), 90.

83 "the first real step": Jones (1919), 86.

83 "Always you are cursing": condensed from Jones (1919), 91.

84 6 grains of calomel: Jones (1919), 91.

84 "It was no use": Ibid.

84 had they been held in Hospital House: Hill (1975), 83.

84 developing a thought-reading act: Ibid.

84 Toward the end of January 1918: Jones (1919), 92.

84 abandon his plan: Ibid.

84 "I have only seen": condensed from Jones (1919), 92–93.

85 "Once the lady learned the reason": Jones (1919), 93. In going on to tell the Pimple that the lady in question was "Princess Blavatsky," Jones is allowing himself a delicious inside joke: "Madame" Helena Blavatsky (1831–91) was a renowned Russian spiritualist and self-professed mystic. She was a founder, in 1875, of the Theosophical Society, a pantheistic quasi-religious movement rooted partly in Eastern philosophies. (The movement continues to attract followers today.) See, e.g., "Helena Blavatsky, Russian Spiritualist," *Encyclopedia Britannica*, britannica.com /biography/Helena-Blavatsky.

85 A few days later: Jones (1955), 231.

85 had never met the Commandant: Jones (1919), 94.

85 "was an amazing interview": Jones (1955), 231.

85 "Before we go into": Jones (1919), 95; italics added.

86 "What did it matter": Jones (1955), 231.

CHAPTER SEVEN: THE REGARD OF FLIGHT

87 "A well-constructed story": W. Lance Bennett and Martha S. Feldman, *Reconstructing Reality in the Courtroom: Justice and Judgment in American Culture* (New Brunswick, N.J.: Rutgers University Press, 1981), 68.

87 "I had had enough": Jones (1919), 97.

87 had been training in secret: Ibid.

87 "There were probably many": Ibid.

87 "He possessed . . . qualities": Jones (1919), 97–98.

88 Edward Ormond Waters Hill: Cedric Hill biographical information per Hill (1975) and Darryl Bennet and Neville Parker, "Hill, Cedric Waters (1891–1975)," in John Ritchie, ed., *Australian Dictionary of Biography Volume 14: 1940–1980* (Melbourne: Melbourne University Press, 1996),

online via National Centre of Biography, Australian National University, Canberra, adb.anu.edu.au/biography/hill-cedric-waters-10502/text 18635.

88 **20,000-acre cattle station:** Hill (1975), 7.

88 **"was wonderfully free":** Ibid.

88 **"walking miles through the bush":** Ibid.

88 **Sent to Brisbane:** Ibid.

88 **"sluggish at his work":** Quoted in Bennet and Parker (1996).

88 **He learned more:** Hill (1975), 7.

88 **moved to New Zealand:** Hill (1975), 7–8.

88 **He was painfully shy:** Hill (1975), 11, 13.

88 **built a biplane glider:** Hill (1975), 8.

88 **Returning to Australia:** Ibid.

88 **considered one of the foremost:** See, e.g., Lewis Ganson and Dai Vernon, *Dai Vernon's Tribute to Nate Leipzig* (London: Harry Stanley Unique Magic Studio, n.d.)

88 **"The amazing thing":** Ganson and Vernon (n.d.), 17.

88 **"He was deadly sure":** Ganson and Vernon (n.d.), 19; italics added.

89 **a maker of optical lenses:** Nate Leipzig, "Thirty-Six Years as a Magician," *The Sphinx: An Independent Magazine for Magicians*, 38:11 (January 1939), 208.

89 **a watchmaker and engineer:** Max Dessoir, "Hermann the Magician: Psychology of the Art of Conjuring," introduction to H. J. Burlingame, *Magician's Handbook: Tricks and Secrets of the World's Greatest Magician, Herrmann the Great* (Chicago: Wilcox & Follett, 1942), 22; Dessoir's essay was originally published in 1885.

89 **took several lessons:** Hill (1975), 8.

89 **Moving to Sydney:** Ibid.

89 **the eighty shearing machines:** Ibid.

89 **a fully functioning military air corps:** Ibid.

89 **Royal Engineers Balloon Section:** "A Brief History of Farnborough Aviation Site, Part 1: The Early Days, 1901–1914," Farnborough Air Sciences Trust, airsciences.org.uk/briefings.html.

89 **In war there is always:** John E. Johnson, *Full Circle: The Tactics of Air Fighting, 1914–1964* (New York: Ballantine Books, 1964), 2.

89 **FN "Australia's early involvement":** Peter Dennis, Jeffrey Grey, Ewan Morris, and Robin Prior, eds., with John Connor, *The Oxford Companion to Australian Military History* (Melbourne: Oxford University Press, 1995), 67.

90 **"Aviation is a useless":** Quoted in "A Brief History of Farnborough Aviation Site, Part 1: The Early Days, 1901–1914," Farnborough Air Sciences Trust, airsciences.org.uk/briefings.html.

90 **179 planes:** Ibid.

90 **bought a second-class passage:** Hill (1975), 9.

90 **His mother had outfitted:** Ibid.

90 **In London, he reported:** Hill (1975), 11.

90 **Weeks went by:** Hill (1975), 11ff.

90 **his funds were running low:** Hill (1975), 14ff.

90 **lost a precious £4:** Hill (1975), 14.

90 **He began to worry:** Hill (1975), 15–16.

90 **went at least once a week:** Hill (1975), 11.

90 **He also struck up:** Hill (1975), 16–17.

91 **"I am in the process":** Hill (1975), 16.

91 **On the Friday:** Hill (1975), 17.

91 **"You haven't joined up yet":** Ibid.

91 **"Gosh, you are beautiful":** Ibid.

91 **It was a white feather:** Ibid.

91 **He seethed all weekend:** Ibid.

91 **"I did not see":** Hill (1975), 18.

91 **Brooklands aerodrome:** Hill (1975), 17.

91 **arrived in 1915:** *En-dor Unveiled*, 51.

91 **Maurice Farman Longhorns:** Hill (1975), 19.

91 **"a top speed":** Ibid.

91 **well suited to stunt flying:** Hill (1975), 22.

92 **"if there was the slightest breath":** Hill (1975), 20.

92 **He could see:** Hill (1975), 23.

92 **"This discrepancy":** Hill (1975), 20.

92 **At the end of June:** Hill (1975), 23.

92 **It came as a bit of a shock:** Ibid.

92 **In July 1915:** Hill (1975), 23–24.

92 **"I felt very much":** Hill (1975), 24.

92 **He was ordered to report:** Ibid.

92 **he was taught map reading:** Hill (1975), 27.

92 **"which did not seem":** Ibid.

93 **Vickers Gun Bus:** Ibid.

93 **In September 1915:** Hill (1975), 28.

93 **Toward the end of the year:** Hill (1975), 30.

93 **forty-two hours and five minutes:** Ibid.

93 **sailing for Egypt in December:** Ibid.

93 **Hill entertained his comrades:** Ibid.

93 **fitted to carry three bombs:** Hill (1975), 33.

93 **The pilot carried:** Ibid.

93 **Only later was a mount:** Ibid.

93 **"With this arrangement":** Ibid.

93 In late February 1916: Hill (1975), 38.

93 Other pilots from his unit: Hill (1975), 36–37.

93 We had no approved: Hill (1975), 37.

94 on February 26, 1916: Hill (1975), 38.

94 dropping live 18-pound bombs: Ibid.

94 At dawn on the twenty-seventh: Ibid.

94 "I had not flown": Ibid.

94 their fire was rarely accurate: Hill (1975), 39.

94 fell 20 yards wide: Ibid.

95 "making rude faces": Ibid.

95 "drunk as an owl": Hill (1975), 40.

95 he never touched the stuff: Ibid.

95 Hill continued making: Hill (1975), 40–41.

95 at 4:00 A.M. on May 3: Hill (1975), 41.

95 in his BE2c: Hill (1975), 43.

95 The British had begun building: Paul Cotterell, *The Railways of Palestine and Israel* (Abingdon: Tourret Publishing, 1984), 17–18.

95 Had the day been clear: Hill (1975), 42.

95 dense cloud cover: Ibid.

95 "the whole Turkish Army": Ibid.

95 he heard several bullets: Ibid.

95 "I must land": Ibid.

96 "By the time I reached": Hill (1975), 42–43.

96 Which way?: Paraphrased from Hill (1975), 43.

96 "It seemed to me": Ibid.

96 found that the engine sump: Ibid.

96 some 300 yards away: Ibid.

96 "it almost broke my heart": Ibid.

96 a "terrific bang": Ibid.

96 "feeling as naked": Hill (1975), 43–44.

96 I was across: Hill (1975), 44.

97 "big lead bullet": Ibid.

97 Spying a piece of wood: Ibid.

97 "After about an hour's work": Hill (1975), 45.

97 20 yards southeast: Ibid.

97 "I had to keep": Ibid.

97 At twelve-thirty: Ibid.

97 until, at two-thirty: Hill (1975), 45–46.

97 At three o'clock: Hill (1975), 46.

97 held his empty gun: Ibid.

97 "The Arabs to the south east": Ibid.

97 weighed killing him: Hill (1975), 46.

97 **he was taken:** Ibid.

97 **FN the only news source permitted:** Holyoake (2013), 153–54.

98 **ringed by Arab men:** Ibid.

98 **The Arabs thronged round him:** Ibid.

98 **An hour later:** Ibid.

98 **They set out walking southward:** Hill (1975), 46–47.

98 **an officer, six men:** Hill (1975), 47.

98 **camping for two nights:** Ibid.

98 **"I almost blush":** Hill (1975), 47.

98 **"When I dismounted":** Hill (1975), 48.

98 **The next morning:** Ibid.

98 **"These few days":** Ibid.

98 **the two–day trip:** Hill (1975), 49.

98 **"a filthy house":** Ibid.

98 **among them Arthur Holyoake:** Holyoake (2013), 127.

98 **dispatched by train on May 12:** Ibid.

98 **once been a prison:** Hill (1975), 50.

98 **the journey largely mirrored:** Hill (1975), 50–51.

98 **five days in an empty house:** Hill (1975), 50.

99 **held for six weeks:** Hill (1975), 51.

99 **"a fairly clean hotel":** Ibid.

99 **"a filthy one":** Hill (1975), 51.

99 **they grew so weak:** Ibid.

99 **on July 11, 1916:** Holyoake (2013), 137.

99 **now had lice:** Holyoake (2013), 142.

99 **arrived on July 16:** Ibid.

99 **walk to the Russian lines:** Hill (1975), 53.

99 **"the general feeling":** Ibid.

99 **"I saw clearly":** Hill (1975), 53.

99 **he spent his days:** Ibid.

99 **"Any demonstration":** Gustav Kuhn, *Experiencing the Impossible: The Science of Magic* (Cambridge, Mass.: MIT Press, 2019), 11.

100 **more than a century ago:** Robert-Houdin lived from 1805 to 1871.

100 **"A thorough understanding":** Quoted in Burlingame (1942), title page.

100 **"To the psychiatrist":** Douglas McG. Kelley, "Mechanisms of Magic and Self-Deception: The Psycho-Logical Basis of Misdirection; an Extensional Non-Aristotelian Method for Prevention of Self-Deception," 54; italics added. In M. Kendig, ed., *Papers from the Second American Congress on General Semantics: Non-Aristotelian Methodology (Applied) for Sanity in Our Time* (Chicago: Institute of General Semantics, 1943), 53–60.

100 **According to Robert-Houdin:** Lamont (2013), 39–40.

100 **FN He published a nonfiction book:** Douglas M. Kelley, *22 Cells in Nuremberg: A Psychiatrist Examines the Nazi Criminals* (New York: Greenberg, 1947).

101 **"If you go to the theatre":** Lamont (2013), 44.

101 **"Create a belief":** Dessoir (1942), 39.

101 **FN In an 1889 article:** Max Dessoir, "Die Parapsychologie," *Sphinx* 7 (June 1889), 341; quoted in English translation in Wolfgang G. Bringmann, Helmut E. Lück, Rudolf Miller, and Charles E. Early, *A Pictorial History of Psychology* (Chicago: Quintessence Publishing, 1997), 71.

102 **the winter and early spring:** Hill (1975), 54–55.

102 **"thought of nothing":** Hill (1975), 53.

102 **"Anyone who tried":** Hill (1975), 54.

102 **In May:** Hill (1975), 55.

102 **he ran a mile:** Ibid.

102 **with forty pounds:** Hill (1975), 56.

102 **"If I succeeded":** Ibid.

102 **planned to leave in June:** Hill (1975), 56.

102 **through the basement:** Hill (1975), 61–62.

102 **7-foot wall:** Hill (1975), 61.

102 **days before his planned exodus:** Hill (1975), 58.

102 **"I know all your plans":** Ibid.

102 **his compatriots were watching:** Hill (1975), 59.

102 **"I felt terribly miserable":** Ibid.

103 **¼-plate films:** Ibid.

103 **also managed to smuggle:** Ibid.

103 **by cryptogram:** Ibid.

103 **body was a wooden box:** Hill (1975), 60.

103 **"The lens and shutter":** Ibid.

103 **"a masterpiece of ingenuity":** Jones (1919), 97.

103 **On January 30, 1918:** Jones (1919), 93, 98.

103 **"I asked him what risks":** Jones (1919), 98.

103 **"I know," I said:** Ibid.

104 **They shook hands:** Jones (1919), 99.

104 **Jones, by agreement:** Jones (1919), 98–99.

CHAPTER EIGHT: IN CONFIDENCE

105 **would not be anatomized formally:** Maurer (1999).

105 **"I have two small mites":** Jones (1919), 28.

105 **FN Jones's son Bevan:** *En-dor Unveiled*, 15.

106 **would refuse all profits:** Jones (1919), 95.

107 "It would have been simple": Jones (1919), 100.

107 the heyday of belief in thought reading: See, e.g., Barry H. Wiley, *The Thought Reader Craze: Victorian Science at the Enchanted Boundary* (Jefferson, N.C.: McFarland & Company, 2012).

107 1870s through the 1910s: Wiley (2012), 9.

107 said to have begun in 1873: Wiley (2012), 38.

107 John Randall Brown: Ibid.

107 Brown soon became: Wiley (2012), 44.

107 "Naturally, not all demonstrations": Wiley (2012), 44–45; italics added.

108 the American neurologist George M. Beard: George M. Beard, "The Physiology of Mind-Reading," *Popular Science Monthly* 10 (February 1877), 459–73.

108 "the general fact that mind": Beard (1877), 459.

108 "it [was] demonstrated": Ibid.

108 "muscle-reading": Beard (1877), 462.

108 The operator, usually blindfolded: Beard (1877), 460.

108 throughout the United States and Britain: Wiley (2012), 2.

109 "If one should question": Mark Twain, "Mental Telegraphy: A Manuscript with a History," *Harper's New Monthly Magazine* (December 1891), 98.

109 since the 1870s: Twain (1891), 95.

109 he had held off publishing: Ibid.

109 "that minds telegraph thoughts": Ibid.

109 I made this discovery: Ibid.; italics added.

109 FN "cases of impression received at a distance": *Oxford English Dictionary*, quoting Frederic W. H. Myers, a founding member of the Society for Psychical Research, writing in *Proceedings of the Society for Psychical Research* 1 (1882).

109 FN The word supplanted earlier terms: Trevor Hamilton, "Frederic W. H. Myers," *Psi Encyclopedia*, psi-encyclopedia.spr.ac.uk/articles /frederic-wh-myers.

110 "a leg-pull for the benefit": Jones (1919), 100.

110 Hill knew from his study: Jones (1919), 100–101.

110 FN an actual magnetic telegraph: Richard Zacks, "The 19th-Century Start-Ups That Cost Mark Twain His Fortune," *Time* (April 19, 2016), time.com/4297572/mark-twain-bad-business.

111 On the afternoon: Jones (1919), 101.

111 three days after: Ibid.

111 singing, clog dancing: Ibid.

111 "As some of you know": Ibid.

111 Much applause followed: Ibid.

111 **"Quickly," he might admonish:** Jones (1919), 102, 373.

111 **"Tell me," Hill continued:** Ibid.

111 **"Now, do you know":** Ibid.

111 **"A few suspected a code":** Jones (1919), 102.

111 **three months of clandestine practice:** Hill (1975), 84.

111 **"There is nothing harder":** [Tony] Corinda. *13 Steps to Mentalism* (Cranbury, N.J.: D. Robbins & Company, 1996; originally published 1968), 238; italics in original.

112 **Jones and Hill's code:** Table adapted from Jones (1919), 373.

112 **a list of eighty objects:** Hill (1975), 84.

114 **"I raised many a good laugh":** Ibid.

114 **nearly 500 objects:** The table shown here, adapted from Jones's book, contains eighty items. Jones (1919), 373, states that this table represents about one-sixth of the total telepathy code.

114 **preface his question with the word "Now":** Hill (1975), 84.

114 **several prisoners told Hill:** Jones (1919), 105.

114 **told them that his limit:** Ibid.

114 **let the two of them use:** Ibid.

114 **"As a *quid pro quo*":** Ibid.

114 **above the senior officers' woodpile:** Ibid.

114 **"Here we could meet":** Ibid.

114 **On the evening of February 2:** Jones (1919), 102.

114 **always addressed as "Sir":** Jones (1919), 186.

114 **he beseeched the Spook:** Jones (1919), 102–3.

115 **The Spook promised:** Jones (1919), 104.

115 **on February 6, 1918:** Jones (1919), 107.

115 **they feared discovery by their compatriots:** Jones (1919), 106.

115 **Either scenario:** Ibid.

115 **it might insulate their countrymen:** Ibid.

115 **transmitting war news by telepathy:** Jones (1919), 106–7.

115 **"The glass . . . spelled out":** Jones (1919), 108.

116 **"You must live together":** Jones (1919), 108–9.

116 **Jones and Hill were horrified:** Jones (1919), 109.

116 **"Hill could only cover":** Ibid.; capitals in original.

116 **He feared reprimand:** Ibid.

116 **offer other prisoners the chance:** Jones (1919), 110.

117 **Eleven days went by:** Ibid.

117 **The Pimple was livid:** Ibid.

117 **On February 17:** Ibid.

117 **orchestrated it with care:** Ibid.

117 **The Spook repeated:** Jones (1919), 110–11.

117 "There is a watermark": Jones (1919), 111.

117 The Spook then ordered: Ibid.

117 Moïse. "We have done it": Jones (1919), 111–12.

117 FN Jones retained verbatim transcripts: Jones (1919), 103n.

118 the identical watermark: Hill (1975), 91n.

118 "Last night at the stated time": Jones (1919), 112.

118 Jones and Hill grew terrified: Ibid.

118 "Can Hill and I withdraw?": Ibid.

118 "If you withdraw now": Ibid.

118 "cold, giddy, and shivering": Ibid.

118 "The Spook says": Jones (1919), 113.

118 "That is why": Ibid.

118 FN "that even I": Jones (1919), 114.

119 He asked the Pimple not to tell: Ibid.

119 "We were making": Jones (1919), 113–14.

119 The Spook proceeded: Jones (1919), 114–15.

119 Should Kiazim fail: Jones (1919), 115.

119 "You promise not to tell": Jones (1919), 113.

119 broke it the moment he left: Ibid.

119 several more thought-reading shows: Hill (1975), 92.

119 including the susceptible Doc O'Farrell: Jones (1919), 117.

120 borrowed O'Farrell's medical books: Ibid.

120 biliary colic: Jones (1919), 122.

120 no arrest came: Jones (1919), 120.

120 "Moïse arrived": Hill (1975), 96.

120 It also threatened: Jones (1919), 119.

120 Three séances were required: Jones (1919), 118.

120 March 5: Jones (1919), 120.

120 The Pimple came: Jones (1919), 121.

120 planned to back out: Ibid.

120 "We sat down": Ibid.

120 Moïse wrote down: Jones (1919), 121–22.

120 FN This was normally accomplished: Hill (1975), 107.

121 the Spook was silent: Jones (1919), 122.

121 "What will you do?": Ibid.

121 bearing his transcript: Jones (1919), 123.

121 "There goes our last chance": Ibid.

121 Lieutenant Jones: Jones (1919), 123–24.

121 Jones and Hill reported: Jones (1919), 124.

121 four chosen comrades: Ibid.

121 "What is telepathy?": Ibid.

121 **"It is not known":** Ibid.

122 **"Lieut. Jones showed":** Quoted in Jones (1919), 125.

122 **"Jones said he did not":** Quoted in ibid.

122 **had made certain to implicate:** Jones (1919), 126.

122 **outwardly raging:** Ibid.

122 **"I never thought":** Ibid.

122 **FN Jones had built in:** Jones (1919), 129; Hill (1975), 98.

123 **"began with a graphic picture":** Jones (1919), 137–38.

123 **Then he told us:** Jones (1919), 138.

123 **The senior British officer:** Ibid.

123 **Once they had gone:** Jones (1919), 138–39.

123 **"The Commandant thought it":** Hill (1975), 100.

123 **sentries arrived:** Jones (1919), 139.

123 **Kiazim shook hands:** Ibid.

123 **"Remember, my friends":** Ibid.

CHAPTER NINE: VILLAINOUS OOO

124 **"Absurd as it may seem":** Jones (1919), 145.

124 **"We no longer":** Ibid.

124 **was entirely empty:** Jones (1919), 140.

124 **moved from room to room:** Ibid.

124 **meals would be sent over:** Jones (1919), 149.

124 **Hill built a new one:** Jones (1919), 152.

124 **the mediums had apprised:** Jones (1919), 151, 154.

124 **"Received a card":** *En-dor Unveiled*, 170.

125 **"I have received orders":** Ibid.

125 **a fine new stove and loads of wood:** Jones (1919), 154.

125 **"was delighted to do it":** Jones (1919), 155.

125 **agreed to tackle them:** Jones (1919), 105–6.

126 **On the Spook's orders:** Jones (1919), 163n.

126 **two small tin cans:** Hill (1975), 93.

126 **an Armenian-French dictionary:** Jones (1919), 117.

126 **a Turkish gold lira:** Hill (1975), 93.

126 **filled the main compartment:** Ibid.

126 **There was no third clue:** Hill (1975), 93.

126 **During their first winter:** Hill (1975), 94.

126 **out of long, straight boards:** Ibid.

126 **Under cover of darkness:** Ibid.

126 **Yozgad Ski Club:** Ibid.

126 **Jones and Hill became:** Jones (1919), 92; Hill (1975), 94.

126 **about three-quarters of a mile apart:** Hill (1975), 94.

126 **A week into the mediums' solitary confinement:** Jones (1919), 163.

126 **"what a lot of practice":** Jones (1919), 184.

126 **need to be constantly vigilant:** Jones (1919), 152.

126 **"No real con man":** Geoffrey O'Brien, "A Nation of Grifters, Fixers, and Marks: David Maurer's *The Big Con*," *Social Research: An International Quarterly* 85:4 (Winter 2018), 728.

126 **they would have to sustain:** Jones (1919), 163.

126 **FN official point-to-point race:** Jones (1919), 142.

126 **FN the camp bookmakers:** Ibid.

127 **only bit by bit:** Jones (1919), 163ff.

127 **"treasure séance":** Jones (1919), 164.

127 **on March 14, 1918:** Ibid.

127 **four and a half hours:** Per Jones (1919), 164, the séance lasted from 5:30 to 10:00 P.M.

127 **"The Spook gave an outline":** Hill (1975), 102.

127 **£28,000:** Jones (1919), 154.

127 **at a later séance:** Jones (1919), 186.

128 **Trance-talk was very difficult:** Jones (1919), 187–89.

128 **on the Spook's orders:** Jones (1919), 190.

128 **"For some time":** Ibid.

128 **A man carrying a letter:** Jones (1919), 191.

129 **"I am afraid":** Jones (1919), 191–92.

129 **The house they had described:** Jones (1919), 192.

129 **supplied a detailed account:** Ibid.

129 **"was half crazed":** Ibid.

129 **ghost of the Armenian treasure owner:** Jones (1919), 165.

129 **"OOO closes his thoughts":** Ibid.

129 **what magicians call an "out":** Lamont and Wiseman (2008), 79.

129 **"gets the magician out of trouble":** Ibid.

130 **"are also of particular use":** Ibid.

130 **"Leave that damned 'D' alone!":** Jones (1919), 38.

130 **"Though OOO himself":** Jones (1919), 195

130 **Napoleon Bonaparte:** Ibid.

130 **"I have found out":** Jones (1919), 168.

130 **"When the glass begins":** Ibid.

130 **"Moïse said afterwards":** Jones (1919), 170.

130 **"T-H-R-E-E C-L-U-E-S":** Ibid.

130 **"named the place":** Adapted from ibid.

130 **"in a S-E-P-A-R-A-T-E":** Adapted from Jones (1919), 170.

130 **"I am BEATEN":** Jones (1919), 171.

130 **OOO and his minions, he explained:** Ibid.

130 **AAA, YYY and KKK:** Jones (1919), 172.

131 **OOO went to AAA:** Ibid.

131 **Without the friends' real names:** Jones (1919), 171.

131 **However, he would add:** Jones (1919), 195.

131 **in five days' time:** Jones (1919), 173.

131 **"The Pimple's only criticism":** Ibid.

131 **the short con:** See, e.g., Maurer (1999), 3.

131 **only in 1849:** Johannes Dietrich Bergmann, "The Original Confidence Man," *American Quarterly* 21:3 (Autumn 1969), 570.

131 **aka Samuel Thompson:** Bergmann (1969), 561, 569.

131 **For the last few months:** *New York Herald*, July 8, 1849; quoted in Bergmann (1969), 561.

132 **Herman Melville's last novel:** Herman Melville, *The Confidence-Man: His Masquerade* (New York: Dix, Edwards & Company, 1857).

132 **April 1, 1857:** Christopher W. Sten, "The Dialogue of Crisis in 'The Confidence-Man': Melville's 'New Novel,'" *Studies in the Novel* 6:2 (Summer 1974), 166.

132 **"so well known in the 1850s":** Bergmann (1969), 561.

132 ***The Rogue's Lexicon***: George W. Matsell, *Vocabulum: Or, The Rogue's Lexicon* (New York: George W. Matsell/National Police Gazette, 1859).

132 **A fellow that by means:** Matsell (1859), 20–21. Also quoted in Bergmann (1969), 574.

133 **known as the long con:** See, e.g., Luc Sante, introduction to Maurer (1999).

133 **"All confidence games":** Maurer (1999), 3–4.

133 **"Mark" or "chump":** Maurer (1999), 298.

133 **"roper," or "outsideman":** Maurer (1999), 299, 303.

133 **"insideman":** Maurer (1999), 296.

133 **"Insidemen," Maurer writes:** Ibid.

133 **"big store":** Maurer (1999), 285.

133 **"manager":** Maurer (1999), 298.

133 **"fixer":** Maurer (1999), 294.

133 **a nostalgic ode:** O'Brien (2018), 728.

133 **Maurer anatomized:** Maurer (1999), 4.

133 **FN In 1974, Maurer filed:** "David W. Maurer Is Dead at 75: An Expert on Underworld Slang," *New York Times*, June 14, 1981, 43, via United Press International.

134 **"the wire":** Maurer (1999), 309.

134 **At a racetrack:** See, e.g., Maurer (1999), 16ff.

134 **"Big-time confidence games":** Maurer (1999), 101; italics in original.

135 **[The mark's] every probable reaction:** Maurer (1999), 101–2.

135 **FN "All this was in":** O'Brien (2018), 728.

136 **the centerpiece:** See, e.g., O'Brien (2018), 734.

136 **They all knew:** Memoirs including Mousley (2005) and Sandes (1919) make this clear. Jones himself (1919), 193, writes of his knowledge of a strafe at Kastamuni.

136 **escape from Kastamuni in 1917:** Jones (1919), 193; Sandes (1919), 438.

136 **a notice was posted:** Mousley (2005), 272.

136 **about 200 prisoners:** Neave (1937), 251.

136 **"were quartered in":** Neave (1937), 251–52.

136 **When the officers:** Neave (1937), 193–94.

137 **would also need documentary proof:** Jones (1919), 147.

137 **"Kiazim was not":** Ibid.

137 **no more than seven paces:** Jones (1919), 148.

137 **"Discovery would be dangerous":** Ibid.

138 **about a foot square:** Jones (1919), 147.

138 **"vest-pocket" Kodak:** Ibid.

138 **on the pretext of helping:** Ibid.

138 **"Now," he told Jones:** Jones (1919), 150.

138 **on their first night:** Jones (1919), 147.

138 **"For fifteen minutes":** Jones (1919), 150.

138 **"You'll have to talk":** Ibid.

138 **"to *pose* the blighters":** Ibid.; italics in original.

CHAPTER TEN: THE TREASURE TEST

139 **on March 27:** Jones (1919), 198.

139 **would be unable to discern:** Jones (1919), 199.

139 **It rained again:** Ibid.

139 **hail and sleet:** Ibid.

139 **Kiazim and the Cook:** Ibid.

139 **"The Turks were now":** Jones (1919), 195.

139 **three unexposed frames:** Jones (1919), 148.

140 **"secret object":** Jones (1919), 197.

140 **conditions included these:** Table adapted from Jones (1919), 197–98.

141 **At the last séance:** Jones (1919), 198.

141 **"'The clue,' the Spook warned us":** Ibid.

141 **dawned bright and clear:** Jones (1919), 199.

141 **At high noon:** Jones (1919), 200.

141 **the local graveyard:** Ibid.

141 **spied KKK:** Ibid.

140 FN "The Commandant kicked": Jones (1919), 197.

141 "About half-way up": Ibid.

142 "Can't snap 'em": Ibid.

142 Jones had impressed: Jones (1919), 65ff.

142 "Head-Hunting Waas" of Burma: Jones (1919), 65.

142 Hill collapsed to the ground: Jones (1919), 200.

142 six paces away: Ibid.

142 sufficiently in tune: Jones (1919), 187, 200–201.

142 Kiazim to his right: Jones (1919), 200.

142 lit a ritual fire: Ibid.

142 he heard a click: Ibid.

142 "Watch the fire!": Ibid.

142 "The bird!": Jones (1919), 201.

143 "Curiously enough": Ibid.

143 the Cook broke his shovel: Ibid.

143 "Spread the clean white handkerchief": Ibid.

143 "All the light": Jones (1919), 202.

143 "The emblem of death": Ibid.

143 "on the verge of tears": Ibid.

143 "Ha! ha! ha!": Ibid.; italics in original.

143 The pantomime he went through: Ibid.

143 cut himself once more: Ibid.

143 "The Commandant shook hands": Jones (1919), 203.

144 the Spook warned the group: Ibid.

144 so that OOO couldn't "control": Ibid.

144 Kiazim promptly doubled: Ibid.

144 Hill locked himself: Ibid.

144 Jones paced up and down: Ibid.

144 Kiazim was clearly recognizable: Jones (1919), 204.

144 that of YYY: Jones (1919), 206.

144 four miles from camp: Jones (1919), 205.

144 Jones regaled his captors: Jones (1919), 206.

145 they could not escape: Ibid.

145 Returning to camp: Jones (1919), 207.

145 The Spook was soon running: Jones (1955), 233, makes this point.

145 Kiazim had begun attending: Jones (1919), 211.

145 now turned to the Spook: Jones (1955), 233.

145 He had already slapped: Jones (1919), 173–74.

145 deputized to learn: Jones (1919), 167.

145 "The Turks were now": Jones (1919), 209.

145 On April 1: Jones (1919), 207n.

145 **received a cipher telegram:** Jones (1919), 207.

145 **OOO's work:** Jones (1919), 208–9.

145 **In early 1918:** Jones (1919), 175.

145 **pack of Turkish greyhounds:** Johnston and Yearsley (1919), 59.

145 **foxes and hares:** Ibid.

145 **that he would square everything:** Jones (1919), 177.

145 **"the most useful":** Johnston and Yearsley (1919), 59.

146 **"Some of the happiest":** Johnston and Yearsley (1919), 59–60.

146 **such organizations were forbidden:** Jones (1919), 176.

146 **The Spook said It wanted:** Jones (1919), 176–77; italics added.

146 **"Would the Superior like":** Jones (1919), 179.

146 **the Spook dictated:** Jones (1919), 179ff.

146 **hear their comrades cheering:** Jones (1919), 182.

146 **FN The greyhounds, Jones wrote:** Jones (1919), 177n.

147 **if they were ever to request:** Jones (1919), 137.

147 **they asked for quinine:** Jones (1919), 210.

147 **Hill slipped a small package:** Ibid.

147 **to simulate madness:** Jones (1919), 98, 151.

147 **"night and day":** Jones (1919), 211.

147 **as long as six hours:** Jones (1919), 234.

147 **"spelling out an answer":** Jones (1919), 275.

147 **Kiazim had requested:** Jones (1919), 211.

147 **entirely in Armenian capitals:** Ibid.

147 **the Spook's grudging assistance:** Jones (1919), 212ff.

147 **"south" and "west":** Jones (1919), 213.

148 **Held one way:** Ibid.

148 **"The Spook told the Turks":** Jones (1919), 213.

148 **"Straightforward answers":** Jones (1919), 212.

148 **AAA, the Spook had learned:** Jones (1919), 196.

148 **first tried to discover:** Jones (1919), 213.

148 **"Because his mind":** Jones (1919), 196.

148 **"We had the greatest difficulty":** Jones (1919), 213–14.

149 **"It is that damned OOO":** Jones (1919), 214.

149 **The risks, the Spook reminded them:** Ibid.

149 **as long as the mediums remained:** Ibid.

149 **There were other methods:** Jones (1919), 196.

149 **"I had not spent":** Jones (1919), 225.

149 **"Advocacy . . . is an art":** Iain Morley, *The Devil's Advocate: A Spry Polemic on How to Be Seriously Good in Court,* third edition (London: Sweet & Maxwell, 2015), 8.

149 **skills of a thespian:** Morley (2015), 20.

150 **controlling the order, pace, and weight:** Morley (2015), 16.

150 **"The whole system collapses":** Morley (2015), 28; italics in original.

150 **"No one likes":** Morley (2015), 42–43.

150 **"have a little something":** Quoted, e.g., in Dennis Coon and John O. Mitterer, *Introduction to Psychology: Gateways to Mind and Behavior*, twelfth edition (Belmont, Calif.: Cengage, 2010), 19.

150 **Identified in 1949:** Bertram R. Forer, "The Fallacy of Personal Validation: A Classroom Demonstration of Gullibility," *Journal of Abnormal and Social Psychology* 44:1 (1949), 118–23.

150 **named in 1956:** Paul E. Meehl, "Wanted—A Good Cookbook," *American Psychologist* 11:6 (1956), 266.

150 **"The Barnum method":** Marvin D. Dunnette, "Use of the Sugar Pill by Industrial Psychologists," *American Psychologist* 12 (1957), 223.

150 **an introductory psychology class:** Forer (1949), 119.

151 **included these statements:** Forer (1949), 120.

151 **After the papers:** Ibid.; italics added.

151 **"Those who have been gulled":** Henderson (1997), 4–5.

152 **"As it concerns a lady":** Jones (1919), 53.

152 **"Who are you?":** Adapted from Jones (1919), 53ff.; italics in original.

152 **"felt Antony give a little start":** Jones (1919), 53.

152 **Some weeks earlier:** Jones (1919), 53–54.

152 **"Remembering this":** Jones (1919), 54.

152 **"I know two Louises":** Jones (1919), 54.

152 **"A little reflection . . . shows":** Ibid.

152 **The response delighted:** Ibid.

152 **"Go on," he urged:** Ibid.

152 **FN "Antony" was in fact:** Holyoake (2013), 167.

152 **FN As Jones points out:** Jones (1919), 53.

153 **"Long straight road":** Jones (1919), 54ff.

153 **"Tony must have left her":** Jones (1919), 54.

153 **"You told me to go":** Ibid.

153 **Which showed, Jones realized:** Ibid.

153 **Antony began another question:** Ibid.

153 **"Tell me where you are":** Jones (1919), 55.

153 **began moving jerkily:** Ibid.

153 **"Look here, young feller!":** Ibid.

153 **"Tony . . . declared":** Jones (1919), 56.

154 **"An individual has":** David Premack and Guy Woodruff, "Does the Chimpanzee Have a Theory of Mind?," *Behavioral and Brain Sciences* 1:4 (1978), 515; italics in original.

154 **develops in childhood:** There is a vast literature in psychology, philosophy, and neurology on the developmental acquisition of theory of mind.

For an overview, see, e.g., Scott A. Miller, *Theory of Mind: Beyond the Preschool Years* (New York: Psychology Press, 2012).

154 **on the autistim spectrum:** See, e.g., Miller (2012), esp. 8.

154 **"Very young children":** Daniel C. Dennett, "Beliefs About Beliefs," *Behavioral and Brain Sciences* 1:4 (1978), 569.

154 **Little Red Riding Hood:** For commentary on "Red Riding Hood" as it relates to theory of mind, see, e.g., Miller (2012), 1, 25; also Joël Bradmetz and Roland Schneider, "Is Little Red Riding Hood Afraid of Her Grandmother? Cognitive vs. Emotional Response to a False Belief," *British Journal of Developmental Psychology* 17 (1999), 501–14.

155 **"Hill and I objected":** Jones (1919), 215.

155 **At night, in darkness:** Ibid.

155 **on the upper floor:** Ibid.

155 **"Then the Spook announced":** Ibid.

156 **talking all the while:** Ibid.

156 **a tremendous explosion:** Ibid.

156 **"Blind with terror":** Jones (1919), 215–16.

156 **battled some terrible force:** Jones (1919), 216.

156 **"Moïse often told us":** Ibid.

156 **"were really suffering":** Ibid.

156 **"Hill was halfway upstairs":** Ibid.

156 **"Shoo—shoo!":** Ibid.

157 **stifled their laughter:** Ibid.

157 **"Cries of souls in torment":** Jones (1919), 217.

157 **in reality Hill banging:** Jones (1919), 218.

157 **with the pick:** Ibid.

157 **"We protested against":** Ibid.

157 **their best chance of escape:** Jones (1919), 225ff.

157 **in early April:** Jones (1919), 219.

157 **could probably get a good head start:** Ibid.

157 **saying nothing:** Jones (1919), 219.

157 **"Why leave the Turks":** Ibid.

157 **It was Jones:** Ibid.

158 **"'There's another point'":** Jones (1919), 220.

158 **They both agreed:** Ibid.

CHAPTER ELEVEN: THE TELECHRONISTIC RAY

159 **Jones's plan:** Jones (1919), 223ff.

159 **before all returned:** Jones (1919), 230.

159 **"If all went well":** Jones (1919), 225–26.

160 **yearned for the bright lights:** Jones (1919), 230.

160 **a séance in March:** Jones (1919), 185.

160 **"preserves both the past":** Ibid.

160 **unfolded this way:** Condensed from Jones (1919), 230–32; italics in original.

161 **"A glance at a map":** Jones (1919), 232.

161 **"Four Cardinal Point Receiver":** Ibid.

161 **"was a secret method":** Jones (1919), 232–33.

161 **"infinitely preferable":** Jones (1919), 233.

161 **"Asia Minor":** Jones (1919), 234.

161 **the telephone, the phonograph:** Carolyn Marvin, *When Old Technologies Were New: Thinking About Electric Communication in the Late Nineteenth Century* (Oxford: Oxford University Press, 1988), 3.

161 **"Only since the late nineteenth century":** Peters (2000), 1.

162 **"Electricians were amused":** Marvin (1988), 21–22.

162 **That Hello!:** *Reading* (Pa.) *Herald*, reprinted in *Electrical Review* (Nov. 23, 1889), 6; quoted in Marvin (1988), 196.

163 **invented in 1895:** Grove (1997), 142.

163 **ideas about the ether:** See, e.g., Sconce (2000), 66, and Simone Natale, "A Cosmology of Invisible Fluids," *Canadian Journal of Communication* 36 (2011), 268.

163 **"As Kafka notes":** Peters (2000), 30; italics added.

163 **audible static was construed:** Peters (2000), 212.

163 **Get on to the surface:** Jones (1919), 233–34.

164 **"I am so glad":** Jones (1919), 234.

164 **In early April:** Jones (1919), 219.

164 **their commandant and interpreter:** Ibid.

164 **while Changri's commandant took over:** Jones (1919), 221.

164 **The Spook ordered Kiazim:** Ibid.

164 **a possible stone:** Ibid.

164 **"was very grateful":** Ibid.

164 **"The Cook, especially":** Jones (1919), 236.

164 **"The link between spiritualism":** Lamont (2013), 150.

165 **dry bread and tea:** Jones (1919), 250.

165 **"increase clairvoyant powers":** Jones (1919), 155.

165 **"to give us a 'starved look'":** Jones (1919), 155n.

165 **weak, thin, and exhausted:** Jones (1919), 261.

166 **"general paralysis of the insane":** Jones (1919), 336.

166 **delusions that he was a Turk:** See, e.g., Jones (1919), 252, 340ff.

166 **acute religious melancholia:** Jones (1919), 336.

166 **"Kiazim was greatly pleased":** Jones (1919), 226.

166 **neither bathed nor shaved:** Jones (1919), 227.

166 **Kiazim now allowed:** Jones (1919), 226.

166 "GO AWAY!": Jones (1919), 227.

166 Many comrades: Ibid.

166 deliberately, insufferably rude: Jones (1919), 227.

166 "Our condition": Jones (1919), 227–28.

167 "the camp thought us crazy": Jones (1919), 226.

167 Unswept and unaired: Jones (1919), 250.

167 "carried enough morphia": Jones (1955), 236.

167 ropes and straps: Ibid.

167 halfway to Cyprus: Ibid.

167 "We thought we could carry": Jones (1919), 220.

167 "scores of times": Jones (1919), 237.

167 a group of Yozgad prisoners: Jones (1919), 193.

167 The mediums' plan: Jones (1919), 194–95, 224–25.

168 "The Spook had told": Jones (1919), 237.

168 "We paid dearly": Ibid.

168 simply as "X": Jones (1919), 237ff.

168 A close friend: Jones (1919), 237.

168 the camp's black sheep: Jones (1919), 194.

168 what he thought was a salutary lie: Jones (1919), 238.

168 The Pimple brought them: Ibid.

168 "He knows you are too weak": Jones (1919), 239.

168 Kiazim believed that X: Jones (1919), 240.

168 "He thinks this is a warning": Jones (1919), 239–40; italics in original.

168 "He is troubled": Jones (1919), 240.

169 "distrusted us not at all": Ibid.

169 "was superlatively afraid": Jones (1919), 240–41.

169 Kiazim now refused: Jones (1919), 242.

169 to take the news blithely: Jones (1919), 241–42.

169 in despair: Jones (1955), 236.

169 "Hill," he wrote: Ibid.

169 Their only recourse now: Jones (1919), 243.

CHAPTER TWELVE: CERTIFIABLE

170 they had had a plan B: Jones (1919), 98, 151.

170 need to be committed: Jones (1919), 260.

170 They discussed their prospects: Jones (1919), 243.

170 He offered to improve: Ibid.

170 "I like to think": Ibid.

170 "Well, Bones": Jones (1919), 243–44.

170 the treasure hunt was still on: Jones (1919), 260.

170 Despite the Spook's warnings: Jones (1919), 264.

171 **"To the Light of the World"**: Jones (1919), 248–49.

171 **"Ye're a pair"**: Adapted from Jones (1919), 255; italics in original.

171 **FN Major Edward John Baylay**: historicgraves.com/christchurch/co -cccf-0006/grave.

171 **FN Deposed in 1909**: I am indebted to Yücel Yanıkdağ for this observation.

172 **"If ye do it"**: Jones (1919), 273–74.

172 **"within limits"**: Jones (1919), 256.

172 **on April 13**: Jones (1919), 250.

172 **Major Osman and Captain Suhbi Fahri**: Jones (1919), 251.

172 **sabotage their room and persons**: Jones (1919), 250–51.

172 **"that our eyes"**: Jones (1919), 250.

172 **which always made him ill**: Ibid.

172 **"he had the horrible"**: Jones (1919), 251.

172 **"Elliman's Embrocation"**: Jones (1919), 250.

172 **"for Horses, Dogs"**: *The Uses of Elliman's Embrocation for Horses, Dogs, Birds, Cattle* (Slough: Elliman, Sons & Company, 1898).

173 **Jones writing frenziedly**: Jones (1919), 251.

173 **sat motionless beside**: Ibid.

173 **stood frozen in the doorway**: Ibid.

173 **"Captain Suhbi Fahri tiptoed"**: Ibid.

173 **Among the questions**: Adapted from Jones (1919), 251–53.

173 **"I grew more and more excited"**: Jones (1919), 252.

174 **"The two doctors"**: Jones (1919), 252–53.

174 **"certificates of lunacy"**: Jones (1919), 253.

174 **"imposing documents"**: Ibid.

174 **a sentry was assigned to their room**: Jones (1919), 254.

174 **On April 14**: Jones (1919), 256.

174 **dictated, at his request**: Ibid.

174 **"Somewhere amongst"**: Ibid.

174 **For over a year**: Ibid.

175 **On April 16**: Jones (1919), 259.

175 **Haidar Pasha Hospital**: Ibid.

175 **"Hurrah!" he cried**: Ibid.

175 **"We were working now"**: Jones (1919), 261.

175 **FN "of a character so useful"**: Ibid.

CHAPTER THIRTEEN: TWO LUNATICS, 500 POUNDS OF BUTTER, AND A GREAT DEAL OF FLOUR

179 **If they failed**: Jones (1919), 260.

179 **held a frenzy of séances**: Jones (1919), 260ff.

179 control the mediums into acting: Jones (1919), 260–61.

179 "Thus," Jones wrote: Jones (1919), 261.

179 O'Farrell made covert daily visits: Ibid.

179 It made a strange picture: Jones (1919), 261–63.

180 Kiazim had kept: Jones (1919), 265.

180 Wanting to destroy: Ibid.

180 to implicate Kiazim further: Ibid.

180 a vise and a hacksaw: Ibid.

180 from a local goldsmith: Ibid.

180 the Spook ordered Hill: Ibid.

180 Per the Spook's instructions: Ibid.

180 "to provide us": Ibid.

180 told them what to do: Jones (1919), 343ff.

181 On April 24, 1918: Jones (1919), 267.

181 the Spook impressed: Jones (1919), 267–68.

181 "He kept his promise": Jones (1919), 269.

181 was roundly despised: Jones (1919), 265–66.

181 the Spook began massaging: Jones (1919), 266.

181 The Pimple agreed: Ibid.

181 At 10:00 A.M. on April 26: Jones (1919), 271.

181 two best carts: Ibid.

181 five-day, 120-mile ride: Jones (1919), 272n.

181 the two sentries: Jones (1919), 272.

181 tied discreetly with the rope: Jones (1919), 274.

181 the spook-board: Jones (1919), 275.

181 500 pounds of butter: Jones (1919), 281.

181 He planned to sell it: Ibid.

182 Ever since Major Osman: Jones (1919), 270.

182 Playing his part: Jones (1919), 271–72.

182 "a florid and affectionate": Jones (1919), 272.

182 crying that he reviled: Hill (1975), 143.

182 who had been charged: Jones (1919), 272.

182 "The Turks," Jones wrote: Jones (1919), 273.

183 sat on a stone: Hill (1975), 142.

183 "but once, when he glanced": Jones (1919), 273.

183 the mediums couldn't risk: Jones (1919), 275.

183 as the glass disclosed: Ibid.

183 twisting the button of his coat: Ibid.

183 On day two: Jones (1919), 276.

183 the Pimple drilled the mediums: Ibid.

183 "Sir!" he exclaimed: Ibid.

183 "The Spook reminded him": Jones (1919), 277.

183 **he would "control" the mediums:** Ibid.

183 ***"Mon Dieu!":*** Jones (1919), 276.

183 **The Spook reproved:** Ibid.

183 **"We decided to put on":** Hill (1975), 144.

183 **FN believed to denote Denck Ma'arden:** *En-dor Unveiled,* 57n.

184 **The plan horrified:** Jones (1919), 277.

184 **an Ottoman Jew:** Jones (1919), vii.

184 **"The term cult":** Singer (2003), xxiv.

184 **"A cultic relationship":** Singer (2003), 7.

184 **wide spectrum of beliefs:** Singer (2003), 13ff.

184 **interviewed thousands:** Singer (2003), 385.

184 **"at least ten":** Singer (2003), 13.

184 **"neo-Christian religious":** Singer (2003), 13–14.

184 **FN "a typical Ottoman Jew":** Jones (1919), vii.

184 **FN "all the natural intelligence":** Jones (1919), 68.

184 **FN "He was not, I suppose":** Jones (1919), 305.

185 **top-down authoritarianism:** Singer (2003), 8.

185 **by means of magicians' tricks:** Singer (2003), 163.

185 **tend to feel disenfranchised:** Singer (2003), 31.

185 **"false promises and bogus ideology":** Singer (2003), xvii.

185 **locales that are isolated from ordinary life:** Singer (2003), 114.

185 **times of social unrest:** Singer (2003), 30.

185 **"can be hoodwinked":** Singer (2003), xxv.

185 **akin to a long con:** Singer (2003), 54.

185 **"The key to successful":** Singer (2003), 52.

185 **On April 29:** Jones (1919), 279.

185 **His echelon had been allowed:** Ibid.

185 **"My second entry":** Jones (1919), 279–80.

185 **Hill caught sight:** Jones (1919), 280.

186 **Mardeen had been ravaged:** Ibid.

186 **"My Turkish being already":** Ibid.

186 **Hill was mooning:** Jones (1919), 280–81.

186 **Bekir and Sabit:** Jones (1919), 273.

186 **When the Pimple told them:** Jones (1919), 281.

186 **the finest in Mardeen:** Ibid.

187 **nearly came to believe:** Hill (1975), 147.

187 **the only vacancy:** Jones (1919), 282.

187 **"strong enough to hold":** Ibid.

187 **Hill immediately sat:** Ibid.

187 **11 feet high:** Ibid.

187 **Opposite the door:** Jones (1919), 282–83.

187 **it was the pretext:** Jones (1919), 283.

187 **Pretending he was reading:** Ibid.

188 **they considered him harmless:** Ibid.

188 **the coffee room had closed:** Ibid.

188 **Bekir offered to buy:** Ibid.

188 **Protocol would demand:** Ibid.

188 **At ten o'clock:** Jones (1919), 284.

188 **a Turkish gold lira and an Indian rupee:** Ibid.

188 ***It's up to you:*** Ibid.

188 **Hill squeezed Jones's arm:** Ibid.

188 **"Ask Bekir":** Jones (1919), 284–85.

189 **barely a yard in front:** Jones (1919), 285.

189 **"It is good":** Ibid.

189 **a look of deep boredom:** Ibid.

189 **storing each one in his pocket:** Ibid.

189 **"More!" Bekir cried:** Ibid.

189 **"Would you like to see":** Ibid.

189 **"Then step outside":** Ibid.

189 **He was to stand outside:** Jones (1919), 277.

189 **"Moïse was terrified":** Hill (1975), 146.

189 **taking one of the candles:** Jones (1919), 286.

190 **which Hill had fashioned:** Jones (1919), 283.

190 **"Ready?":** Jones (1919), 286.

190 **"Take the strain":** Ibid.

190 **Holding the rope:** Ibid.

190 **"I could not see":** Ibid.

190 **"To anyone desirous":** Jones (1919), 286–87.

191 **Hill on the bed:** Jones (1919), 287–88.

191 **Buckets of ice water:** Jones (1919), 288.

191 **loud and abusive:** Ibid.

191 **he shook his fist:** Ibid.

191 **about the murderous Major Baylay:** Jones (1919), 290.

191 **beat him up:** Jones (1919), 288.

191 **"Send us to bed":** Jones (1919), 290.

191 **"Had the crowd":** Ibid.

191 **The next morning:** Jones (1919), 293.

191 **righteously denied:** Ibid.

191 **wrote up a report:** Ibid.

191 **signed by several witnesses:** Ibid.

191 **told Jones and Hill privately:** Jones (1919), 290.

191 **"A telegraphic report":** Jones (1919), 293.

192 **They left Mardeen:** Ibid.

192 **augmented by a local policeman:** Ibid.

192 **"We were handed on":** Ibid.

192 **On the road that night:** Ibid.

192 **On May 1:** Jones (1919), 295.

192 **a 200-pound bag of flour:** Jones (1919), 299.

192 **the evening of the sixth:** Ibid.

192 **tiny third-class compartment:** Hill (1975), 154.

192 **the "BBB":** Hill (1975), 144.

192 **for the journey:** Jones (1919), 300.

192 **lapsed gradually into trance-talk:** Hill (1975), 154.

192 **Clue 3, AAA revealed:** Jones (1919), 302.

192 **wild with joy:** Ibid.

192 **might have dug the clue up:** Jones (1919), 302.

192 **FN On reaching the capital:** Ibid.

193 **OOO could well be lying:** Ibid.

193 **if all else failed:** Ibid.

193 **The Spook then made:** Jones (1919), 302ff.

193 **leading the entire world:** Jones (1919), 305.

193 **The Pimple wept:** Jones (1919), 306.

193 **two and a half days:** Jones (1919), 300.

193 **a half mile from the station:** Jones (1919), 307.

193 **each swallowed his last 20 grams:** Ibid.

193 **acting on the "delusion":** Ibid.

193 **ordered a whisky and soda:** Ibid.

CHAPTER FOURTEEN: THE MAD WARD

194 **a military hospital:** N[icholas] Senn, "Military Surgery in Turkey," *Journal of the American Medical Association* 29:12 (Sept. 18, 1897), 566–67.

194 **Established in the mid-nineteenth century:** Senn (1897), 567.

194 **in Scutari:** Ibid.

194 **"good modern institutions":** *Report on the Treatment* (1918), 4.

194 **the night of May 8, 1918:** Jones (1919), 302.

194 **relieved of the food:** Jones (1919), 308.

194 **Jones never saw his again:** Ibid.

194 **Hill managed to hold on to:** Ibid.

194 **his magnum opus:** Ibid.

194 **"a vest, a pair of pants":** Ibid.

194 **the "nervous ward":** Ibid.

194 **a dimly lighted room:** Ibid.

194 **a time-honored con:** See, e.g., William Francis Drewry, "Feigned Insanity: Report of Three Cases," *Journal of the American Medical Association* 27:15 (Oct. 10, 1896), 798.

194 **"He disguised his sanity":** 1 Samuel 21:13.

195 **afterward in book form:** Nellie Bly, *Ten Days in a Mad-House. Or, Nellie Bly's Experience on Blackwell's Island: Feigning Insanity in Order to Reveal Asylum Horrors* (New York: N. L. Munro, 1887).

195 **fearsomely difficult:** Drewry (1896).

195 **fearsomely difficult to detect:** Ibid.

195 **"one of the most difficult":** From the alienist Connolly Norman (1853–1908); quoted in Drewry (1896), 798.

195 **"there is no established":** Drewry (1896), 801.

195 **seen clearly from the door:** Jones (1919), 308.

195 **The Ottoman officer:** Ibid.

195 **"It was obvious":** Hill (1975), 160.

195 **about thirty large notebooks:** Jones (1919), 350.

195 *Scheme for the Abolition of England:* Jones (1919), 340.

195 **refused all nourishment:** Hill (1975), 157.

195 **three days without sleep:** Jones (1919), 309.

195 **the "insane look":** Ibid.

195 **imprisoned at Kastamuni:** Mousley (1922), 185ff.

196 **In the middle of the night:** Mousley (1922), 358.

196 **took him into his confidence:** Mousley (1922), 358.

196 **"He was a daring actor":** Mousley (1922), 360.

196 **sent back to Yozgad:** Jones (1919), 301.

196 **far worse would be:** Ibid.

196 **they could be committed:** Hill (1975), 160.

196 **"Pretend to be":** Jones (1919), 270–71. Feigning insanity to report on conditions in a New York City madhouse, the journalist Nellie Bly grappled with a similar fear (1887, 8): "Who could tell," she wrote, "but that the strain of playing crazy, and being shut up with a crowd of mad people, might turn my own brain, and I would never get back."

196 **the sound of blows:** Jones (1919), 309.

196 **"being pounded back to bed":** Jones (1919), 309.

197 **He would hear that sound:** Ibid.

197 **Ihsan Bey:** Jones (1919), 311.

197 **"The Turkish War Office":** Jones (1919), 266–67.

197 **"I launched into":** Jones (1919), 312.

198 **"Your name":** Condensed from ibid.

198 **"Measles, scarlet fever":** Jones (1919), 312–13.

198 **"Enver Pasha is very particular":** Jones (1919), 313.

198 **"Do you ever smell"**: Jones (1919), 316.

198 **"I leant forward"**: Ibid.

199 **"You are mad"**: Jones (1919), 317.

199 **"I don't know whether"**: Ibid.

199 **"I've been examining"**: Ibid.

199 **The doctor seemed puzzled**: Jones (1919), 318.

199 **Talha Bey**: Ibid.

199 **Talha asked Jones**: Ibid.

199 **"I saw what the sly fellow"**: Ibid.

199 **"Oh, yes!"**: Ibid.

199 **"Where did they inject you?"**: Ibid.

199 **"In the thigh"**: Jones (1919), 318–19.

199 **"Not more than once"**: Jones (1919), 319.

199 **"Oh yes"**: Ibid.

199 **"Dear me!"**: Ibid.

199 **"I managed to look"**: Ibid.

199 **"Malaria!"**: Ibid.

199 **Talha went away satisfied**: Ibid.

200 **"What is the book"**: Condensed from Hill (1975), 158–59.

200 **Hill replied gloomily**: Jones (1919), 320.

200 **people "alienated"**: See, e.g., Morton G. Miller, "The Problem of Drug Abuse: Alienation and the 'Alienist,'" *Military Medicine* 134:8 (August 1969), 577.

201 **as far back as the 1500s**: Julien Bogousslavsky and Thierry Moulin, "From Alienism to the Birth of Modern Psychiatry: A Neurological Story?," *European Neurology* 62 (2009), 257.

201 **in the early 1800s**: Bogousslavsky and Moulin (2009), 257.

201 **viewed as a moral failing**: Miller (1969), 584.

201 **"the victory of psychiatry"**: Rhodri Hayward, "Demonology, Neurology, and Medicine in Edwardian Britain," *Bulletin of the History of Medicine* 78:1 (Spring 2004), 37.

201 **disorders thought to result**: Bogousslavsky and Moulin (2009), 257–58.

201 **commonly referred to a neurologist**: Bogousslavsky and Moulin (2009), 258.

201 **advocated humane treatment**: See, e.g., T. L. Wright, "Some Prominent Features Common to Drunkenness and General Paralysis of the Insane," *Journal of the American Medical Association* 14:25 (June 21, 1890), 887.

201 **"nanny for troublesome adults"**: Thomas Szasz, "The Origin of Psychiatry: The Alienist as Nanny for Troublesome Adults," *History of Psychiatry* 6 (1995), 1.

201 **confinement in insane asylums:** See, e.g., Roger K. Blashfield, "Pre-Kraepelin Names for Mental Disorders," *Journal of Nervous and Mental Disease* 207:9 (September 2019), 727.

201 **treatments might include:** Camilla M. Haw, "John Conolly and the Treatment of Mental Illness in Early Victorian England," *Psychiatric Bulletin* 13:8 (1989), 440.

201 **"an extremely poisonous alkaloid":** Haw (1989), 440.

201 **"antimony, mercury":** Ibid.

201 **along the lines of the kingdom-phylum-class:** Blashfield (2019), 729.

201 **a classification based on etiology:** Ibid.

201 **more than a dozen competing taxonomies:** Blashfield (2019), 726, identifies sixteen systems in use before World War I.

202 **a taxonomic free-for-all:** See, e.g., Blashfield (2019), 727–29.

202 **the father of modern psychiatry:** See, e.g., A[lexander] Bonkalo, "Emil Kraepelin (1856–1926)," *Canadian Medical Association Journal* 74 (May 15, 1956), 835.

203 **"conspicuous degenerations":** Wright (1890), 886.

203 **they did not take root:** Vamik D. Volkan, "Turkey," in John G. Howells, ed., *World History of Psychiatry* (New York: Brunner/Mazel Publishers, 1975), 392.

203 **"the founding father":** Volkan (1975), 391.

203 **Trained in Germany:** Yanıkdağ, personal communication.

203 **planned to be an obstetrician:** Salgirli (2011), 288n.

203 **a pasha's son:** Ibid.

203 **At the time the field entailed:** Ibid.

203 **hundreds of scientific papers:** Volkan (1975), 392.

203 **chairman of the department of psychiatry:** Ibid.

203 **the first Turkish-language:** Ibid.

203 **in 1914 helping to found:** Fatih Artvinli, Şahap Erkoç, and Fulya Kardeş, "Two Branches of the Same Tree: A Brief History of Turkish Neuropsychiatric Society (1914–2016)," *Archives of Neuropsychiatry* 54 (2017), 364–71.

203 **"the greatest authority":** Jones (1919), 321.

203 **an expert in particular:** Fatih Artvinli, "More than a Disease: The History of General Paralysis of the Insane in Turkey," *Journal of the History of the Neurosciences* 23:2 (2014), 131ff.

204 **later that first morning:** Jones (1919), 320.

204 **"During our stay":** Jones (1919), 321.

204 **stopped at Jones's bed:** Ibid.

204 **"Ihsan Bey does not":** Jones (1919), 321–22.

205 **Osman withdrew:** Jones (1919), 322.

205 **They would test his blood:** Ibid.

205 **I had hoped:** Jones (1919), 322–23.

205 **"I protest":** Jones (1919), 323.

205 **Ihsan said with a grin:** Ibid.

205 **Would they care:** Ibid.

205 **negotiated the figure down:** Ibid.

205 **An orderly cleared:** Ibid.

205 **"If it had not been":** Ibid.

205 **stabbed into his back three times:** Ibid.

205 **"I danced":** Ibid.

205 **"I knew the diagnosis":** Jones (1919), 336.

206 **"a treatment quite as trying":** Jones (1919), 323.

206 **In mid-May:** Ibid.

206 **Jones was brought in first:** Jones (1919), 324.

206 **"I replied":** Ibid.

206 **Jones had planted:** Jones (1919), 326n.

206 **an untidy scrawl:** Ibid.

206 **I, Elias Henry Jones:** Ibid.

206 **FN Developed in 1906:** Sara Stevens, "Diagnosing Syphilis with the Wassermann Test," STD Resource Center (2015), stdaware.com/stds/syphilis/treatment/wassermann-test.

207 **The drawing, too:** Jones (1919), 325–26n.

207 **"Did you do this drawing":** Jones (1919), 325–26.

207 **"Do you know what":** Jones (1919), 326.

207 **A murmur ran through:** Ibid.

208 **given the Pimple a code:** Jones (1919), 331.

208 **the Pimple had bowed:** Ibid.

208 **The day after:** Ibid.

CHAPTER FIFTEEN: NEAR DEATH

209 **The previous day:** Jones (1919), 237.

209 **Madame Paulus:** Ibid.

209 **"I see you are reading":** Jones (1919), 328.

209 **"Here are some flowers":** Ibid.

209 **"It is wicked to eat much":** Adapted from Jones (1919), 329.

209 **"May I write":** Adapted from ibid.

210 **"You will be going home soon":** Adapted from Jones (1919), 330–31.

210 **almost in tears:** Jones (1919), 331.

210 **They felt guilty:** Jones (1919), 331; Hill (1975), 167.

210 **"Our task was":** Jones (1919), 334.

210 **Unable to procure:** Jones (1919), 340.

210 **"Had we known"**: Ibid.; italics in original.

210 **In July**: Jones (1919), 343.

210 **"The Commandant is being"**: Jones (1919), 344–45.

210 **"Everything is going wrong!"**: Adapted from Jones (1919), 343–44.

211 **"As soon as the Commandant"**: Jones (1919), 344.

211 **the delight that exhibition**: Ibid.

211 **"Everything's all right"**: Adapted from Ibid.

211 **"Tell me about yourself"**: Jones (1919), 347.

211 **the Spook had promised the Pimple**: Jones (1919), 305.

211 **"live a righteous and austere life"**: Ibid.

211 **"I obey the Spook"**: Jones (1919), 347.

211 **"I don't know"**: Ibid.

212 **"What's Choctaw like?"**: Ibid.

212 **"*Hwch goch*"**: Ibid.

212 **"A red sow"**: Jones (1919), 347n.

212 **"*Mon Dieu!*"**: Jones (1919), 347.

212 **Osman instructed the orderlies**: Jones (1919), 339.

212 **It was, the doctor assured him**: Ibid.

212 **Jones drank it down**: Ibid.

212 **hoarding hard-boiled eggs**: Hill (1975), 193.

212 **"The man fled"**: Hill (1975), 194.

212 **Jones managed to slip**: Jones (1919), 349n.

212 **One night he donned**: Hill (1975), 195.

212 **shouting, whistle-blowing pandemonium**: Ibid.

213 **he was nearly shot**: Jones (1919), 349n.

213 **he began raving**: Ibid.

213 **he was drugged**: Ibid.

213 **I had to be ready**: Jones (1919), 340–41.

213 **Hill's task was harder still**: Jones (1919), 341ff.

213 **he had read the entire book**: Jones (1919), 341.

214 **"It was the most wonderful exhibition"**: Jones (1919), 341–42.

214 **in late July**: Hill (1975), 177.

214 **Hill developed severe dysentery**: Hill (1975), 176ff.

214 **influenza and a fever of 103**: Jones (1919), 337n.

214 **to see Enver Pasha**: Hill (1975), 177.

214 **allowed themselves to hope**: Ibid.

214 **train, boat, and cart**: Ibid.

214 **it had no facilities**: Jones (1919), 338n.

214 **after thirty-six hours**: Ibid.

214 **"It amounts to this"**: Ibid.; italics in original.

215 **"could hardly crawl"**: Hill (1975), 180.

215 **at least two months**: Ibid.

215 **"Judging by the attitude":** Hill (1975), 181.

215 **that Hill was dead:** Jones (1919), 343.

215 **"It was a good job":** Ibid.

215 **days in inward misery:** Ibid.

215 **Hill would languish:** Jones (1919), 336.

215 **captured near Baghdad:** White (1990), 44ff.

215 **Imprisoned at Afion Karahissar:** White (1990), 148ff.

215 **foot and ankle injuries:** White (1990), 232–33.

216 **I stared in amazement:** White (1990), 235–36.

216 **"Don't speak to him":** White (1990), 236.

216 **the bed next to Hill's:** Ibid.

216 **At about 2:00 A.M.:** White (1990), 237–38.

216 **Whenever Hill stared:** White (1990), 238.

216 **"I shall ask you":** Ibid.

217 **"gave me the opportunity":** Ibid.

217 **He implored Hill:** Ibid.

217 **"I have made up my mind":** Ibid.

217 **"When he next bent":** Ibid.

217 **In early August:** Hill (1975), 182.

217 **for prisoners discharged:** *Report on the Treatment of British Prisoners of War in Turkey*, 4.

217 **more than seventy pounds:** Jones (1919), 338.

217 **"sat like a ghost":** Hill (1975), 183.

217 **the five-hour journey:** Ibid.

217 **excruciating pain:** White (1990), 245.

217 **flung into the road:** Hill (1975), 183.

217 **"I always looked":** Ibid.

217 **Armenian religious school:** White (1990), 247.

217 **hundreds of British, Indian:** Ibid.

217 **seething with vermin:** Ibid.

217 **the rotten boards of his bedstead:** Ibid.

217 **A few days later:** Hill (1975), 185.

218 **he was watched unremittingly:** Hill (1975), 186.

218 **most likely an Ottoman doctor:** Ibid.

218 **on August 17:** Hill (1975), 187.

218 **another stop at Psamatia:** Hill (1975), 186–87.

218 **"The general 'messing about'":** Hill (1975), 187.

218 **"more like 'tearing'":** Hill (1975), 188.

218 **a blunt rusty razor:** Ibid.

218 **another "patient" in the bath:** Ibid.

218 **"so emaciated":** Jones (1919), 353.

218 **was left there, naked:** Ibid.

218 "The object of the Turks": Jones (1919), 353.

218 less than a hundred pounds: Jones (1919), 338.

218 Jones did not recognize him: Hill (1975), 190.

218 the Pimple caught sight: Hill (1975), 198.

218 "I am going to punish": Adapted from Jones (1919), 348.

219 visited again in August: Ibid.

219 "There has been a big escape": Ibid.

219 "I could have shouted": Ibid.

219 "Neither Kiazim": Jones (1919), 343; italics in original.

219 under deeper suspicion: Jones (1919), 348ff.

219 no longer allowed outside: Jones (1919), 349.

219 whenever Jones entered: Jones (1919), 350.

219 "That evening": Jones (1919), 349; italics in original.

219 Bathing in the hammam: Ibid.

219 "I wished joy": Jones (1919), 350.

219 "a letter from Yozgad": Jones (1919), 353.

219 Not Kiazim: Jones (1919), 351.

220 "What that letter was": Jones (1919), 353.

220 on August 7, 1918: Ibid.

220 to the Mediterranean: Johnston and Yearsley (1919), 62.

220 Kiazim cursed: Hill (1975), 198.

220 he strafed the camp: Jones (1919), 353ff.

220 with the influenza pandemic: Berna Arda and Ahmet Acıduman, "Pandemic Influenza 1918–19: Lessons from 20th Century to the 21st from the History of Medicine Point of View," *Lokman Hekim Journal* 2:3 (2012), 16.

220 twelve deaths in all: Jones (1919), 358.

220 applied only to a strafing: Jones (1919), 355.

220 "Never for a moment": Ibid.; italics in original.

220 Matthews had escaped: Ibid.

220 Price was among the twelve: Jones (1919), 358.

220 believing they could be used: Jones (1919), 355.

220 turned one of the images over: Jones (1919), 355–56.

220 "The negative showed": Jones (1919), 354.

221 "the camp": Jones (1919), 354–55.

221 appeared to have been written: Jones (1919), 353.

221 "quite undeserved discomfort": Jones (1919), 354.

221 officially certified for exchange: Hill (1975), 190.

221 "What Mazhar Osman Bey's": Jones (1919), 336.

221 in late September: Jones (1919), 356.

221 The Spook explained: Ibid.

222 partly, he later learned: Hill (1975), 200.

222 **"That," he wrote:** Ibid.

222 **On October 10:** Jones (1919), 356.

222 **the two-day journey:** Hill (1975), 199.

222 **the British hospital ship *Kanowna*:** Hill (1975), 200.

222 **on November 1:** Ibid.

222 **continued to look for him:** Hill (1975), 201.

222 **had convinced the Ottoman authorities:** Jones (1919), 356.

222 **the second exchange ship:** Jones (1919), 356–57.

222 **a few days after Hill's:** Jones (1919), 357.

CHAPTER SIXTEEN: PERSUASION

223 **"influence technicians":** Taylor (2017), 312.

223 **"compliance professionals":** Robert B. Cialdini, *Influence: The Psychology of Persuasion* (New York: Collins Business, 2007; originally published 1984), esp. xii.

223 **FN the American foreign correspondent Edward Hunter:** Edward Hunter, *Brain-Washing in Red China: The Calculated Destruction of Men's Minds* (New York: Vanguard Press, 1951), and *Brainwashing: The Story of Men Who Defied It* (New York: Farrar, Straus & Cudahy, 1956). An analysis of Chinese indoctrination efforts considered by scholars to be more evenhanded than Hunter's is Edgar H. Schein, "The Chinese Indoctrination Program for Prisoners of War: A Study of Attempted 'Brainwashing,'" *Psychiatry* 19:2 (1956), 149–72.

223 **FN Sources differ on whether Hunter:** Cf., e.g., Kathleen Taylor, *Brain Washing: The Science of Thought Control* (Oxford: Oxford University Press, 2017; originally published 2004), 3, and Marcia Holmes, "Edward Hunter and the Origins of 'Brainwashing,'" Birkbeck College Hidden Persuaders Project, bbk.ac.uk/hiddenpersuaders/blog/hunter-origins-of-brainwashing.

224 **any of three ways:** Taylor (2017), xiii.

224 **manipulate his subject's brain:** Taylor (2017), 350ff.

224 **"weapons of influence":** Cialdini (2007), esp. 1ff.

224 **"*know what isn't so*":** Thomas Gilovich, *How We Know What Isn't So: The Fallibility of Human Reason in Everyday Life* (New York: The Free Press, 1993; originally published 1991).

224 **"Magical illusions are possible":** Robert Edmund Bernhard Jr., *The Psychology of Conjuring* (Stanford, Calif.: self-published, 1936), 4.

224 **"No one can take advantage":** Ralph Keyes, *The Quote Verifier: Who Said What, Where, and When* (New York: St. Martin's Griffin, 2006), 115.

225 **"Belief is the normal":** Bernhard (1936), 10.

225 **indoctrination by slow, subtle steps:** See, e.g, Thomas Gilovich, Dacher

Keltner, Serena Chen, and Richard E. Nisbett, *Social Psychology*, fifth edition (New York: W. W. Norton & Company, 2019), 306.

225 **"In most human endeavors"**: Thomas Gilovich, personal communication; italics added on "mostly."

225 **FN For precisely this reason**: Matthew L. Tompkins, personal communication.

226 **"The Commandant was our friend"**: Jones (1919), 215.

226 **"the techniques of *verbal control*"**: Philip T. Goldstein, *Verbal Control: A Treatise on the Under-Exposed Art of Equivoque* (n.p.: self-published, 1996; originally published 1976), 1; italics added.

226 **"It is absolutely necessary"**: Ibid.; italics added.

226 **"Also known as"**: James L. Clark, *Mind Magic and Mentalism for Dummies* (Chichester: John Wiley & Sons, 2012), 358.

226 **"The best way to get"**: Jones (1919), 228.

227 **"Get on to the surface"**: Jones (1919), 233.

227 **"I am so glad"**: Jones (1919), 234.

227 **"You see,"**: Jones (1919), 240.

227 **Jones never did learn**: Jones (1919), 336.

227 **"When examining evidence"**: Gilovich (1993), 50–51.

228 **"To them . . . I made"**: Jones (1919), 226–27; italics in original.

228 **"conjuring in disguise"**: the remark, attributed to the nineteenth-century Scottish magician John Henry Anderson, is quoted in Barton Whaley, "Toward a General Theory of Deception," *The Journal of Strategic Studies* 5:1 (1982), 179.

229 **"Con games never remain"**: Maurer (1999), 55.

229 **"Conforming to the dictates"**: Cialdini (2007), 218; italics added.

229 **a transit camp in Alexandria**: Hill (1975), 201.

229 **From there, they shipped**: Ibid.

230 **barely more than two weeks**: Jones (1919), 357.

230 **solitary graves in the hills**: Jones (1919), 358.

230 **"Amongst the dead"**: Ibid.

230 **"Freedom was our lodestar"**: Jones (1919), 340.

EPILOGUE: AFTERLIFE

231 **During the long convalescence**: *En-dor Unveiled*, 56.

231 **"When we reached England"**: Jones (1919), viii–ix.

231 **"An Irish Gentleman"**: Jones (1919), vi.

231 **Jones served briefly**: *En-dor Unveiled*, 56.

231 **attached to the Middle East Committee**: David Roberts, *Bangor University, 1884–2009* (Cardiff: University of Wales Press, 2009), 17.

231 **In the early 1920s**: *En-dor Unveiled*, 56.

231 **a large house in north Wales:** *En-dor Unveiled,* 57; "Elias Henry Jones," The Home Front Museum, Llandudno, Wales, https://homefrontmuseum .wordpress.com/tag/elias-henry-jones.

232 **In 1924, at forty:** *En-dor Unveiled,* 57.

232 **he and Hill maintained:** *En-dor Unveiled,* 56.

232 **From 1927 to 1933:** "Elias Henry Jones," *The University of Glasgow Story.*

232 **socially progressive Welsh nationalist:** Kenneth O. Morgan, *Rebirth of a Nation: Wales, 1880–1980* (New York: Oxford University Press, 1981), 132.

232 **In 1933 he was appointed:** *En-dor Unveiled,* 58.

232 **"His style of working":** Ibid.

232 **a 2014 edition:** E. H. Jones, *The Road to En-dor: Being an Account of How Two Prisoners of War at Yozgad in Turkey Won Their Way to Freedom,* foreword by Neil Gaiman (London: Hesperus Press, 2014).

232 **"My dearest dear":** *En-dor Unveiled,* 57.

232 **eighteen-year-old Arthur:** *En-dor Unveiled,* 58; "Elias Henry Jones," Home Front Museum; "Jones, Arthur Bevan," Losses Database, International Bomber Command Centre, losses.internationalbcc.co.uk/loss /214872.

232 **one of the youngest pilots:** "Jones, Arthur Bevan," Losses Database, International Bomber Command Centre.

232 **On occasion:** *En-dor Unveiled,* 58.

232 **"Harry was ill":** Ibid.

232 **In May 1942:** Ibid.

232 **They had agreed:** *En-dor Unveiled,* 58–59.

232 **He died of pneumonia:** *En-dor Unveiled,* 59.

233 **Hill returned to England:** Hill (1975), jacket biography.

233 **He served over the years:** Ibid.

233 **attaining the rank of group captain:** Bennett and Parker (1996).

233 **In 1921, in Egypt:** Ibid.

233 **parents of a daughter:** Ibid.

233 **just over fifteen days:** E[dward] P. Wixted, "Hinkler, Herbert John (Bert) (1892–1933)," in Bede Nairn and Geoffrey Searle, eds., *Australian Dictionary of Biography,* volume 9, *1891–1939* (Melbourne: Melbourne University Press, 1983), online via National Centre of Biography, Australian National University, Canberra, adb.anu.edu.au/biography/hinkler -herbert-john-bert-6680.

233 **Flying from dawn:** "Dramatic Air Race Ends," *The Age* (Melbourne, Australia), Oct. 20, 1930, 9:7.

233 **after twelve days:** "Pioneering Flights—To and from Australia," *A Fleet-*

ing Peace: Golden Age Aviation in the British Empire, http://ata.afleeting
peace.org/index.php/pioneering-flights/10-pioneering-flights/120
-pioneering-flights-englandaustralia.

233 **his wing clipped a fence:** "Dramatic Air Race Ends," 9:8.

233 **suffering smashed wings:** Ibid.

233 **Hill was unhurt:** Ibid.

233 **During World War II:** Hill (1975), jacket biography.

233 **retiring from active service in 1944:** Bennett and Parker (1996).

233 **An avid rifle and pistol shot:** Ibid.

233 **RAF revolver champion:** "Dramatic Air Race Ends," 9:7.

233 **Inner Magic Circle:** Ibid.

234 **Considerable interest was aroused:** "The May Social," *The Magic Circular* 23:266 (Oct. 19, 1929), 155. I am indebted to Matthew L. Tompkins
for furnishing me with Hill's *Magic Circle* clippings.

234 **March 5, 1975:** Ibid.

234 **three letters to Jones:** Jones (1919), 359–65.

235 **had answered none:** Jones (1919), 359.

235 **"I have a lot of news":** Jones (1919), 359–61.

235 **teaching English and French:** Jones (1919), 361.

235 **"I am very anxious":** Jones (1919), 362.

235 **FN As Jones points out:** Jones (1919), 362n.

236 **"I am now in the employ":** Jones (1919), 364–65; italics added.

236 **"not so much":** Jones (1919), 359; italics added.

237 **"The Commandant sent":** Holyoake (2013), 180.

237 **Kiazim, Holyoake added:** Ibid.

237 **The outcome of the court-martial:** Jones (1919), 364n. I have attempted via sources in Turkey to find surviving archival records of the
court-martial, to no avail.

237 **"the leading psychiatrist":** Yanıkdağ (2014), 176.

237 **In 1933 he was named:** "Obituary: Mazar Osman Uzman," *The Lancet*,
September 29, 1951, 599.

237 **his death in 1951, at sixty-seven:** Ibid.

237 **"his international repute":** Ibid.

237 **FN An ardent eugenicist:** See, e.g., Yücel Yanıkdağ, *Healing the Nation:
Prisoners of War, Medicine and Nationalism in Turkey, 1914–1939* (Edinburgh: Edinburgh University Press, 2014; originally published 2013),
228–29.

237 **FN he forced his sisters:** Sanem Güvenç Salgirli, "Eugenics for the Doctors: Medicine and Social Control in 1930s Turkey," *Journal of the History of Medicine and Allied Sciences* 66:3 (July 2011), 290n.

238 **a marked copy:** Ibid.

238 **"most prized possessions":** Ibid.

238 **In return:** Ibid.

238 **one of his earliest publications:** Türesay (2018), 188.

238 **the 1910 monograph:** Ibid., 181.

238 *Spiritizma Aleyhine*: Ibid.

Index

Page references in *italics* refer to illustrations.

ABOUT THE TYPE

———————

This book was set in Walbaum, a typeface designed in 1810 by German punch cutter J. E. (Justus Erich) Walbaum (1768–1839). Walbaum's type is more French than German in appearance. Like Bodoni, it is a classical typeface, yet its openness and slight irregularities give it a human, romantic quality.